THE ART OF MARKETING MORTGAGES

For my wife Lesley,
and my sons,
Timothy and Joshua

THE ART OF MARKETING MORTGAGES

STEPHEN KNIGHT

COLLINS & BROWN

First published in Great Britain in 1997 by Collins & Brown Limited, London House,
Great Eastern Wharf, Parkgate Road, London SW11 4NQ

Text copyright © Stephen Knight 1997
Copyright © Collins & Brown 1997

135798642

British Library Cataloguing-in-Publication Data
A catalogue record for this book is available at the British Library

ISBN 1 85585 491 0

Edited, designed and typeset by Book Creation Services Ltd, London

Printed and bound in Great Britain by The Bath Press

CONTENTS

I am indebted to
Britannia Building Society
for generously sponsoring
this book

ACKNOWLEDGMENTS

I am extremely grateful to my colleagues, Godfrey Blight, Tony Fisher and Judy Lawrence for their considerable help in connection with Chapters 5, 6 and 7 respectively. Warmest thanks are also due to my secretary, Kerensa Porter, for typing the entire manuscript and cheerfully putting up with a considerable number of redrafts.

Other friends and business connections who provided great assistance in compiling this book, either by acting as "readers/critics", or by providing expert comment are: Lucian Camp; Ian Darby; Barry Field; Michael Kelly; John Meakin; Peter Smith; Ben Thompson and Simon Tyler.

Invaluable assistance in bringing this book to publication has been given by Cameron Brown, John Meakin (again!) and Hal Robinson.

A very special vote of thanks must go to the expert contributors to Chapter 8 who generously gave their invaluable views and predictions.

The press cuttings featured in Chapters 1–3 are reproduced with the kind permission of the publications named. The illustration for case study no. 28 in Chapter 4 has been reproduced with the kind permission of GB Investments. The other case studies in that chapter have been reproduced with the kind permission of Corporate Marketing Services Limited, DMB&B Financial, John Charcol Limited and Private Label Mortgage Services Limited. The illustrations in Chapters 5 and 6 are either the author's own work, or have been reproduced with the kind permission of Corporate Marketing Services Limited, DMB&B Financial and Private Label Mortgage Services Limited.

PRESENTATION OF PRODUCT MATERIAL

Some of the product advertising and marketing material featured in this book has been re-set and scaled down to fit the black and white quarto format. In this process, some or all of the regulatory material has been deleted so that the main commercial points about the product can be featured with greater prominence.

PART ONE

Company Biography

1

1985–1988
FROM CONCEPT TO LAUNCH,
AND AN EVENTFUL FIRST YEAR

I f I was naming the company now, I wouldn't call it Private Label. Branding was pivotal to our original plans, but today it is peripheral. We've thought about changing the name to more accurately capture what we do today, but the disadvantages outweigh the advantages. A decade later, and one in which we have been lucky enough to win some awards, the company name is so well recognised by its two different types of customer – lenders and mortgage intermediaries – that it is here to stay.

The origins of the idea of Private Label can be traced back to the early summer of 1985. Although at that time I was in charge of a number of Citibank branches, only getting involved in mortgages insofar as they were one of the products being sold at local level, I had retained the interest in the market on a wider level that had been with me throughout my career. I had become particularly interested in the fragmentation of the market which permitted lenders, administrators and originators to separate their functions. Although I had no master plan in place at that time, this seemed to me to be a development full of potential.

A company that was crucial to these developments was Mortgage Systems Ltd (MSL). Frustrated by lenders' inability to write a computer programme to administer his innovative index-linked mortgage idea, mortgage broker Michael Kelly had formed the Index-Linked Mortgage and Investment Company Ltd to undertake the administration on behalf of lenders. The idea of subcontracting portfolio management quickly caught on and MSL was born from these modest beginnings, eventually undertaking mainly the administration for straightforward vanilla loans.

In the early summer of 1985 I therefore applied for the job of General Manager with MSL. I had no intention of taking the job if offered, but if you want to learn more about a company then applying for a job there is the best way. I had, however, met my match in Michael Kelly. As he now admits, Michael saw me without any intention of offering me the job if I had wanted it. Michael had been intrigued by some of the sales and marketing ideas I had put across at the first interview with the agency, and was keen to discuss these with me.

It seems that we both got something valuable out of the encounter. Certainly, a friendship was started which has endured to this day. And it was to Michael that I turned first, in October 1986, with my idea of linking a sales and marketing company with a funder and an administrator to produce a mortgage programme. But first, back to Citibank.

I had been promoted to the job of UK Sales and Marketing Director of Citibank, then the largest foreign bank player in the residential mortgage market, in the autumn of 1985. Shortly after my appointment I was given the task of chairing a strategy group reporting to the New York head office on what steps Citibank should take to grow its mortgage business over the ensuing five years. Coming out of the day-to-day business on a regular basis, to meet with talented colleagues for the purpose of taking an objective look at the market in which you operate, was a new discipline for me.

My previous training with two building societies had given me a professional qualification, and a certain freedom to innovate. But I had never previously been subject to the discipline of carrying colleagues with an idea, accommodating their opinions, and compromising to reach the best, most thoroughly researched conclusion. It was a fascinating process for me, and one of the many management disciplines for which I owe a debt of gratitude to Citibank.

Citibank had pioneered the idea (before my arrival in the job) of distributing mortgages in low-cost volume through the intermediary market via a small panel of life assurance companies. The relative exclusivity of the panel kept the volumes going, not least because the members wished to keep their competitors out. Building societies were still making customers queue for mortgages, so a readily available source of finance was a valuable tool for insurance companies seeking business from mortgage intermediaries.

In 1985, Bank of America (as it then was) copied the Citibank idea. There then followed a series of launches from the "new wave" centralised lenders, such as National Home Loans, The Mortgage Corporation (TMC) and Household Mortgage Corporation Plc (HMC). My instinct is always to leave a market when others start to enter in a big way, so I began to turn my mind in the strategy group to other opportunities, particularly the distribution potential of the small to medium-sized insurance companies who were feeling squeezed out by these new lender launches.

Because they couldn't each promise to achieve £100m of annual distribution (typically the benchmark at that stage), the salesforces of

> I became increasingly engaged by the idea that a sales and marketing company ...could tap the demand...available from the small to medium-sized insurance companies

the small to medium-sized insurance companies were not getting access to the new centralised lenders which were at that time starting to revolutionise the market. Moreover, the whole life company panel concept – whilst fresh to the newer lenders – was becoming outdated in my view, and was starting to creak with inflexibility. For example, we couldn't offer an exclusive to one life office because that would confuse the market and upset the other panel members. I thought that if we could persuade each insurance company to "brand" its own mortgage programme, then any number of parallel exclusives could be offered, and we could then start to look at running a series of branded programmes with smaller life offices. The *total* volume achieved by a group of these smaller life offices would add up to a viable sum.

Some of this thinking found its way into the strategy paper, but most did not. Neither my project colleagues, nor my superiors at the bank, were particularly impressed with my line of thinking. As I revisit my thoughts of January 1986, I do, however, find one quote which is very instructive when related to the business I launched on my own some 20 months later:

"The mortgage market is seen as growing in real terms and one of increasing demand/supply interaction, dynamic, diverse, profitable and highly competitive. It is breaking into component parts of ORIGINATOR, SERVICER and FUNDER. An Originator will find and sell to the customer; a Servicer will process the loan application, complete the security and collect the repayments and a Funder will supply the funds. An institution can be one, two or all three and still build a profitable business. Citibank has to decide which or all of the services to provide."

As 1986 wore on, I became increasingly engaged by the idea that a sales and marketing company, working with one of the new off balance sheet funding structures, and a third-party administrator, could tap the demand I was sure was available from the small to medium-sized insurance companies. I hope that this did not distract me too much from the job in hand because I achieved record new business results for Citibank in 1986. Later that year I also received a promotion to the bank's Executive Committee – the policy-making board for Citibank's five UK consumer businesses. But the feeling that I wanted to do something on my own was growing.

This wasn't helped by the frenetic mortgage market of 1986. I had been approached by many headhunters, and had attended several interviews for senior level mortgage jobs. At many of these I had taken psychometric tests, which said nice things about my ability, and nasty things about my employability. The net message was one from which I could not escape: maybe it was time to go it alone.

SOWING THE SEEDS

In the autumn of 1986 I started to gather my thoughts together in a meaningful way and, on 17 October of that year, I arranged to share my outline ideas with Michael Kelly over a cup of coffee at the Institute of Directors. The fact that Michael had taken a brand new concept and sold it to conservative institutions made him the ideal person to talk to about my own new concept. I would need a flexible third-party administration company to run a myriad different schemes, each personalised according to the insurance companies' preference. A new type of sales and marketing company would hold the whole programme together and invent the products, with funding provided from an off balance sheet structure. In that way origination, administration and funding would be segmented by one overseeing company who would front the operation. The flexibility and price advantages of this structure seemed to me to be very exciting indeed.

Michael was enthusiastic about the idea. He not only offered me the full support of MSL, but also his own personal support, to the point of being prepared to invest his own money if required. It was seven months before I was able to meet somebody else who was equally enthusiastic about the idea from the perspective of supplying the mortgage funds. But that first meeting with Michael certainly set me on my way.

The next stage was to put together a business plan and some financials. I turned to an old friend who had recently started his own chartered accountancy practice in south London. Stephen O'Neill was perfectly entitled to say that he had other priorities when I asked him to work with me in putting the financials together, but my outrageous request for Stephen to work without payment until and if the project ever took off was "beyond the call". That Stephen readily agreed to my request, and is still my personal accountant today, is another endorsement of two core lessons which have been ever-present in my life. First, nobody survives without friends. Second, be a friend when the other person needs you, not when it suits you.

My first meeting with Stephen was on Saturday, 1 November 1986. We subsequently put some numbers together which meant that, as we went into 1987, I was in good shape to start thinking about funding.

It was at this stage in the project that my naivety really started to show. I found out that institutions were (rightly) sceptical about executives with big jobs who are trying to fund a business plan whilst keeping their employment going as additional security. The majority were also suspicious of personality-led ideas, the most often repeated quote being: "If this was a good idea, then a large institution would have thought of it!". I lost count of the number of people who said that my concept would not work.

> two core lessons have been ever-present in my life. First, nobody survives without friends. Second, be a friend when the other person needs you, not when it suits you

The obvious pigeon-hole for me to be pushed into was to acquire venture capital. But this clashed with one of my core themes. I only needed a small part of the interest margin and general insurance commissions to make Private Label work. Most of the income would go to those providing the capital, such as the funding structure and the third-party administration. But I wanted to own outright the small bit of the margin that Private Label was to enjoy. So I pressed on in January and February 1987, suffering knock-back after knock-back.

I still maintain great respect for Citibank, which taught me so many management, credit policy and banking disciplines – a training for which I remain eternally grateful. But it was clear that all the time I stayed with the bank, the question of whether I had the "bottle" to actually launch this company was constantly on the agenda. It therefore had to be removed, with my business plan substituted.

Then, as happened so many times subsequently in the early years of Private Label, Michael Kelly stepped in. By that time my friendship and discussions with the people at MSL had extended to include Michael's wife, Dee, and his legal director, Barry Field. Michael and Barry were the two other directors when I incorporated Private Label as a new company on 5 February 1987. Dee Kelly, who acted as Finance and Personnel Director of MSL, was (and is) a shrewd businesswoman who, together with Barry Field, was always close behind Michael in his innovative wake, making sure that his ideas and new ventures made financial and legal sense. It was therefore of great comfort to me that Michael, Dee and Barry were unanimous in their offer of an alternative way.

I would join MSL as a consultant. From that base, I would be free to develop the plans for Private Label and talk to funders and distributors. At the same time I would be expected to do a selling job for MSL, bringing in more business. If for any reason Private Label did not get off the ground, then there was the fall-back of a senior level sales and marketing job at MSL. It was on this basis, therefore, that I handed in my notice at Citibank towards the end of March, leaving on Friday, 17 April 1987.

A NEW POSITION

At MSL, my first duty was to earn my keep. I was immediately thrust into a round of pre-booked meetings and presentations that I willingly undertook. MSL was a happy and successful place to be at that time. I must admit that, for a while, the role of self-employed consultant, operating from such a friendly base, caused me to reconsider whether I wanted to go ahead with the Private Label idea. I know that Michael, Dee and Barry would have preferred me to have joined them at that time, but it was characteristic of their generosity that they offered to provide any help they could when I said that I was determined to stick to the original game plan.

Meetings with potential lenders and distributors continued. On 15 May 1987 I had a meeting with Nick Deutsch of First Mortgage Securities Ltd (FMS). Like Michael Kelly, Nick was an entrepreneur who had sold a new concept to a number of institutions.

15

He ran a series of off balance sheet structures made available to insurance companies for origination purposes. This is exactly the structure that I thought I could improve upon. In theory the funders knew about funding and the insurance companies knew about origination, but the subsequent failure of these structures showed that something was missing. Our ultimate long-term survival showed that we were well placed to provide the missing product design/marketing flair that would motivate everybody to sell the products, and position them favourably against the competition.

It was perhaps inevitable that, if I was to get Private Label off the ground, it would take like-minded businessmen to see the opportunity. The big institutions themselves would always be the "second party" in. I continued to meet with other lenders, but – increasingly – FMS looked to be the one. On 23 June 1987 I sent FMS a formal proposal, which was knocked into shape and tabled at the FMS board meeting on 6 August 1987. After such a long and tortuous build-up, I could hardly believe that we were so near to launch. But the FMS board approved the proposal and, on 10 August 1987, I held the very first project meeting to discuss the launch of Private Label Mortgage Services Limited. Whilst Michael and Barry were very interested and active non-executive directors, I knew I needed to get somebody else on board very quickly, because so far there was only me. Fortunately, I knew the person I wanted.

never skimp on promotional material. Always punch above your weight and make whatever you are doing look important and classy

When I was Sales & Marketing Director of Citibank, one person on my team had shone out as somebody really special. Godfrey Blight was quick, bright, strong-minded and a brilliant salesman. It was a massive gamble for somebody who had received two promotions at Citibank in the six months or so since I had gone, to join a new venture like Private Label. Fortunately Godfrey said that he wanted to take the challenge, and the rest, as they say, is history. Godfrey has been my partner-in-crime ever since.

Our first challenge was to produce a corporate brochure by which we could explain our new concept to interested parties. We were breaking the mortgage process down into three component parts – funding, administration and sales and marketing – then putting all the pieces back together again in order to provide a cohesive programme for small insurance companies to take off the shelf and brand. We argued that an insurance company would deal only with the sales and marketing department of a new centralised lender, for example, and they would have the same consistency of contact with us. Behind the scenes, however, *we* would subcontract the key elements rather than have them all in-house.

This was not an easy concept to put across. Indeed, to this day, I still have trouble trying to describe to people at parties what Private Label actually does. But, with the help of a creative agency, we managed to represent the position graphically. We spent thousands of pounds on that initial corporate brochure, money that came straight from my personal building society account! However, it reinforced something that has stayed with me to this day: never skimp on promotional material. Always punch above your weight and make whatever you are doing look important and classy.

We signed up three small insurance companie with whom I had been talking in my capacity as a consultant at MSL: Crusader Insurance, Liberty Life and Provident Mutual. Each company had appointed a manager to pursue a strategy to increase its mortgage presence, and our off-the-shelf package obviously appealed. At the last moment, FMS delivered Irish Life to us – a company with whom they had been in direct conversation – thereby enabling us to launch Private Label officially on 14 October 1987 at a press conference in London with four medium-sized insurance companies already signed. We still regard the date of that press conference as being our official launch.

PRIVATE LABEL IS LAUNCHED

With three separate companies combining to produce one integrated mortgage package, I felt that we needed to do a bit more in order to make this look and behave cohesively. I therefore invited Nick Deutsch to become a director of Private Label, whilst I became a director of the funding vehicle, the innovatively named FMS No. 3 Limited. The CVs of all the directors appeared in the original corporate brochure, with Michael, Nick and I sitting together at the press conference table at the launch. With the help of a PR agency, we had trailed the launch a week earlier, and organised a personal profile of me during the week of launch, in *Money Marketing*. This publicity undoubtedly allowed us to take off far more quickly than the modest size of our operation actually warranted.

If we had been superstitious, of course, then we would have given up after what happened within a few days of our launch. On Friday,

Private Label gets its team all together

PRIVATE LABEL Mortgage Services has appointed Stephen Knight as chairman and managing director, Nicholas Deutsch, Barry Field and Michael Kelly as directors and Godfrey Blight as head of sales.

Knight is a former vice-president of Citibank where he was responsible for the distribution and marketing of mortgages in the UK.

Deutsch is founder and managing director of First Mortgage Securities. His business experience includes London merchant banking and 10 years with McKinsey & Co.

Field is the legal director of Mortgage Systems. Prior to his appointment in 1985, he spent 15 years as a partner in a Hampshire based firm of solicitors.

Kelly is founder and chairman of Mortgage Systems which he has built into the country's largest independent manager of mortgage portfolios.

Blight has joined Private Label Mortgage Services from Citibank where he was a senior account manager in the mortgage banking division.

Money Week, 22 October 1987

Knight signs up four firms

Stephen Knight, the ex-sales and marketing director of Citibank Savings' mortgage division, will this week launch his own mortgage lending company, called Private Label Mortgage Services.

The company has signed up four insurance companies - Crusader, Liberty Life, Provident Mutual and Irish Life - to market mortgage schemes through intermediaries. It is also holding talks with other insurance companies and building societies (Money Marketing, last week).

Knight, who will be chairman and managing director of the new company, hopes to offer between £200m and £250m of funds in the firm's first year.

The funding will be off-balance sheet and will come from First Mortgage Securities. Administration will be carried out by Mortgage Systems. FMS managing director Nick Deutsch, Mortgage Systems chairman Michael Kelly and Mortgage Systems director Barry Field will join the company's board.

Knight says: "We will guarantee a dedicated tranche of funds to insurance companies and also guarantee not to demand a share of life or pension commission. Unlike National Home Loans, we will allow companies to offer exclusive mortgage schemes under their own name."

Knight is the principal shareholder with a stake of £100,000.

Money Marketing, 15 October 1987

Mortgage venture ready for take-off

Stephen Knight, the ex-sales and marketing director of Citibank Savings mortgage division, is believed to be setting up his own mortgage lending company which would market products through intermediaries.

Knight, who is currently working as a mortgage consultant from Mortgage Systems, is understood to have been working on the project since he left Citibank in April (Money Marketing, April 2).

The new company is understood to be on similar lines to National Home Loans and the Household Mortgage Corporation.

But unlike NHL and HMC, which carry out their own funding and administration, Knight's company will employ a specialist mortgage funding vehicle and administrator to carry out these functions.

Money Marketing, 8 October 1987

Private Label taps a gap in the market

PRIVATE Label Mortgage Services is not a name which you are likely to hear unless you are in the business of mortgages.

The idea of the company, dreamt up by 33-year-old Stephen Knight, is that medium sized insurance companies and even building societies can market mortgages in their own names with funding and administration provided by Private Label.

Knight has spent 11 years working for building societies and in 1984 became a vice-president of Citibank, in charge of mortgages: "Mortgages are all I know about. They are my life."

While at Citibank, Knight conducted a survey of the mortgage market in which he predicted the rise of the new lenders - the so called special purpose finance vehicles. He also believed that he could see a gap in the market: these vehicles would not take medium sized insurance companies on board as passengers.

The reason for this was twofold. First the mortgage lenders demanded quotas of business from the insurance companies which were too big for some to handle. And second these companies could not win a triple A credit rating.

The mortgage lenders required a quality credit rating in order to securitise mortgages on the international capital markets. Standard & Poor's, the world's leading credit rating agency likes to do things thoroughly. It needed to know that the insurance companies were capable of paying off the endowment to cover the cost of the mortgage at the end of 25 years. Unfortunately it did not have a rating for Britain's medium sized insurance companies.

Knight's breakthrough came when Standard & Poor's agreed to give a pool of mortgages a high rating, as long as no one company originated more than 25 per cent of the mortgages.

In April this year Knight left Citibank and set himself up as a mortgage consultant working freelance for Mortgage Systems, the mortgage administration company. He used those six months to put a package of ideas to various insurance companies and to run a feasibility study for Private Label.

Stephen Knight has sold a new idea to insurance groups, as Hugh Fraser discovered

He discovered a variety of grievances. The companies did not like using building societies, as it was felt they were their competitors in the savings market. They wanted their own name on the package in order to enhance their corporate image. They were not happy about guaranteeing an interest spread to the mortgage lenders, even at times when the lending rates moved against them. Nor were they happy about fees for setting up a mortgage product.

Knight felt that insurance companies were moving into a position to call the shots: "For too long they have acted as voluntary, free distributors of other people's mortgage products."

First Mortgage Securities agreed to supply funds of the right size in order to attract medium sized companies, and Mortgage Systems agreed to let them tap into their cost effective processing system. Private Label brought these two services together.

Knight describes his products as off-the-shelf mortgages. All the insurance company has to do is set up a central information point to answer customer queries.

So far four insurance companies have been signed up - Liberty Life, Irish Life, Provident Mutual and Crusader - with another 15 companies holding discussions with Knight. There is a further, unexpected source of interest - building societies.

Financial Adviser, 19 November 1987

Mounting interest in Private Label option

by Kate Rankine

Private Label Mortgage Services, the company which allows life offices and building societies to offer exclusive mortgage schemes under its own brand name, is currently holding talks with ten more insurance companies.

Private Label Mortgage Services has already signed up Crusader, Liberty Life, Provident Mutual and Irish Life in a £200m off-balance-sheet funding deal with First Mortgage Securities.

The companies each have funding of £50m from FMS No3, a special-purpose finance vehicle set up exclusively for Private Label by FMS. Mortgage administration is handled by Mortgage Systems in Hampshire.

Private Label managing director Stephen Knight says: "We have been inundated with insurance companies contacting us. They seem to like the idea." He adds that the board will discuss increasing the funding available and may have to restrict its current panel to between six and eight companies.

Crusader, Liberty Life, Provident Mutual and Irish Life will offer two mortgage schemes through intermediaries. There is a standard variable rate mortgage, with an interest rate of 11.15 per cent and a self-certified "non-status" scheme with an interest rate of 11.5 per cent.

Liberty Life began marketing the schemes last week and the other three companies will launch later this month.

Money Marketing, 5 November 1987

Societies debated at Lords

A MOTION proposed by Stephen Knight, chairman of Private Label Mortgage Services, that building societies have lost their way was recently heard at the House of Lords.

The debate was organised by the Chartered Building Societies Institute and sponsored by Baroness Falkender. Roger Anderson, editor of *Money Marketing*, chaired the meeting and the motion was opposed by Mark Boleat, director general of the BSA.

Mr Knight made three main points on why building societies have lost their way. He said they had lost their business to new lenders, failed to respond to new legislation and competition, and as a result had moved into conflict areas.

He also claimed that the legislation they had fought for had only contributed further to their undoing. Capital adequacy and wholesale funds limits are inappropriate, he said. Societies left the market open to new lenders by not offering choice, failing to use securitisation and turning their backs on financial intermediaries. Now that they have moved into conflict areas, such as unsecured lending and estate agency, they were putting their image at risk. In short, he summed up saying societies are jacks of all trades and masters of none.

"Societies have been remarkable in the way they have responded to new market conditions," said Mark Boleat in his response to the motion. Now that the cartel had broken up there was no longer one industry but numerous organisations going off in their own direction, he commented.

Building societies have moved into new areas because the market requires it and, because of their strong customer base, they have done extremely well.

He pointed out that societies had made record profits last year at a time of stiff competition, even taking consideration of the City crash.

He said that they have moved into estate agencies because they are able to collect good business through them and that building societies will improve the image of estate agencies.

A total of 13 voted for the motion and 99 voted against, resulting in the motion being declared lost.

Building Societies Gazette, June 1988

Knight sells Private Label to Abaco

by Pamela Atherton

Stephen Knight has sold Private Label Mortgage Services to Abaco Investments just ten months after launching the company.

The link-up will allow Private Label to bring forward its plans to diversify its products and distribution channels, according to PLMS chairman and managing director Knight.

On price, Knight will say only that he has been paid a small sum initially and that the company will be independently valued in 1990.

The company should fit well with Abaco's existing businesses, which include John Charcol, Provincial Trust, Mortgage Systems and Lloyd's broker Burgoyne Alford.

PLMS mortgage lending - running at £35m in July - will now be funded by Banque Paribas through its subsidiary Paribas Lombard Mortgages at an interest rate of 11.35 per cent. The administration of the mortgage portfolios will continue to be handled by Mortgage Systems.

Charles Wishart of Abaco, Michael Kelly of Mortgage Systems and Private Label sales manager Godfrey Blight will join the Private Label board.

Knight comments: "Abaco opens doors to more funding and, with the prime movers in the mortgage market on board, the synergy will be terrific. Massive expansion will be possible."

One of the first areas of diversification will be the establishment of a consultancy division. "We will provide sales and marketing expertise to insurance companies and financial institutions that wish to become mortgage consultants in the market. We are also keen to expand our building society division," says Knight.

Money Marketing, 11 August 1988

Private Label

Private Label Mortgage Services has passed the £150m mark for new business since the beginning of the year, and is on target for its original forecast of £250m by 31 December.

Private Label's entire panel of 11 insurance companies has switched new applications to Paribas Lombard Mortgages, the Banque Paribas subsidiary which now funds Private Label's new business.

Earlier this month it was announced that Abaco investments had acquired, for an undisclosed sum, a controlling interest in Private Label with Stephen Knight, the founder and chairman, maintaining a substantial ongoing stake.

"We are delighted to have within the group such a successful and innovative company as Private Label," said Charles Wishart, the Abaco managing director, who has joined the Private Label board.

Substantial further expansion is planned in the areas of new distribution, new products and consultancy.

Money Week, 13 September 1988

Michael and Dee Kelly

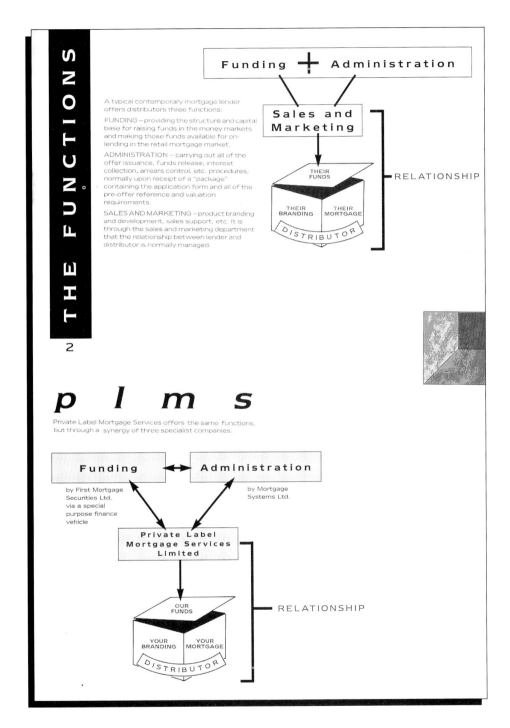

THE FUNCTIONS

2

A typical contemporary mortgage lender offers distributors three functions:

FUNDING – providing the structure and capital base for raising funds in the money markets and making those funds available for on-lending in the retail mortgage market.

ADMINISTRATION – carrying out all of the offer issuance, funds release, interest collection, arrears control, etc. procedures, normally upon receipt of a "package" containing the application form and all of the pre-offer reference and valuation requirements.

SALES AND MARKETING – product branding and development, sales support, etc. It is through the sales and marketing department that the relationship between lender and distributor is normally managed.

Private Label Mortgage Services offers the same functions, but through a synergy of three specialist companies:

Funding by First Mortgage Securities Ltd. via a special purpose finance vehicle

Administration by Mortgage Systems Ltd.

Extract from Private Label's first corporate brochure, released for the first time at a press conference on 14 October 1987.

THE·PEOPLE

10

The Board of Private Label Mortgage Services Limited

Stephen C. Knight
— Chairman & Managing Director

As founder of Private Label Mortgage Services Limited, Stephen Knight is using the skills and experience acquired from fifteen years of specialisation in the UK mortgage market. Having spent the first eleven years in the building society industry he joined Citibank – one of the world's largest banks – and as Vice-President responsible for the distribution and marketing of mortgages in the UK he took their portfolio past £1 billion, lending almost exclusively through third party distributors. Stephen Knight has been associated throughout his career with a number of mortgage product and marketing initiatives and is a frequent speaker at mortgage conferences and a regular contributor of specialist articles to the trade press. He is a graduate by professional examination of the Chartered Building Societies Institute, a Member of the Institute of Marketing and of the British Institute of Management.

Nicholas S. Deutsch
— Director

As founder and managing director of First Mortgage Securities Limited, Nicholas Deutsch has developed the concept of special purpose finance vehicles in the UK and is acknowledged as one of the City's leading experts on mortgage securitisation. His business experience includes London merchant banking and ten years with McKinsey & Co., management consultants, specialising in commercial and investment banking. Nicholas Deutsch is a graduate of Cambridge University [in economics] and of the New York Graduate School of Business Administration.

Barry J. Field
— Director

As legal director of Mortgage Systems Limited, Barry Field has developed a unique insight into the legal implications and requirements arising from new types of mortgage product and contractual relationship. Previously a partner for fifteen years in a Hampshire based firm of solicitors Barry Field became a full-time director of Mortgage Systems Limited in 1985. He is a graduate in law of Birmingham University.

Michael J.R. Kelly
— Director

As its founder and chairman, Michael Kelly has built Mortgage Systems Limited into the country's largest independent manager of mortgage portfolios currently acting for some twenty diverse financial institutions. Michael Kelly has become well-known for not only developing new products and concepts for the UK mortgage market on behalf of his clients, but also for developing the sophisticated computer software in order to administer them. He is a graduate in engineering of Cambridge University.

N.B. Mortgage Systems Limited has a consultancy contract with Private Label Mortgage Services Limited entitling it to appoint at its discretion up to two non-executive directors to the latter's board which is currently being exercised.

Extract from Private Label's first corporate brochure, released for the first time at a press conference on 14 October 1987.

THE SYNERGY 11

Private Label Mortgage Services Limited

– formed principally to specialise in the marketing and distribution of UK mortgages, it is the company responsible for founding and promoting the lending schemes mentioned in this brochure and its principal shareholder is Mr. S.C. Knight.

First Mortgage Securities Limited

– formed to provide special purpose finance vehicles to fund and hold mortgage assets originated by third parties, eventually refinancing through the issue of mortgage backed securities. It is capitalised at £20 million by shareholders' funds provided by Morgan Grenfell, Bank of Scotland, G.E.C. Financial Holdings and F. & C. Enterprise Trust. FMS No.3 Ltd – the special purpose finance vehicle available exclusively for Private Label Mortgage Services Ltd – is owned by a trust with charitable and benevolent objects. The directors are Mr. B.N.A. Weatherill [Trustee], Mr. N.S. Deutsch and Mr. S.C. Knight. The company has been established, capitalised and MIRAS registered, and medium term bank financing and pool insurance has been put in place.

Mortgage Systems Limited

– incorporating the Index Linked Mortgage and Investment Company Ltd which was formed in 1979. It is now the country's largest independent manager of mortgage portfolios with assets under management fast approaching £1 billion. In 1986 a 55% equity holding was acquired by Abaco Investments plc; the balance of shares remaining in the private ownership of the principal directors.

Extract from Private Label's first corporate brochure, released for the
first time at a press conference on 14 October 1987.

16 October 1987 the UK was hit by the worst storm for many a year, with trees struck down all over the country. I for one was unable to get to work on what was only the second full day of Private Label's existence following the press conference. But there was worse to come. On Monday, 19 October 1987 UK shares had more money wiped off their value in one day than ever before or since in the equities market. A stormier first launch week could not have been imagined!

Godfrey hit the ground running when he officially joined on 2 November 1987. He would account manage the four initial insurance companies, whilst I would split my time between their launches and signing up new companies. We had some teething problems with the administration and in ensuring that the mortgage demand we created was in line with the lender's credit policy. Some summit meetings were necessary during those few months, but, in hindsight, it all went off relatively smoothly.

In November 1987 we generated 22 applications, and we were proud of every one of them. In December 1987 we generated 57 applications. As I write this chapter, we consider it a bad day at Private Label if we do not generate 100 applications *in a day*. But Godfrey and I often reflect on whether we enjoy today's applications as much as we did those of the early days.

Just as I had begun to accept that I had finally launched Private Label, I found that we were faced with the most fundamental strategic review of the business within two months. I had continued to see various potential insurance companies during November and December 1987 following the initial publicity, and it was quite clear that we could sign ten as opposed to the four with which we originally launched. The problem was that Godfrey and I could barely service the existing four, let alone launch six others.

The first year budget provided for no extra staff recruitment. Moreover, although I had guaranteed a £100,000 overdraft line to the company, that was all I had in the world at that time. Whilst it was good to have the small to medium-sized insurance company strategy validated in this way, we had little choice but to turn the extra custom down unless we could think of something which had not been a part of our initial plans. And then it came to us.

We would charge the insurance companies a fee. It seems odd, all these years later, when we are paying insurance companies and other mortgage intermediaries more than £100,000 per month to distribute our products, that there was a time when the insurance companies were prepared to pay us. But it happened, and the initial fee that we charged ranged from £10,000 to £25,000.

What this fee income did was to provide the company with immediate extra capital, which we reinvested in people and premises. We approached two of our ex-colleagues at Citibank and recruited Tony Fisher and Tim Hoad to our cause. Tim left us for pastures new a few years later, but Tony is still with us today, now in the role of Marketing Manager. The fees also meant that we could establish our base in central London, as opposed to MSL's offices in Fleet, Hampshire. Luxuries like secretaries and marketing agencies were hired as we went into the spring of 1988, having by then signed 11 insurance companies to our "off-the-shelf, ready-to-brand" mortgage programme.

The biggest life company to sign with us at this time was General Accident (GA). We had entertained vague notions that, having established our company over a few years, we would attract the interest of some of the larger players. But it was evidence of how quickly our integrated programme had established itself in the market that a company like GA had wanted to join, and GA quickly established itself as the number one distributor.

> On Monday 19 October 1987 UK shares had more money wiped off their value in one day than ever before or since in the equities market. A stormier first launch week could not have been imagined!

All these years later, the mortgage market has changed fundamentally, but back then, the main commodity was availability. In one calendar quarter of 1988 the new style lenders captured 50 per cent of new business. After spending over 100 years building up a near-monopoly of the mortgage market, the building societies had surrendered this position to the centralised lenders almost overnight.

The building societies had traditionally channelled all of their marketing and sales resource into the competitive savings market. Depending on how successful they were in any particular year, that is the amount of mortgage money they had available. If this was insufficient for demand then people queued. This was the prime factor that led to the growth of centralised lenders and off balance sheet programmes of the type we helped to pioneer.

Price also played an important part. Funding wholesale, processing centrally and distributing via intermediaries for no payment, saved an enormous amount of money versus the building society model. This meant that the mortgage rate being offered by the new style lenders was at least 0.25 per cent, and sometimes more, below the typical building society mortgage rate. People signed up to the concept that these new structures were for the modern mortgage borrower and that a building society mortgage was "old hat". Of course, it all ended in tears a few years later, but that was the thinking of the time.

Insurance companies needed access to mortgage funds so that their life and pension products could be presented as part of a mortgage package – always an easier sale. Moreover, there was a rush at that time to sign up salesmen and tied agents. Access to competitive mortgage funds was often a factor in determining whether somebody would sign up with a particular insurance company. We were able to give the small to medium-sized insurance companies (and some large ones like GA) access to the same sort of rates and products from which they were excluded under the life company panel deals set up by the high profile lenders such as National Home Loans, The Mortgage Corporation, etc. Indeed, the structure of our programme meant that we could personalise each insurance company's arrangement a little according to taste. With the insurance companies taking the branding, the scheme could be presented as their own in-house mortgage deal, leaving us very much behind the scenes, as our "Private Label" name implied.

> the scheme could be presented as [the insurance companies'] own in-house mortgage deal, leaving us very much behind the scenes, as our "Private Label" name implied

Our role was on the sales and marketing side. The four of us, as it then was, would tour the country helping the insurance company fieldstaff to sell the product, producing scripts, sales aids and analysis of competitor products in very much the same way as we do today. It still amazes me all these years later when I see lenders' sales staff running through the criteria for their particular mortgage product at a valuable field meeting. Introducers can read the criteria from the product information: what they want are scripts, sales angles and marketing help, which is how we have often maintained an edge and generated new business where larger competition has struggled.

Our growth in those first few months was, of course, helped by the withdrawal of double Miras in the 1988 Budget, forward-dated to July. This created a crazy market. House prices were increasing by £5000 or £10,000 during the pre-offer process, with valuers prepared to back the newly negotiated prices. Everybody agrees with hindsight that this period was disastrous for future house prices, but for us it produced more first-year growth than we had expected in our most optimistic predictions.

The fee income poured in as we launched *11* insurance companies. It had never been budgeted that we would be in profit during the first couple of years because we had to wait for the mortgage assets to build up. In what turned out to be an important decision, I had rejected a large up-front fee from the lender in favour of a share of the interest margin and commissions, allowing earnings to build up on an annuity basis over the years. We could not have been more happy as we ran our tiny business from pleasant offices just off the Strand, except for one looming problem. It is a lesson which is as indelibly printed on my mind today as it became then.

STORMY WEATHER

Following the FMS board meeting on 6 August 1987, a project sheet was produced under which the responsibility for drawing up a formal Heads of Agreement was down to FMS. At that time, the Private Label board was meeting monthly and, at each successive meeting, the minutes record that this document was slowly being worked up by FMS and Barry Field into a formal agreement. As Nick Deutsch was a director of Private Label, and I was a director of the lending vehicle, we had agreed to launch without there being a formal contract. The commercial issues – or so we at Private Label thought – had all been ironed out and agreed between colleagues: all that was left was to capture them in a formal document.

The trouble with drawing up an agreement six months *after* launch is that it gives both sides an opportunity to review the partnership with the benefit of experience. This always leads to difficulties. The time to strike an agreement is *before* launch. At that point, both sides want to do the deal and nobody has the advantage of hindsight. It is a mistake I have never made since. Every move that Private Label makes with lenders or distributors is now documented to a level which sometimes frustrates our business partners!

The final draft of the FMS funding contract was one that, with full support from Michael, Barry and Godfrey, I was not prepared to sign. Losing my only funding nine months after launch was a deeply unattractive proposition, but it still looked better than the alternative. FMS therefore said, on 16 May 1988, that Private Label would have to find itself another funder. With 11 insurance companies having invested in their own branded schemes, and with all of Private Label's finances at that stage guaranteed by me, I was under no illusion as to the consequences of this announcement.

I remember that particular day for another reason. The Chartered Building Societies Institute, as it then was, had booked a private room at the House of Lords for that evening so that the motion "This House believes that building societies have lost their way" could be debated. I had been invited to propose the motion, with that eloquent debater Mark Boléat, then Director-General of the Building Societies Association, opposing. My recollection is that I was able to set aside the day's excitement in order to give a fair performance. But I lost the vote by 99 votes to 13, so perhaps I wasn't very good after all!

It is still not clear whether the "find another funder" message was an FMS negotiating tactic or a final decision. Certainly, business proceeded as normal afterwards, with applications coming in, and completion cheques going out. I had decided, however, that the FMS relationship had irretrievably broken down and I set about trying to find a new funder with some urgency.

> Losing my only funding nine months after launch was a deeply unattractive proposition, but it still looked better than the alternative

As usual, Michael Kelly was there to help. Banque Paribas, the French investment bank, had already by then launched itself into the UK mortgage market. A series of subsidiaries had been established, the ultimate aim of which was the same as most of the other investment or merchant bank structures at that time, namely securitisation. However, unlike the off balance sheet vehicles established by FMS, Paribas was prepared to initially take the assets on balance sheet, which provided many funding and credit advantages. My first meeting with Paribas was on 26 May 1988, a mere ten days from the FMS decision, and I hit it off immediately with the two executives in charge of UK mortgages, David Griffith and Charles Greenwood.

We did not want to make the same mistake as before. Therefore, whilst it was possible to agree commercial terms after two or three meetings, it took the best part of six weeks for solicitors to agree the wording of a 100-page funding contract. By the time the solicitors were well into their work, however, there was another excitement: a deadline to work to.

We were told by FMS that funding would be withdrawn from two particular insurance companies in respect of all applications started after the end of July 1988. Again, I do not know whether this was a tactic, but the deadline motivated us all, and we made it with two days to spare, signing with Paribas on 29 July 1988. This enabled me to call all of our insurance companies together for an "important announcement" on 2 August 1988. In keeping with our philosophy of punching above our weight, we booked the Ritz Hotel for a very positive and upbeat presentation on the new facilities we had negotiated with Paribas. There was no mention at that meeting of any problem with FMS: rather, the addition of a new funder was announced and accepted as the most obvious logical next step for Private Label's development.

> the addition of a new funder was announced and accepted as the most obvious logical next step

It helped that, via Paribas, we could offer keener rates and more flexible criteria terms than we had with FMS. The insurance companies responded enthusiastically to the move, and all 11 agreed to immediately transfer new business to the Paribas arrangement. The fact that the subsidiary funding our business had been called "Paribas Lombard Mortgages Limited", so as to have the same "PLM" initials as our company, was a nice touch from the bank, and made it look as though the new arrangement had been a long time in the planning.

On the afternoon of the Ritz presentation, I hand-delivered a satisfying letter to the directors of FMS stating that, in accordance with their request of 16 May 1988, I had indeed "found another funder". By a stroke of luck, both Nick Deutsch and Gareth Jones were on holiday at the same time, and new business had been going to Paribas for quite a few days before they returned. The letter also contained another announcement that caused some surprise. Private Label had been acquired by Abaco Investments Plc.

On 29 April 1988, amidst all the trauma of our funding contract negotiations with FMS, I had received a call to go and see Cameron Brown and Charles Wishart of Abaco. Cameron was a co-founder of Abaco, set up in the early 1970s to acquire owner-managed financial services companies so as to create an entrepreneurial group of synergising businesses. Charles Wishart had been one of the founding directors of John Charcol, one of Abaco's first acquisitions, and was then working for Abaco. Abaco had already by then acquired MSL, Hamptons, Burgoyne Alford and many others in addition to John Charcol. The proposal at this meeting was that Abaco acquire Private Label.

I was both flattered and astonished. The idea that a major public company would wish to bid for our business, which was barely nine months old, was extraordinary. An "earn out" arrangement, promising a generous guaranteed multiple of 1990's pre-tax profits was on offer, generating a cash sum greater than any I had ever thought about, albeit towards the lower end of the sums Abaco was used to paying out.

My initial reaction was that I wanted to paddle my own canoe for a few years yet. But it became increasingly clear in the subsequent negotiations with Paribas – which had a strong corporate connection with Abaco – that this new funder would prefer us to be part of a larger group. My fellow directors were also concerned that, bearing in mind what was planned for 2 August 1988, it might be better to have the resources of Abaco behind us if FMS decided to object. Thus I agreed to the terms offered and, within our first year of business, we became a subsidiary of Abaco.

> Paribas were a delight to work with: straightforward, friendly and very much seeking the partnership approach

In the end, there were no significant problems from FMS. Negotiations went on for many months about outstanding payments due to us which, at one stage, we agreed to forfeit if FMS would strike a more competitive existing borrower interest rate. But thanks to the patience and perseverance of Barry Field, in a valuable background role that he was to play for us time and time again, the terms were finally settled. An early chapter in our business life, so promising at the outset, but so disappointing at its conclusion, finally passed into history.

LIFE WITH ABACO

Abaco were true to their word and never once interfered in the day-to-day running of our business. For our part, we most definitely benefited from the synergising opportunities coming the other way. We signed fellow Abaco subsidiary John Charcol as a branded distributor (our first non- insurance company), and participated in regular product "brainstorming" sessions with other Abaco subsidiaries, some of which bore fruit the following year. Paribas were a delight to work with: straightforward, friendly and very much seeking the partnership approach. Business volumes steadily increased and we appointed five new insurance companies, taking the total to 16, finishing our first year in business with a £79,000 pre-tax profit, against an original expectation of a substantial first year loss.

We were therefore in good shape, and very happy, as we approached the challenges of 1989, a year of higher interest rates and the start of the era of deferred interest mortgage products.

2

1989–1992
ANOTHER CHANGE OF OWNERSHIP AND WHOLESALE GIVES WAY TO RETAIL FUNDING

T he contrast between the years 1988 and 1989 could not have been more vivid. Whereas in 1988 we had diffi- culties with our only lender, having to tread water in order to transfer the funding and survive, the floodgates were now open, enabling us to give full vent to our product innovation. Paribas, whilst being cautious like all banks (for example, we hardly ever received a letter that was not signed by two executives), was nevertheless friendly and open to ideas. The bank had an appetite to build its sterling asset book, and we were well placed to provide the ideas and the distribution.

No sooner had we launched with Paribas than we started work on researching some new product ideas. Given today's product prolifer- ation, it seems incredible now that we were surviving at that time on one product – an ordinary variable rate mortgage with a self certifi- cation option. The rest of the market – particularly the likes of The Mortgage Corporation Ltd, Household Mortgage Corporation Plc, National Home Loans, Mortgage Express and so on – were moving ahead quickly. Through product innovation, we had to catch up and, if possible, get into the lead.

The mortgage market thinking of the time was that, in order to keep the housing market going, customers should be given some relief against rising interest rates. The deferred interest mortgage was therefore born, under which borrowers could pay at a competitive rate, with the difference between the pay and charge rates adding to the loan. This difference – so it was predicted – would become lost in the continuing double digit compound growth in property prices.

We were not to know at the time that the recession of the 1990s would be the worst in the history of the housing market, sending property prices plummeting. With the benefit of hindsight, any deferred interest product was a bad deal. But some were worse than others, and hopefully our approach demonstrated that it was possible to exercise a degree of foresight, even then.

The worst deferred interest product I came across at the time was a 7654321 deal. This permitted the customer to defer 7 per cent in year one, 6 per cent in year two and so on, reducing by 1 per cent each year over 7 years. The reader will not need me to calculate the way in which that sort of formula will add to the original debt. We chose the more modest formula of 3 per cent for 3 years, and took the precaution of having Mortgage Systems Ltd (MSL) state on the offer of advance what the outstanding debt would be after three years. Neither we nor Paribas, therefore, had any of the subsequent complaints so common in the 1990s amongst borrowers who had not understood the deal they had bought.

Yet another factor in our favour at this time was the very structure of our operation. Paribas was only interested in providing the funding and holding the assets. We were required to arrange all of the various block policies, including the Mortgage Indemnity Guarantee cover (MIG). The correspondence shows that it was a painful process at the time, but we nevertheless had meeting after meeting, and wrote letter after letter, to Sun Alliance, ensuring that every move we made was signed off in writing by the MIG insurers. I did not do this in anticipation of a recession, because that was the last thing on my mind at that time. I took this action because our funding structure meant that we were acting as agents for the lender, and I wanted to ensure that our backs were covered.

It all seemed perfectly logical to us, but – rather like our more conservative approach to deferred interest mortgages – it paid us back in spades when the recession hit. Probably the biggest problem in the mortgage market in the recession was indemnity insurers not knowing the risks that had been underwritten on their behalf by mortgage lenders. The subsequent non-availability of MIG cover in circumstances where the lenders thought they were insured, contributed massively to factors such as uncertainty, losses and market withdrawals. It is one of our proudest achievements that this did not apply to any of our schemes, because there was neither a product nor a feature that we offered which was not pre-approved in writing by the MIG insurers.

As we entered 1989 we were deep in three-way discussions with Paribas and Sun Alliance on several innovations which we wanted to introduce at a conference for all of our distributors in February 1989. The low start 3 per cent deferral for three years was the flagship deal, and the first new product innovation to be introduced by Private Label. However, we had also devised a 100 per cent product where a normal 90 per cent loan would be provided by Paribas, with a 10 per cent top-up by Provincial Bank Plc (another Abaco subsidiary).

A split loan of this type was not in itself a major innovation, but our proposed delivery was. We persuaded the top-up lender to accept

> the process was as smooth as a split loan can ever be

the first lender's application form, together with copy references, and to send its mortgage offer to the first lender, so that both offers could then be issued together. Not only could an attractive weighted average interest rate be marketed, generally undercutting the market, but also the process was as smooth as a split loan can ever be, with one application form producing, at the end of the processing line, one envelope containing both mortgage offers.

At that time we were distinguishing between "products" and "features" just as the motor car industry distinguishes between the basic car and the optional extras. Premium Reserve was the first of these "features", establishing a fund to cover the first three or five years' life assurance premiums. The feature could be used in conjunction with the ordinary level interest mortgage, or the Low Start product. It enabled the seller of an endowment mortgage to offer customers the opportunity to have their first few years' life assurance premiums covered and paid direct to the assurance company by the lender, with all the commission certainty that brought about. Over 80 per cent of new mortgages then being written were on an endowment basis, with customers and the press believing that only the unsophisticated borrowers took repayment loans. Premium Reserve was therefore a major attraction to the intermediary market, and we were the first to offer it in that form.

SALES CONFERENCE TIME

All of these new deals were eventually agreed and we held our first ever large-scale sales conference on 7 February 1989. Although we were by then 16 months old as a business, we could not afford to fund the scale of conference we were seeking to put on, with 200 delegates. Embracing our standard policy of punching above our weight, we had reserved a large room at a Heathrow hotel and booked the services of Rory Bremner to provide an after-lunch cabaret. In 1989 Rory was not the famous TV face that he is today, but he was nevertheless well known enough to influence the decisions of potential attendees to come to our sales conference.

Having devised the package, we then sold tickets, even though the principal content of the conference was for us to launch new products! The records show that not only did we achieve 170 delegates on that day, but we also made a modest profit. I hasten to add that all of our sales conferences in subsequent years have been free of charge to those attending. But necessity prevailed in February 1989. It also taught us about some of the techniques necessary to get "bums on seats" at sales conferences, including having some entertainment, which we have put to good effect every year since.

The new products accelerated our growth sharply. Not only did new business start building rapidly, but also yet more insurance companies wanted to join our panel, bringing the total to 21. As spring turned to summer, we added further "features", like drawdown (line of credit), and payment holiday (three months' suspended payments), whilst launching yet another new product – Fixed Payment Stabiliser. This product allowed customers to pay at a 9.99 per cent rate, and to continue with that payment, or adjust it on the serving of one month's notice, unless and until alarm bells rang in connection with the loan-to-value ratio.

With a range of new products, an increasing insurance company panel, and mortgage applications all coming thick and fast, we were establishing ourselves as a serious competitor to the other centralised lenders of the time, even though we were in practice a tiny business. One of the by-products of this era is that we became accepted by many intermediaries as a centralised lender – an image which we had subsequently to fight hard to change. But at the time it suited us, because centralised lenders were still "flavour of the month".

SPREADING OUR WINGS

One of our principal competitors at the time was The Mortgage Corporation (TMC). I normally approach competitors to see if there is a way of working together. Usually there is not, but sometimes a gem of an idea appears. It was in this way that I met Ray Pierce, then number two at TMC, for lunch on 15 March 1989. It was a meeting which would bear fruit a couple of years later.

At the time we were flirting with the idea of operating as a consultancy as well as undertaking our mainstream business. We acted as consultants to Capital Home Loans when they first launched into the UK mortgage market, and also for National Bank of Kuwait during their brief foray into mortgages. But consultancy proved to be a distraction which created fee income rather than enduring assets, and it is not a side to our business that ever really took off.

An interesting new distributor was Solicitors Financial Services (SFS), the company set up by Sedgwicks to provide financial services support to Scottish solicitors. Godfrey and I spent a week touring Scotland trying to persuade the local solicitors to use a branded off balance sheet mortgage programme. In many cases this was too much contemporary thinking to take in at one time, and there were two or three meetings where solicitors turned up, shovelled the buffet food into their briefcases and went, without hearing what we had to say. In truth, to maximise new business in Scotland you have to be a Scottish institution. It's a great market north of the border, but we did not crack it with SFS, and haven't cracked it with any other Scottish distributor since.

> This was still a crazy, booming market, and Private Label was fast emerging as a high profile, if still small, player

By the summer of 1989 we were ready to expand our sales team with the first non ex-Citibanker, and Rod Hamilton-King joined us on 14 August 1989. Whilst business was going from better to fabulous, however, I was now facing challenges in relation to our involvement with Abaco.

British and Commonwealth Holdings Plc (B&C) had for some time held a minority stake in Abaco, and had not up to that stage interfered in the running of their business. In 1989, however, B&C increased its investment and started to take a greater interest in Abaco's day-to-day affairs, seeking to curtail its acquisition activities in certain areas so as to align with B&C's intentions. We were probably the smallest subsidiary that Abaco had at that time, and we only became aware of the issues when we learned that Cameron Brown – one of the original Abaco founders – had resigned, with John Charcol completing a management buy-out away from Abaco.

Cameron had invested in the new holding company which had purchased John Charcol, to be known as Mortgage Group Holdings Plc (MGH). MGH had the intention of building a group of businesses focused on the UK mortgage market where maximum synergy could be obtained. We were the first port of call for MGH, because, whilst part of Abaco, we had synergised with John Charcol more than any other of our fellow subsidiaries in relation to products and distribution opportunities.

Like most deals of this type, a resistance to change clouds the first few meetings from the point of view of the proposed seller. But it gradually became clear to me that we could prosper more as part of MGH than we could by staying with B&C. Also, the guys at MGH were very flattering in their wish for us to join with them, offering me a cash and shareholding package which would eventually make me equal largest shareholder, a group board director and – if not fabulously wealthy – certainly "comfortable". The key was how to extract myself from B&C.

Fortunately at that time, B&C had more important things than us on its mind. We were a small subsidiary where the owner-founder was still managing the business – always an awkward formula unless the personalities are close. B&C said that as long as they could claim a dividend for 1989, and a relatively modest cash payment from me, I could buy back the business. I then set about running parallel negotiations with solicitors during November and December 1989 in a series of top secret discussions where, more than once, I temporarily forgot which set of negotiations I was in. Fortunately, nobody noticed because if B&C had got wind of the price I was selling at, they would never have let me buy the business back so cheaply!

The deal was eventually done on 12 December 1989 and Private Label then became a wholly owned subsidiary of MGH, a status it has enjoyed ever since. It is an interesting exercise to form a business, and then sell it twice in two years. But this was still a crazy, booming market, and Private Label was fast emerging as a high profile, if still small, player. Meanwhile, the following year, B&C went bust, meaning that I would never have achieved my proposed earn-out. Who said that luck counts for nothing in business?

ENTERING THE 1990s

The mood of the market swung significantly as we moved into 1990. The major demand was for fixed rates and, with a falling yield curve, it was possible to give borrowers some certainty, as well as a flavour of the sort of lower rates the market expected (and would subsequently get) over the coming couple of years. We had another one of our large set-piece sales conferences booked for February 1990 and – such was the continuing appetite of Paribas – we persuaded the bank to let us have a one-year fixed rate for launch at those conferences at "cost". In fact, the 13.75 per cent one-year fixed rate we were seeking was slightly below the cost of funds at the time and, in order to secure the deal, we agreed to rebate back to the bank some of our earnings in order to bring the product back to break even. A 13.75 per cent one-year fixed rate does not sound very exciting now, but compared with a 15.4 per cent average building society rate, and with the wholesale-funded lenders charging between 15.95 and 16.95 per cent, it was a very big deal at the time, as subsequent volumes showed.

We also had something else of importance to announce at our sales conferences. As our list of distributors had increased, so the range and type of mortgage demand had diversified. Although Paribas had not undertaken any securitisation issues, its criteria was to AAA standard, just in case. Many applications, particularly where the status or the overall proposition required a degree of flexibility, had to be rejected and were snapped up by building societies. It was clear to us that, if we were able to sign up with one of the more flexible medium-range societies, we would provide an important in-fill to our overall product offering, and take another significant step forward in the company's development.

The introduction to Leeds & Holbeck Building Society came from Paribas. There was an immediate meeting of minds between David Pickersgill, then Assistant General Manager (Finance), and myself as to the opportunities that would arise from our two organisations working together. The Society had already formed a series of subsidiaries with which to attack the intermediary market and one of these – Leeds & Holbeck Mortgage Corporation Limited – would be allocated to exclusively fund the Private Label programme. Our common application form would be accepted and we would be able to offer building society-type criteria, alongside the best centralised lender rates, in one package. We did not know it at the time, but this was to become a model for multi-lender programmes of the future.

The deal was not, however, concluded without a hitch. With our sales conferences due to start on Friday, 23 February 1990, Godfrey and I travelled to Leeds ten days before for the official signing ceremony. All terms of the contract had been agreed, and the bound copies were laid out on the board table ready for signing. As we waited in the room for the arrival of Arthur Stone, the Leeds & Holbeck Chief Executive, there was no hint of what was to follow. But when Arthur came in, we knew something was wrong.

It appears that Arthur had not been consulted as fully as he would have liked by his executives as to the contract's content. At that time, Arthur Stone *was* the Leeds & Holbeck. Instead of completing the formalities, we therefore had to go through all of the changes Arthur required and then go away and have the solicitors prepare a new contract. We had no choice, because everybody was booked to come to the sales conferences and, by then, our distribution list had grown even larger. We did, however, make use of the photographer and pretended to sign the contract, because we needed the picture for publicity purposes. This was the first agreement of its type between a wholly owned subsidiary of a building society and an organisation like Private Label and we wanted to get our PR agency working overtime on the announcement.

We eventually signed a day or so before the sales conferences, and *after* the sales scripts had been agreed. Many of Arthur's new points were unworkable (e.g. no new distributors) and quietly, over time, we agreed ways around various issues with the society's executives. But certainly at that time I was beginning to wonder whether we were jinxed in relation to getting contracts signed. Fortunately we have never had a problem since, so I guess the problems were down to the turbulence to be expected by a small company when dealing with larger institutions.

The ability of one single source, on a common application form, to offer both building society and centralised lender funding was quite a revolution at the time, and those sales conferences of 1990 remain the most successful we have ever undertaken. For the entertainment, we hired a comedian and scriptwriter who is a personal friend. My wife and I first met Terry Morrison when he was appearing live with Hale & Pace, but Terry had by now branched off on his own. Whilst I had announced at the conferences our new six-point customer security plan, designed to show that there would be no cross-selling of life and pension products to customers introduced via our programme, Terry appeared as a training manager for the fictitious Ford Anglia Building Society. In the guise of a cockney street trader, Terry unveiled the imaginary building society's six-point "customer nicking plan". Through the medium of humour we were promoting the fact that a customer handed to a local building society branch might be cross-sold other investment products, whereas this would not happen with Private Label.

> this was the first agreement of its type between a wholly owned subsidiary of a building society and an organisation like Private Label

At that time, customer security was important to intermediaries. Subsequently, when the recession hit, philosophical points like that went off the agenda as intermediaries battled for survival. From being one of our main initial marketing thrusts when we launched

Private Label, customer security is now something we rarely promote, research indicating that it is of little interest to mortgage intermediaries. We still hang on to it as a matter of principle, however, asking all of our lenders to guarantee not to cross-sell life and pension products to customers that come to them via our programme. But I often wonder today how much it really matters to our distribution customers.

Demand took off spectacularly following those February 1990 sales conferences. The 13.75 per cent one-year fixed rate exceeded £150m of new business on its own, representing what was for us an unprecedented new business volume. Indeed, we had to wait until 1997 before any individual product beat that level. On the day the product closed – Friday, 11 May 1990 – we received 167 fully completed application packages ready for offer. This remains a Private Label record for the number of complete application packages ready for offer on any one business day.

At the 1990 sales conferences we also tried our first mortgage incentive. It is difficult to imagine any sales environment outside of the mortgage market where you would see over-supply without a sophisticated incentive programme for distributors. But nobody, to my knowledge, has ever got mortgage incentives right, and I certainly count myself amongst that number. Perhaps the answer is that there is too little proximity between a complicated mortgage sale and the ultimate achievement of an incentive so that the two cannot work well in tandem.

Whilst at Citibank I had toyed with the idea of introducer fees. In 1986 I instituted what now seems to be the ridiculously modest concept of a £40 per completion introducer fee. My competitors of the time reacted angrily and I did little to conciliate, which I now recognise to be an act of immaturity. In any event, the scheme failed because nobody was particularly interested in these fees: indeed, one major insurance company returned a cheque to us for nearly £40,000, saying that it had no line on which to credit the income! After that experience I did not want to introduce procuration fees again, particularly as I was seeking a one-off incentive to give a sales push to the 1990 conferences. I did not want anything that would be a hostage to fortune.

In the end, we chose an unusual package which had been offered to us for entertainment purposes, but which we could not justify without some form of incentive being involved. It was a full day out involving a chartered plane from Luton Airport to Reims, in the heart of champagne country. A tour of a well-known champagne house, with a talk on the champagne-making process, would greet our arrival, followed by a five-course gourmet lunch and then the trip home. We said that the four insurance companies achieving most volume under any of the new products launched at the 1990 sales conferences would be able to nominate their top four salesmen to come on the trip. Since the products we were launching at the sales conferences sold well in their own right, this probably ended up being an entertaining package after all.

On the day of the trip itself, we had our own boarding gate at Luton airport. As holiday passengers queued in June 1990 for their flights to Majorca and Benidorm, the "Private Label flight to Reims" took its place on the board with equal prominence – a very strange sight considering we were still a tiny company. This pleasant sensation was in contrast to two particular problems we had on that trip which would always make me think twice about repeating it. Of the four life companies that won the incentive programme, three used self-employed direct salesforces. Things are much more professional now in the financial services market, but then the professionalism was not so consistent.

> nobody, to my knowledge, has ever got mortgage incentives right, and I certainly count myself amongst that number

The first problem we encountered was when one of the award-winning salesmen turned up at the airport with his wife. Apparently they had only recently been married and she was very jealous of him going on this trip, even though it was quite clearly a business-only arrangement. She had turned up at the airport in the expectation that we would be embarrassed into letting her board the plane with him. We were embarrassed, but there was nothing we could do to help. Every seat in the small, chartered double-propeller plane was taken and the poor lady had to go back home to Surrey. Her husband was clearly not too put out, however, because he still came on the trip.

When we arrived at Reims, the party from one particular direct salesforce then decided that it wanted to stay at the airport. Considering that the noisy flight was the least pleasant aspect of the day's programme, this was an extraordinary decision. The whole point of the trip was to see champagne-making in progress, whilst having a gourmet lunch. But they insisted on staying in the bar at the tiny Reims airport, which is where we found them when we returned for the flight home. Of course, by that time, they were more than a little inebriated. We were barely ten minutes into the return flight when I received a complaint from the captain that the back of the

Private Label offers more comfort to introducers

Private Label, the company which provides branded mortgages for 13 life companies and two brokers, issued a six point plan this week to protect the client databases of its introducers.

Chairman Stephen Knight claimed that it went "far further than any one else in the market to give intermediaries comfort when they introduce a client to a mortgage lender".

The six undertakings are binding on Private Label and its financial backers and Mortgage Systems, the company which administers its mortgages. The undertakings are passed on by insurance companies on Private Label's panel to their intermediaries. The six Private Label undertakings include:

● No cross selling of financial products.

● Separate databases for Private Label's introducers.

● If a client asks for a redemption figure on a mortgage, this will be copied and sent to the introducer.

● If a new lender's reference is required by the client this will be delayed while a notice is sent to the introducer.

● A request for a further advance will be referred to the introducer.

● Any query on a policy will be referred to the introducer.

Mortgage Systems, a fellow member of the Abaco group with Private Label, aims to introduce the same six point plan. It has a number of funding sources which will have to agree to the plan before this can go ahead.

Money Week, 25 January 1989

Deferred interest link-up

Gresham Life and Prolific are offering deferred-interest mortgages in a link-up with Private Label Mortgage Services.

Borrowers can defer 3 per cent interest, paying 10.95 per cent for three years. Repayments can be further reduced by using the Premium Reserve service, which defers endowment payments for five years.

No references are needed for loans up to 70 per cent of valuation.

Income multiples for the deferred-interest loan are 3.5 times principal income plus second or 2.75 times joint.

A 100 per cent mortgage is also offered. It is split into two loans. Banque Paribas provides 90 per cent of the loan at 13.45 per cent, while Provincial Bank supplies the remaining 10 per cent at 15.95 per cent. Admin will be by Mortgage Systems.

Minimum loan is £18,500 and maximum is £150,000. Income multiples are three times principal income plus second, or 2.5 times joint.

Money Marketing, 23 February 1989

Scottish solicitors plan TV ad push

by Jill Insley

Scottish solicitors are planning a TV ad campaign promoting mortgage products and independent financial advice.

Solicitors Financial Services, a co-operative of Scottish solicitors, is launching a £100,000 TV and press campaign to promote financial products offered by its members.

SFS provides advice through a link with Sedgwick Financial Services and has just completed a deal with mortgage marketing company Private Label Mortgage Services. This will provide four different mortgages to SFS members through a panel of 35 life offices.

Private Label managing director Stephen Knight says the mortgages on offer include fixed and deferred-interest schemes as well as a 100 per cent option.

David McLetchie, SFS director and partner in solicitors firm Tods Murray, says the move follows the Government's decision to allow banks, building societies and insurance companies to offer conveyancing to their customers.

Mortgages will be SFS branded. Every mortgage offer - apart from 100 per cent loans - will include an extra 1.5 per cent of the loan value as a contribution to legal costs to be paid to solicitors on completion. The first 12 months' payments will be adjusted to pay back the legal costs contribution.

The ad campaign is expected to run for five weeks from late March, although McLetchie says this may be delayed to avoid the current slump in the mortgage market.

Money Marketing, 18 January 1990

Solicitors to launch range of home loans

by Eric Baird

In a determined attempt to fend off hotter competition from banks and building societies, whose activities will soon extend to conveyancing, Scottish solicitors have formed their own financial services group and yesterday announced plans to launch their own range of home loans.

It is a move the public should welcome, because the effect will be to widen the choice. Better still it reduces the risk of home-buying becoming the preserve, if not the monopoly, of a few large groups which have already bought up the largest estate agency chains.

The new home loans should be available shortly from any of the 260 offices of Scottish firms who have joined the Edinburgh-based Solicitors Financial Services. A co-operative, it was set up two years' ago to provide independent advice and services.

"The solicitor will handle the whole transaction, from initial consultation to handing over the keys," said vice-chairman David McLetchie, who has been heavily involved in planning the scheme.

"We think it will give the solicitor a winning edge over our likely competitors," he added.

Effectively it widens the choice for member firms, who will continue to arrange home loans through established sources, particularly if clients indicate a special preference for them.

"As perhaps one of the last bastions of genuine independent financial advice, our members are now better equipped than ever to put together the best financial package," claimed Mr McLetchie.

There are four new home loan schemes in the SFS Mortgage range, with seven optional variations. They have been devised by a specialist company, Private Label Mortgage Services, set up in 1987 by managing director Stephen Knight, formerly with Citibank.

"We perform a role no other company does," he said, pointing out that administration and funding were sub-contracted out. Lenders include Banque Paribas and others without a retail presence in the UK.

The scheme launches with a base rate of 12.45% for the standard full status mortgage, fixed until June when the normal variable rate will apply. A low-start mortgage will offer a deferred rate of 12.75% for the first three years.

Among other features is an option to spread legal fees and other outlays over the first year, a secured line of credit for up to five years, and a premium reserve and options plan for self-certification and stabilised payments. Up to 100% loans will be available.

"We have added own brand mortgages to the wide choice already available through member firms, to strengthen our market appeal at a time when competition has never been keener," said Mr McLetchie.

He points out, too, that while rivals will be offering a one-stop house purchase for the first time, Scottish solicitors have always done so and backed it with years of experience.

Glasgow Herald, 25 January 1990

• *Central lender signs funding deal with Leeds & Holbeck BS subsidiary*

Private Label is to offer building society funds

by Hugh Fraser

PRIVATE LABEL has become the first contemporary central lender to offer retail funds raised through a building society branch network.

It has signed a funding deal with the Leeds & Holbeck Mortgage Corporation, a subsidiary of the Leeds & Holbeck Building Society.

The building society funds have more flexible lending criteria than the wholesale funds, which are the normal source for central lenders. This is because wholesale funds have to meet stringent lending criteria to securitise mortgages. In particular, L&H can offer 3.5 times income, high equity finance for non-status loans, loans in Northern Ireland, and 125% of the value of discounted Right to Buy council homes. But the recent rise in mortgage rates means that the building society funds will not be more competitive on rates than wholesale funds.

Private Label's wholesale funds are raised through Banque Paribas. The mortgages from all sources will be available on one application form branded with the distributor's name.

Stephen Knight, chairman of Private Label, stressed that intermediaries and direct salesmen for the life companies on Private Label's panel could access the building society funds without fear of their customers being cross-sold a product. L&H has signed the company's customer security guarantee.

The guarantee also means that brokers will be informed if the customer makes an enquiry about redeeming the mortgage.

L&H set up the subsidiary company specifically to acquire blocks of mortgages from foreign banks, which now want to withdraw from the markets.

David Pickersgill, assistant general manager, said: "Two or three years ago foreign banks saw the UK mortgage market as the place to be, but since the downturn there have not been the high yields available."

Pickersgill said that the Society was waiting for new rules from the Building Societies Commission which would allow the society to rate acquired funds as class one assets.

The Private Label deal has provided an outside source of mortgage origination. Pickersgill said L&H was talking to a number of other central lenders.

Money Week, 28 February 1990

Private Label hails new deal and new owner

by Kevin O'Donnell

PRIVATE Label Mortgage Services, a wholesale funder, has been sold twice in one week and is now owned by Mortgage Group Holdings - the parent company of leading intermediary, John Charcol.

Private Label has also announced a new joint funding deal with a building society, the Leeds & Holbeck, to provide mortgages at 14.85 per cent. It is believed to be the first deal of its kind between a building society and a centralised lender.

Both sales of Private Label were completed at Christmas, although details have only emerged now.

The first sale was by owners British & Commonwealth to Private Label managing director, Mr Stephen Knight, who then sold the business a week later for an undisclosed sum involving cash and shares to Mortgage Group Holdings.

Mr Knight now has a seat on the board of Mortgage Group Holdings and retains his position as managing director of Private Label.

"It made sense to be part of a larger group," Mr Knight said.

John Charcol has expanded rapidly in the past year with new commercial mortgage and financial planning divisions.

Mr Charles Wishart, joint chairman of Mortgage Group Holdings, said his group was not on the acquisition trail but would consider "any interesting opportunities".

Private Label, which works through a panel of life offices and intermediaries, believes its new deal with Leeds & Holbeck Mortgage Corporation, the centralised arm of the building society, is the first of its kind in the UK mortgage market.

Financial Adviser, 1 March 1990

Private Label spotlights unique deal

MORTGAGES

ACCORDING TO **Private Label** chairman, Stephen Knight, its **Fixed Cap and Option mortgage** (FC and O) "is the nearest we've got yet to an all singing, all dancing mortgage".

"To my knowledge, it is the first mortgage product to combine a fixed rate, a forward dated cap and the option to exit without penalty," he said.

There are plenty of fixed rates available, and there are lenders who offer to "cap" interest rates, but in return for these facilities, all charge higher than average redemption penalties.

Although there are no redemption penalties, as such, on the mortgage, there is an up front fee equivalent to one month's interest. It is normally added to the loan at completion.

Knight prefers to describe the fee as "an insurance premium". "What better item to insure than your mortgage rate? In any case, one month's interest, added at the start, is less than the redemption penalties charged by most of our competitors for fixed rate facilities," he said.

There are three key elements combined in the Fixed Cap and Option mortgage.

First, a one year fixed rate of 13.45% (typical APR 14.5%) until 1 October 1991. This rate is about 2.5% below the rate charged by centralised lenders and compares with the 15.95% paid by existing Private Label borrowers on wholesale funded mortgages.

Second, from 1 October 1991, the variable rate is "capped" at 13.45% for a year, a period which is certain to include a general election, if it does not take place before then.

The rate will be no higher than 13.45%, but may be below if interest rates have fallen. Knight believes talk of 11% mortgage rates in the run up to a general election is too optimistic, but believes 13% is possible. From 1 October 1992, the loan reverts to the prevailing variable rate.

Third, there is no redemption charge or notice period throughout the term of the loan, once the "upfront" fee is paid.

Should borrowers find the Private Label mortgage uncompetitive in the future, they can change without penalty.

The Fixed Cap and Option is not only available on standard mortgages, but is available on all Private Label products, notably the Low Start 3,3,3 and the Fixed Payment Stabiliser.

With the 3,3,3, the payment rate is 3% below the charge rate for the first three years. So with FC and O, the payment rate will be 10.45% in the first year and a maximum of 10.45% in the second.

With the Fixed Payment Stabiliser, the borrower chooses a payment rate of 10% plus. With the Fixed Cap and Option, this means the maximum amount of interest that will be rolled up during the first two years can be calculated from the outset.

Fixed Cap and Option is not yet available on an interest only basis, but options such as self certification of income, premium reserve and a three months payment holiday are available. Maximum loan to value on the mortgage is 95% and maximum income multiple is 3.5 x main income (less in the case of certain options). The indemnity premiums "are among the lowest in the business", according to Knight.

Money Week, 19 September 1990

• Branded Home Loans will offer innovative products

Private Label, TMC unveil joint venture

by Damian Reece

PRIVATE LABEL and The Mortgage Corporation (TMC) have unveiled a new joint venture company to launch innovative mortgage products with funding raised on the wholesale market.

The company, Branded Home Loans, expects to generate advances in the region of £500m over the next year using securitised funds raised by the treasury department of TMC. Private Label will use the funds to provide own branded mortgages for 15 life company distributors. The life offices will in turn distribute the mortgage products through intermediaries. In addition to extending its funding arrangements, Private Label will use TMC's Portfolio Services for the mortgage administration of Branded Home Loans (BHL).

BHL will offer a range of "contemporary" products which will include fixed rate mortgages, and mortgages with a cap and collar in addition to having attractive exit options.

Private Label chairman and chief executive, Stephen Knight, said: "Centralised lenders are winning back market share through treasury type products which intermediaries can explain easily to their clients."

The company claimed to have increased its own lending by 70% in 1990 through the use of innovative offers while the monetary sector contracted to one third of its 1989 level.

"To continue with this growth, we had to diversify our funding. TMC is the leading and most highly respected centralised lender in the UK," said Knight. This is the first time TMC has

offered stand alone funding after negotiating the joint venture with Private Label for more than a year. TMC will join Private Label's other funder for its "contemporary" products Paribas Lombard Mortgages.

Intermediaries welcomed the move towards a renewed centralised lender presence in the marketplace which had been lacking over the past year. Mortgage brokers said they were looking for attractive fixed rate products from the lenders whose rates have, on average, been higher than the building societies'.

Mortgage IFA with Greig Middleton, Mandy Witt, said the centralised lenders had to move now after being out in the cold for so long allowing the building societies to establish a comfortable position.

Money Week, 6 February 1991

Private Label and TMC in funding link

by Jill Insley

Private label has formed a new funding venture with The Mortgage Corporation.

TMC's treasury department will secure funds for the venture, Branded Home Loans.

Private Label will then design mortgage products according to the terms of the tranches of money. The products will be distributed by Private Label's panel of insurance companies, which will each brand the mortgages to their own tastes.

The loans will be administered by TMC Portfolio Services.

Private Label chairman Stephen Knight says TMC will

provide unlimited funds for the venture but Private Label will continue to draw funds from Leeds & Holbeck Mortgage Corporation for building-society-type mortgages, Security Pacific for 100 per cent loans, and Paribas Lombard Mortgages for central-lender-style loans.

Knight says: "Private Label's lending increased by 70 per cent to £400m during 1990. To continue this growth, we had to diversify our funding."

TMC chief executive Ray Pierce says Branded Home Loans will provide products to protect borrowers against the state of the market, including fixed-rate, capped and collared loans.

Money Marketing, 7 February 1991

Knight in call for action over fraud

Private Label chairman Stephen Knight has called for stringent action from lenders' marketing departments to stop mortgage fraud.

In a speech at the Council of Mortgage Lenders' seminar on mortgage fraud prevention this week, Knight said there had been an imbalance between marketing objectives and prudent credit policy for some lenders.

He said: "The marketing function is at the front end and does not directly cause fraud. However, it can create or prevent the circumstances under which fraud can thrive."

He said a regular forum between the marketing and credit departments would help the lenders present a balanced and united front to the market and would help them respond quickly to changing economic conditions.

He said his own company does not allow any insurance company to distribute the company's loans unless a written agreement is in place, setting out mutual responsibilities and objectives.

Lenders should be more careful in targeting their market with innovative mortgage products, he said, to reduce the risk of the right product going to the wrong borrower who does not need or is unable to cope with the lending requirements.

Money Marketing, 14 November 1991

Lenders start to face up to the home truths

Last week, we used this space to argue that brokers were being unjustly blamed for the problems faced by smaller building societies and some central lenders.

Lenders, we said, must face up to the fact that they bear the prime responsibility for maintaining sensible lending controls. They should not be allowed to get away with shifting that responsibility to brokers whose business they were all too happy to accept at the time.

It is gratifying to see that the lenders seem to agree with us.

Household Mortgage Corporation managing director Duncan Young points out in his letter on this page that the quality of business which lenders get from brokers is no different from that which walks through the door of the average building society. Some will be good, some bad and some indifferent: it is the lender's job to sort out which is which.

Meanwhile, Private Label Mortgage Services managing director Stephen Knight used his speech this week to the Council of Mortgage Lenders to share a few home truths with his colleagues.

Enthusiastic marketing and a neurotic determination to maintain market share at all costs must not be allowed to overwhelm the need for a prudent lending policy, Knight told the CML. Innovative products are fine, but proper underwriting of those products is paramount.

It may seem that much of what Knight has to say is simply common sense. But, if that is the case, then we must accept that many lenders took leave of their senses during the mid-1980s boom.

Lenders which threw all restraint to the winds during those heady days were certainly foolish enough. But any lender which refuses to put its house in order during the current recession, preferring to pretend that its problems are all someone else's fault, is surely more foolish still.

Money Marketing, 14 November 1991

Urging caution before the recession really bit

Unique loan from Private Label

BY DAMIAN REECE

A TEN YEAR fixed rate mortgage at 9.95% has been launched, designed to take the market by the scruff of the neck, according to its author, **Private Label Mortgage Services.**

Stephen Knight's specialist sourcing and packaging company has raised an undisclosed tranche of money with an equally secretive top 10 building society to offer this product, which he believes carries a unique portability feature.

The 9.95% (APR 10.9%) is fixed until 1 July 2002 which makes it the first sub 10% rate fixed for any reasonable length to be launched. But Private Label has also introduced what it feels is a first in transferability.

"With most fixed rate mortgages, the portability aspect would be lost if a higher loan was required at the next property move, but with Private Label's scheme it is guaranteed that the existing 9.95% element can be transferred on, with a new fixed rate to the same expiry date quoted for any further borrowing. This special arrangement also applies to those borrowers requiring a further advance for a home improvement for example," said the company.

A self certification option is available at a slightly higher rate of 10.95% (APR 11.7%). The funding for the product comes from a building society new to Private Label's panel of lenders. The product itself is being made available through a select group of outlets through which intermediaries can place business.

The life offices involved are Legal & General, General Accident, Scottish Provident, Equity & Law, MGM and Laurentian.

Loans are available from a minimum of £15,500 to a maximum of £250,000 within criteria, at income multiples of three plus one or 2.5 x joint up to 95% of the property value. Loans of more than £250,000 will be available subject to individual negotiation of each case. An arrangement fee of 1% of the loan will be charged and can be added to the advance itself. To qualify for the new rate the lender will require its payment protection cover and buildings and contents insurance to be taken out by the borrower. While the margins being taken on this product by the lender are narrow indeed, at least they are not negative, argued Private Label.

Having witnessed some lenders recently targeting first time buyers with lending rates significantly below deposit rates, Knight believes this is an effective way of building up volumes of business and generating interest in the market while maintaining a profit, be it a significantly reduced one.

"UK borrowers must now make up their minds. Either interest rates are going to defy gravity, and history, and continue falling after the election, or they will revert to form and start rising again at some point. Our new fixed rate offer, launched in the immediate pre-election period, gives borrowers the opportunity to book their places among the sub 10% elite, or take their chances politically and economically," said Knight.

A generous redemption penalty of three months' interest throughout the whole 10 year fixed rate term is also part of the offer.

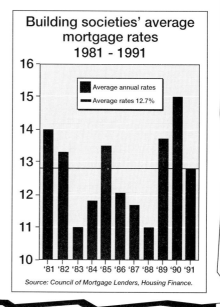

Building societies' average mortgage rates 1981 - 1991

Legend:
- ■ Average annual rates
- ▬ Average rates 12.7%

Source: Council of Mortgage Lenders, Housing Finance.

Money Week, 25 March 1992

Knight offers novel interest rate hedge

STEPHEN KNIGHT'S Private Label mortgage operation has become the first provider to create a product which allows borrowers to hedge their bets against the effects of fluctuating interest rates.

The company's new Bull Bear Mortgage achieves this by placing half the repayment on a fixed rate and half on a variable rate.

Knight said: "The bulls think that interest rates will carry on falling, so they are taking out building society variable rate mortgages with discounts. The bears think that history will repeat itself and that rates will rise again, so they are taking fixed rate offers at anything around 10%. The Bull Bear Mortgage is for the majority of us, who simply don't know what will happen and who therefore wish to hedge both options."

At launch, the rate for both the fixed and variable rates will be 9.99%. The fixed rate lasts until September 1995. The variable element represents a discount of 0.71% from the lender's standard variable rate of 10.7% until end of January 1993. After that, the variable rate will move in line with building society rates generally.

The product will be sold through mortgage intermediaries and Private Label's panel of life office distributors. The confidential funding source for the new product is a top 20 building society which has signed an exclusivity agreement with Private Label barring it from selling it through branches.

Minimum loan is £40,000, maximum £200,000. Redemption penalty is one month's interest during the fixed rate period. The loan to value figures are 95% for purchases and 90% for re-mortgages.

Mortgage brokers welcomed the innovation. IFA Geoff Buckingham said: "It is an interesting and innovative concept that deserves to succeed."

Money Week, 20 May 1992

Private Label's interest double

By Mike Goodman

THE EVER ingenious Private Label Mortgage Services has devised two new products which try to provide borrowers with protection against interest rate rises, yet provide room for manoeuvre if interest rates fall.

Stephen Knight, Private Label chairman, said the assumption that the ERM would produce a gradual reduction in base rate has disappeared.

In fact it is the ERM which is causing the current upward pressure, he said.

"Measured by terms offered to new customers, mortgage rates have already gone up as in August a whole batch of fixed and capped rates below 10% were withdrawn."

Knight described the two products as complementary, as one is a three year cap and collar, the other a six year step down fixed rate. The first provides short term protection against rises in mortgage rates but still offers good value if they fall, the second a long term protection against rate rises coupled with the certainty that payments will fall.

The three year cap and collar offers a 10.95% cap rate and a 6.95% collar rate until 1 September 1995. "This represents an unprecedented 4% differential between the upper and lower limits," said Knight.

In addition, there is a 0.75% discount on the lender's variable rate for the first six months, which means the initial rate is 9.95%.

The £195 arrangement fee is the same as for a normal variable rate loan.

Knight is optimistic that these features address the main reservations intermediaries have about cap and collar schemes.

"In particular, when the initial rate is the same as the capped rate, intermediaries suspect the lender will always set its variable rate at a rate equal to or near the cap. With this product, the initial rate is 1% lower."

The six year stepped down offers an average rate of 9.66% over the fixed period. There is a £395 arrangement fee. The rate is 9.99% for the first three years, 9.49% for the following two years and 8.99% for the final year. The typical APR is 11.6%.

Knight said Private Label used a top 20 building society for the cap and collar and a top 10 society for the six year step down.

Both schemes are portable but the redemption penalty is three months' interest for the cap and collar during the first three years and six months' interest during the first six years for the step down.

The three year cap and collar offers a maximum loan to value of 95% for purchase and 90% for remortgage, while the six year stepped down offers 95% maximum loan to value.

For the cap and collar, the lender insists on arranging home and contents or payment protection for the first two years, and for the step down, it insists on both home and contents and payment protection.

Both products carry a £35 reservation fee but Private Label will warn introducers when two thirds of the funds have been allocated, so they will know when funds are running low.

The products will be available through the 18 life offices on the Private Label panel.

Money Week, 2 September 1992

Rod Hamilton-King (far right) was the first non-Citibanker to join Private Label's sales team.
From the left are Tim Hoad, Godfrey Blight, Stephen Knight and Tony Fisher. Autumn 1989

Arthur Stone (left), Chief Executive of Leeds & Holbeck Building Society, and Stephen Knight, Chairman of Private Label, sign the funding agreement between Private Label and Leeds & Holbeck Mortgage Corporation Ltd – the first agreement of its type in the UK mortgage market. Spring 1990

Signing the funding contract with Branded Home Loans (TMC). Seated are Ray Pierce and Stephen Knight. Standing are Susan Hill, Roland Ward and Janet Milton from TMC. January 1991

Godfrey Blight accepts one of Private Label's Your Mortgage *(formerly* Which Mortgage*) awards for product innovation. Presenting the award is BBC broadcaster John Humphreys. To Godfrey's left is Andrew Stuart, Editor of* Your Mortgage *magazine.*

Judy Lawrence
Previously Head of Administration at Branded Home Loans, now
in a senior management post at Private Label.

The Branded Home Loans trading style used a logo and colour to differentiate it from The Mortgage Corporation.

plane, where these people were seated, was no longer a safe place for the stewardess to go. We had a word with them and they quietened down a bit, with one of our people accompanying the stewardess every time she had to go to that part of the plane. It was certainly a memorable trip and, as ever, a typical Private Label promotion that punched above its weight in terms of image awareness. But I can't say that the incentive achieved much, and I didn't fare much better five years later when I tried my hand again at a spectacular mortgage incentive. More of that later.

MOVING AHEAD

Meanwhile, being part of the same group as John Charcol was paying off in many ways. We started to attract the attention of the larger insurance companies, who had previously assumed that we were small to medium-sized insurance company specialists. The likes of Standard Life, Scottish Provident, Equity & Law and Royal (as the latter two then were known) signed with us. Later in the year we secured a really big prize: Legal & General. We had to take on three more salesmen, the most significant appointment being that of Simon Knight, who is now a main board director of Private Label. There are still people today who think that Simon is a relative of mine (which he isn't), and given that there is only a ten-year age gap between us, I am most offended when people ask whether he is my son!

Two further developments in the summer of 1990 proved that, whilst the depth and nature of the subsequent recession were not predictable by mere mortals like us, there were nevertheless business arrangements which would never make sense, whatever the market conditions. One such arrangement related to a company specialising in Right-to-Buy. Tenants had to pay a fee, and start an endowment policy, before the Right-to-Buy paperwork was complete. Once the mortgage was available, home improvement salesmen went in for their bite of the flesh. This company was extracting many thousands of pounds worth of commission out of the same customer and gearing their business for this apparent constant supply of future income. We did not like the proposition at all. We refused to entertain the deal at a time when many lenders were providing funding for this company.

We took the same view of a firm of brokers who were specialising in remortgages where they, too, were attempting to extract too much money from the same customer. Their business similarly subsequently fell apart. When news of both companies' demise hit the press, we were delighted to be able to report to Paribas at the time that there was no exposure to either organisation. We have made our fair share of mistakes during the years we have been in business, but our reputation in avoiding all the nastier areas of lending has been pretty consistent.

We replaced the record-breaking 13.75 per cent one-year fixed rate deal with a Fixed & Capped product. Rates had fallen a little and we were offering a 12.75 per cent fixed rate for one year, followed by a cap at the same level for the next year. The formula of a fixed rate followed by a cap was one that we would successfully use several times in the following years. It is the right combination for an interest rate environment where rates are high or rising in the short term, but where people see possible rate reductions on the horizon. The new product continued our volume momentum as we saw 1990 out.

As the salesforce had increased, Godfrey was taking more control. I was rarely required in the field, which meant that I could concentrate on the areas which I enjoyed most – product development and lender liaison. Godfrey and I continued to work largely in this way over the years and, if you asked me to name a leading industry exponent on the skills of selling mortgages into the intermediary market, I would not put myself forward. I would unhesitatingly nominate Godfrey Blight. Some four years later, Simon Knight would take on the role of Sales Director, picking up many of the skills that Godfrey has taught him, with more than a few interesting variations of his own. The quality of people we have been able to attract to senior management level within the company has undoubtedly been the cornerstone of the success that has brought us to our current market position.

> We have made our fair share of mistakes...but our reputation in avoiding all the nastier areas of lending has been pretty consistent

I used the extra time on my hands in 1990 to nurture the TMC relationship, which had begun with that Ray Pierce lunch the previous year. I had the idea that we could easily replicate with TMC the arrangement that we were enjoying with Paribas. Whereas the French bank was using MSL to complete the administration loop, TMC had started its own third party administration company and could therefore provide both the funding and administration aspects of the arrangement. My diary shows that I met with the senior people at TMC at least once a month on average during 1990, with neither side entirely sure about two would-be rivals getting together in a joint venture, but both feeling that there could be some synergy. It needed an external event to inject sufficient spark into the negotiations to move on from the "strategic" to "formal contract and launch". This event was to occur on Christmas Eve 1990.

As we went into the final month of the year we were feeling very good about life. We had achieved record volumes and our pre-tax profits were continuing to grow substantially, from £180,000 in 1989 to £600,000 in 1990. At that time, only a small part of our income was represented by an up-front payment from the lender. The majority of our earnings was still derived from a growing portfolio producing interest margin and general insurance commissions. At no time had we contemplated taking our earnings in the form of an up-front fee, because it did not seem logical. Our role was to create longstanding performing assets for the lender, so it was only natural that we should be paid in proportion to our ability to achieve that goal. What we did not know at the time was that we were establishing the structure which would allow us to survive and prosper during the recession.

THE RECESSION

When the recession finally hit us towards the end of 1991, new business plummeted. Rumours abounded at the time that Private Label was struggling in the few years that followed. Certainly our new business didn't grow much, in line with a shrinking market. But the income derived from the portfolio of loans built up during the period 1987–91, and not redeeming, was creating substantial profitability. We could have stayed on the beach throughout 1992 and 1993 and still made a six-figure profit. In practice we maintained a high-profile presence and achieved just under £400,000 per annum pre-tax profit as an average between 1991 and 1995 inclusive. Taking only a small part of our income up front, and not recognising the rest of it until it was paid in cash terms, was one of the most prudent and sensible steps we ever took to establish the financial security of the business.

On Christmas Eve 1990 David Griffith, the Executive Director in overall charge of mortgage lending at Paribas, advised me that auditors were descending from Paris on 2 January 1991 to look at the mortgage book. In fact, delinquency on the various Paribas portfolios we had originated was better than average. But, a couple of months earlier, Paribas had pulled out of the 100 per cent scheme because of its continuing concerns about the UK housing market. This is when the true benefit of having more than one lender on board was revealed, for Leeds & Holbeck picked up where Paribas left off in a very smooth handover. I was, however, incredulous when I was told that our lending with Paribas had, for the first time, at the end of 1990 (some two years after the relationship had started), been converted into francs in terms of assessing the bank's exposure to us. When the figures ran into billions, alarm bells had apparently started ringing.

The cumulative effect of all of these developments made me very concerned to receive David Griffith's Christmas Eve warning. I was so troubled over that Christmas that, on Boxing Day, I faxed a long handwritten commentary to David from home on why the bank should not panic and stay with the market to trade through the problems. But I guess I knew that this was a lost cause because I began to accelerate our TMC discussions as soon as I returned to work in the New Year. Considering we had been speaking to TMC by then for nearly two years, events now moved at an extraordinary pace.

Paribas decided that the bank would exit the UK mortgage market so far as new business was concerned. Although our funding contract effectively required 12 months' notice, Paribas told us on 18 January 1991 that the then existing new business offer would close on 8 February 1991, and not be replaced. Although, technically, funds would continue to be available under the contract, the loans would have to be at the full variable rate. The

> It was an example of how like-minded people who want to do a deal can ensure that everybody else falls into line

market had by then moved on, such that virtually no new business was being achieved without a discount or a subsidised fix. Fortunately, with fantastic co-operation from Ray Pierce, by then Chief Executive of TMC, and Barry Meeks, then Managing Director of TMC Portfolio Services (the third party administration arm), we had got the funding contract in shape and signed the previous day, on 17 January 1991. This contract was considered so important to TMC that I was invited to Leeds Castle to make a presentation to all of the TMC management, after which I was presented with a silver decanter inscribed to the occasion. It was an example of how like-minded people who want to do a deal can ensure that everybody else falls into line, and I remain good friends with both Ray and Barry to this day.

We managed to get the administration in place ready for the new venture to take new business from 1 March 1991. There was a two-week period in February when we effectively had no funding (other than the relatively useless offer of loans at the full variable rate), but somehow Godfrey and his sales team managed to paper over that particular crack and we experienced no problems (and, more importantly, no adverse publicity). The need to obtain replacement funding at short notice on decent terms with one foot over the cliff, however, was not an experience I wanted to go through at all, let alone twice in three years. It is why we work so hard at the present time to maintain live funding contracts with several major lenders simultaneously.

ENTER BRANDED HOME LOANS

We repeated the tried and tested fixed and capped formula when launching our first product with Branded Home Loans, the trading style given to the joint venture between us and TMC. A distinctive green logo was developed to demonstrate that this was a different programme to TMC's. Of course, it meant that Mortgage Systems Ltd (MSL), who had been such a close partner with us throughout our business life to date, would receive no new business under the TMC arrangement. We were able to renew the relationship with MSL a year later when we signed them as our branded, subcontracted packaging arm, and again in 1995 with Kensington Mortgage Company providing funds. However, although the two companies have always remained close, the year 1991 marked the end of an era so far as Private Label and MSL were concerned.

We had no time to organise large-scale sales conferences to announce the launch of Branded Home Loans, although we did fix up some short-notice presentations in London and in the north of England. Thinking laterally, we therefore decided to compensate for the lack of face-to-face contact by producing a video to promote our first TMC product. The idea was that the videos be given free of charge to intermediaries. They would then play them to customers and the videos would sell the deal for them. This meant

> every word of the script, and every flicker of the screen, had to be approved by two sets of lawyers – ours and TMC's

that every word of the script, and every flicker of the screen, had to be approved by two sets of lawyers – ours and TMC's. A great lesson in dancing on a pinhead, if ever there was one.

We survived that process and the video was very well received by all of our distributors. It was such an unusual and high profile thing to do that everybody forgot that there was yet another change of funder, this time from Paribas to Branded Home Loans. We all agreed that Tony Fisher had the best speaking voice amongst us, so Tony went into the studio in order to read the script we had written. We commissioned an advertising agency to produce the promotional material, and Lucian Camp – then of DMB&B Financial – came up with one of the funniest and best pieces of copy I have ever seen in connection with a mortgage product. Under the headline "We've fixed it. We've capped it. And now we're plugging it", Lucian success-fully sold the benefits of the product and ended by inviting interme-diaries to apply for the video with the line "So not only have we fixed it, capped it and plugged it. We've now got it taped".

We quickly built our Branded Home Loans relationship beyond the £100m mark, with the help of some first class processing. The user-friendliness of the individual staff members, and the speed of turnaround, was the best we had ever received, and showed why the centralised lenders were more in tune with the needs of the interme-diary market than the building societies of the time. The person running our particular department at Branded Home Loans was Judy Lawrence, and it was on the strength of this performance that we recruited Judy a year later. I am pleased to say that Judy is still with us in a senior management position.

As we approached the end of 1991, having developed several clever treasury-based products with Branded Home Loans, it became clear that the recession was really starting to bite. Understandably, people were tending to leave their money in building societies, almost irrespective of the rate of interest being paid. This gave the building societies the upper hand on funding – a development which I had seen happen in the recession of the late 1970s and early 1980s. I realised that we would need to get a funding arrangement going with a large building society, if we were to survive the recession. In order that I could concentrate more on signing some building societies, and to more clearly define our day-to-day roles, Godfrey was appointed Managing Director on 1 January 1992, whilst I became Executive Chairman. This coincided with the ideal new lender opportunity.

By the end of 1991, Rod Hamilton-King, our first externally recruited salesman, had left us and applied for a job with the newly formed central lending arm of Britannia Building Society. The person heading that particular operation at the time, Barbara Schonhofer, rang me for a reference. I was happy to give the reference, but what I was more concerned with was meeting Barbara and asking whether Britannia would like to fund our programme. This was not on Barbara's mind when she called, and it was an example of a lesson I had been taught years previously, that is,

"Never accept the other person's agenda. Always feel free to substitute your own."

I met with Barbara at the beginning of January 1992, and there followed a swift series of meetings with her boss, Neil Rawlinson, and his colleagues at the Britannia head office. A funding agreement was signed within a month, and we were able to put to Britannia something that we had been trying to launch for some time, namely a ten-year fixed rate. This happened to suit the treasury position then being held by Gerald Gregory (Britannia's Treasurer). With the interest rate subsidised by the use of compulsory accident, sickness and unemployment insurance and buildings and contents insurance, we managed to get a 9.95 per cent ten-year fixed rate out into the

> the deal you do with one set of people can look completely different to their successors

market just as the 1992 general election was announced. During that campaign, the Conservatives were using the advertising phrase "Double Whammy" to indicate Labour's alleged tax plans. John Charcol took up the phrase and advertised the ten-year fix on the front page of *The Times* on the basis that this deal would see applicants through two general elections. So popular was the deal that we had a queue of couriers snaking outside our building and into the street, bringing reservations on behalf of mortgage intermediaries. We closed out on the deal within a few weeks.

The high volumes achieved obviously meant that we could represent a significant player for Britannia. Understandably, the Britannia senior management therefore wanted to meet with us before signing off a new high-volume product. This took a little time to organise and was a frustrating wait. But we obviously passed muster because the next Britannia product was agreed the day following our meeting, and we launched a step-down fixed rate, allowing customers the opportunity to go down from 9.99 per cent in 0.5 per cent steps to 8.99 per cent over six years. We were fortunate enough to be advertising this product on "white Wednesday" – 16 September 1992 – when interest rates went up, temporarily, by 5 per cent on the one day, preceding sterling's exit from the Exchange Rate Mechanism. Our advert carried the headline "The Chancellor hopes for interest rate cuts over the next few years. We guarantee them", and this product sold out as spectacularly as the ten-year fix. Private Label in partnership with Britannia was obviously a lucky and winning formula, as has been proved time and time again by new business we have undertaken together over the years that have followed exceeding £1 billion

Our timing could not have been better because, in the spring of 1992, TMC was not a nice place to be if you weren't a number cruncher. Ray Pierce and Barry Meeks had left the company to pursue successful careers elsewhere. This left the accountants in charge, and such a formula is always likely to create a lending policy of "The answer's no. Now what was the question?"

By the summer of 1992 we were enjoying considerable success with Britannia and therefore ended our relationship with Branded Home Loans by mutual consent. Another lesson had been learned: the deal you do with one set of people can look completely different to their successors.

In October 1992 we also signed a funding agreement with Bradford & Bingley Building Society. This had come about after several years of on-off discussions. Initially, the only product in which we could interest Bradford & Bingley was to provide the first loan under our 100 per cent product, and then only on a 75/25 per cent first loan/top-up deal, with Sterling Credit providing the second charge advance. This was our third change of lender providing the first loan under our 100 per cent product, as Leeds & Holbeck had by then withdrawn from this 100 per cent arrangement. We were virtually alone in offering a 100 per cent mortgage in the market at that time, and we were able to generate acceptable levels of business for Bradford & Bingley whilst strongly supporting Britannia. At the same time, decent levels of new business were being generated for Leeds & Holbeck on a range of fixed and discounted deals. The result was that, as we went into 1993, we had shifted our entire funding from centralised-type wholesale arrangements to building societies.

AWARD-WINNERS

In addition to signing Bradford & Bingley there was another piece of good news in October 1992. A letter arrived from the Editor of *Which Mortgage* (as it was then called) explaining that its panel of 100 inter-mediaries had voted Private Label as the winner of that year's "Most Innovative Lending Organisation" award. This particular category, which the magazine had originally called "Most Innovative Lender", had been started that year. The title of the award itself had been changed to accommodate the fact that we were not a lender.

These awards are one of those clever marketing ideas that benefit both publication and recipient simultaneously, and we were not shy about announcing in our sales and promotional literature the news that we had won this award. In an overcrowded market where innovation is key, we were very happy that a panel of our customers – mortgage intermediaries – had voted us into this position.

I never dreamt that we would win the award again. To be regarded as the industry's top innovator in the face of fierce competition is not easily sustainable. Yet we did win the award again in 1993, in 1994 *and* in 1995. In fact, we won it for the first four years of its existence, and were only pushed into second place in 1996 by Mortgage Trust with their clever and very innovative Early Payment Plus product. Awards like these – expensive though they are to win, in terms of updating stationery and publicity – are a useful barometer of the impact you are having on your target customers.

CHANGES AFOOT

Whilst all this was going on, it was quite clear that the insurance companies, who had hitherto undertaken all of the pre-offer packaging at their own expense, were no longer prepared to continue on that basis. A major structural plank in the financing of our company, namely insurance companies picking up all of the front end costs, was about to go away, never to return. Although our finances were getting stronger due to our new business success and the stream of earnings being generated from the existing portfolios, we had insufficient capital at that time to launch a major pre-offer packaging service in-house. Moreover, we wanted to learn more about the profit dynamics of such a business before jumping in with both feet. We therefore entered into an 18-month arrangement with MSL (by then known as Homeloan Management Ltd, having been acquired by Skipton Building Society from B&C), which we launched on 12 October 1992.

The new service was voluntary. The insurance companies could continue to package if they wanted to. However, those that no longer wanted to provide this service could send raw cases to HML. The service was badged to Private Label and delivered in our name. It represented no turning back on a significant new development. We were no longer just a "Mortgage Design and Distribution" sales and marketing company: we had now been forced to add pre-offer packaging to our core function. And, again unknowingly, we were the forerunner to a subsequent trend, this time the trend for the launch of so-called packaging companies.

We could, of course, have had the insurance companies deal direct with the lenders. But this isn't my concept of a multi-lender programme that works. We were used to holding the whole programme together, and fronting it. The prospect of lenders offering different service standards to, and dealing directly with, our distributors, with no opportunity for us to switch between lenders, did not appeal. We had no choice but to change the face of our business fundamentally and irrevocably.

CHAPTER

3

1993–1997
A NEW SHAPE AND THE TENTH ANNIVERSARY

T he first challenge of 1993 was an office move. We had outgrown our Brettenham House headquarters, but were determined if possible to stay in the Covent Garden area. In the summer of the previous year, suitable premises to house all of the group had been found in Great Queen Street and, on 25 January 1993, both Private Label and John Charcol moved into the premises where we can still be found today.

From the point of view of the commercial property market, the move was timed perfectly, and for that we have John Garfield – Chairman of John Charcol – to thank. Having lived and worked in central London all of his life, John has a much better feel for a commercial property deal than I, and he secured a reverse premium of staggering proportions. This financial injection into the group in the heart of the recession was a most welcome development.

It was also in January 1993 that the group board asked me to become a non-executive director of John Charcol. This was something that all sides had previously resisted, mainly because Private Label sources its business from the intermediary market and I did not want to create the wrong impression. The fact is that then, as today, John Charcol trades at arm's length with Private Label, with the group deliberately *limiting* the amount of business that the two subsidiaries undertake with each other. This is to maintain the independence of both organisations. But we had been part of the same group as John Charcol for almost all of our existence – firstly with Abaco/B&C, and then with MGH – and had demonstrated that there were no special favours or secrets shared. I therefore joined the John Charcol board in January 1993.

It has been a very happy association. For my part, I have learned a lot more about the needs and interests of the mortgage broker serving the public directly, and have been able to hone even more sharply my product design skills. For their part, my fellow John Charcol directors often say that my structured approach to management has helped their business evolve. But they may be being kind to me. Nonetheless, the association has certainly enhanced the skills base of both organisations, enabling us to better serve our respective customers.

Despite the office move and these extra responsibilities, I was determined that the company would never again be exposed to one funder. We had escaped from First Mortgage Securities to Paribas, only to find that we had to repeat the exercise from Paribas to Branded Home Loans. With our reputation growing, I resolved that 1993 would be the year to introduce some new lenders to spread the load. My business diary records conversations started with no fewer than 14 banks, building societies and centralised lenders over the year. Eight of these negotiations were successful either in 1993 or in the years that followed. We were also the first to sign a contract with a subsidiary of Barclays Bank, as the bank attempted to relaunch a version of its previously successful intermediary-based lending operation, which had been closed in the recession. However, despite the contract being signed, the launch never took place. As this book goes to press, some four years on, Barclays have still not relaunched an intermediary-focused mortgage business.

> the association has certainly enhanced the skills base of both organisations

Inevitably, some of the new lenders were more successful than others. It was in 1993 that we first started talking to the Halifax, but it was not until 1996 that we launched with Halifax Mortgage Services Limited, now one of our largest lenders. We tried very hard to effect a successful launch with all of the new lenders, but inevitably did not quite get our product and distribution ideas aligned with the needs of all of them. The fact is, however, that we ended 1993 with more than double the number of lenders with which we started the year, and this depth of lending is now a permanent feature of our programme.

We continued to specialise in insurance company schemes as the main distribution focus, and were pleased to sign Scottish Life in 1993. Through Scotlife Home Loans, Scottish Life has long specialised in the mortgage market and, after a brief flirtation with Appointed Representatives, has returned to specialise in the market it knows best, namely Independent Financial Advisers (IFAs). Scottish Life is a demanding account, but the company offers a special kind of value added service to IFAs and has rarely delivered less than £50m of new business to us each year since we launched with them in 1993.

An insurance company specialising in the mortgage market was, however, becoming a rarity. Fewer and fewer life offices were seeing mortgages as significant to their growth plans. Indeed, this trend had been one of the reasons that insurance companies were no longer interested in controlling the crucial front end pre-offer process. In previous years our distribution strategy had been to concentrate on a panel of life offices and to tell any intermediaries approaching us directly to re-approach one of the life offices. But a change of distribution strategy was clearly necessary, and would be permitted as we were then in theory able to accept raw applications from the market at large for the first time in our history.

INTRODUCING PREFERRED INTRODUCERS

We started this move tentatively by signing direct with selected brokers, whom we called Preferred Introducers. These were the intermediaries who were allowed to deal with us direct: those not on the list would continue to be referred back to the life offices. We maintain our Preferred Introducer panel to this day, although we are still searching for the formula which really clicks, and which will encourage these introducers to place most of their mortgage business with us.

We had two problems to address before being able to maximise business from the market at large. The first was that research we had commissioned via a marketing agency had revealed that most people in the market still hadn't heard of us, and those that had thought we were a centralised lender. The second was that, without blame on either side, it was proving impossible to subcontract our culture and multi-lender approach to HML.

In the spring of 1993, John Meakin had approached me to discuss the new marketing and advertising firm he had started. Previously with Hill Murray, John was doing what all small businessmen need to do if they are to get their businesses off the ground: contact prospective clients and offer to do something which adds value to their business. In our particular case, John was offering to fund some research into intermediaries' perception of Private Label and to craft an advertising campaign in the trade press, which would enable us to respond to that perception and expand our distribution base.

As I have said, the research showed that the people who knew us felt that we were a centralised lender. The advertising campaign that John Meakin devised to address this problem was one of the cleverest we have ever undertaken, but I am doubtful as to whether it produced much business. Not only was it trying to sell something that we *weren't*, it was also trying to conceptualise in a medium – the trade press – where you have a one-second chance to get readers to look below the headline. To stand any chance of success, the "Popular Misconceptions" advertising campaign needed a budget which would sustain it for longer than the six weeks we were able to afford. Nevertheless, the whole exercise, which I discuss at greater length in Chapter 6, got us thinking about ourselves as a larger business, and about the possibility of advertising in our own name (having hitherto stuck to our "Private Label" principles and placed advertisements only in the names of our distributors).

> **the whole exercise...got us thinking about ourselves as a larger business**

While all this was going on, we had to face up to the other big issue, namely that delegating pre-offer processing to third parties rarely works. Post-offer mortgage administration is a sequence of increasingly automated functions which can work very well through third party administrators. Pre-offer, there is a far greater human and emotional element.

As we signed with each new lender we realised that there was an opportunity to effect switches between them. This might occur where, for example, a new aspect to the status made a particular application unsuitable for the originally chosen lender, but acceptable to another lender on our panel. This concept was alien to HML at the time, and we knew that we could not get that part of our service going unless we ourselves handled the pre-offer stage. We felt that we needed bespoke software so that a computer could tell us whether an application fitted the criteria of any given lender, since no human brain could store, with instant recall, the criteria on behalf of a number of lenders. We also had an idea of how we could teach our sales techniques to good administration people, but this was near to impossible when the key staff concerned were not our own employees.

I was – and, to an extent, still am – a reluctant owner of a factory-type operation. Pre-offer processing is a thankless task, rarely praised and too often at the mercy of third parties' actions: the delaying of references by employers; uncooperative existing lenders trying to prevent their clients remortgaging; inefficient valuers and even your own lenders issuing incorrect offers or suffering backlogs. I knew from the experience with HML that all these things can and do happen, in addition to the mistakes which any company can make in the face of hundreds of telephone calls each day. This is why I hung onto the idea for most of 1993 that we might be able to make it work via HML. But in signing an 18-month contract I was also deliberately leaving the door open to take the processing in-house in the spring of 1994, if we had to.

We took a long hard look at all of the factors, including the processing and profitability dynamics, and decided that we had no choice. We prepared a business plan to launch our own Processing Centre in the spring of 1994 and set about looking for someone to run it. This would call for a completely different set of skills from those we had previously recruited for.

SETTING UP A PROCESSING CENTRE

In the middle of the recruitment process, we were contacted by Barry Searle, who was with HML. Barry was known to us as a "troubleshooter", somebody who was often used by HML to sort out processing problems. He was first introduced to us in that role in 1988, when we encountered some backlogs in the processing of our FMS business. We then worked with Barry again in 1993 as he attempted to bridge the culture gap between our needs, and the service that his employers were able to deliver. HML were looking to move most of their key staff to Skipton, and Barry – reluctant to make the move – applied to us for a sales job. For our part, we saw in Barry just the right person to launch our Processing Centre and he joined us in December of that year, fortunately with the blessing of his previous employers and, indeed, a jointly funded party.

There was therefore very little time off as we went into 1994. Not only did we have to recruit staff and find premises for our new Processing Centre, we also had to specify the bespoke software necessary to provide back-up to a multi-lender programme of the type unique to Private Label. And who better to come to the rescue than Michael Kelly? Michael had ceased to be involved with MSL when it had been taken over by HML and was engaged in various personal business ventures, including a computer software company.

Michael and his team immediately understood our brief and delivered an amazing system to us on time, and at a greatly reduced cost, which served us well for the ensuing three years. The software has now been completely rewritten to cope with the volumes we are now experiencing, but again we used Michael's firm.

Barry Searle proved himself to be an outstanding project manager, juggling the move, the software (and attendant testing), recruitment and the overall launch in such a way that we were able to open our doors on 12 March 1994 fully staffed. We phased in the transfer of distributors from HML, but, by the summer 1994, there were only two companies – Scottish Life and John Charcol – who were themselves undertaking the pre-offer processing. In a couple of years, we had transformed our company from being a niche sales and marketing boutique-type operation to being a processor of mortgage applications, as well as a designer and distributor.

Looking back, it is interesting to note that 1994 was the first in a series of consecutive years where we enjoyed massive new business growth. The idea of there being one company to whom an intermediary can pass an application, with one application form accessing a range of lenders, first started to take off in 1994 when we launched our Processing Centre. It is now the reason why many hundreds of intermediaries pour applications into the top end of our funnel each month. They know that even if the application falls out of bed with the originally chosen lender a mortgage offer can often result from another lender, without the client ever having to complete another form, or write out another valuation fee cheque.

THE FAB FOUR

On the lending side, four individuals representing four different lenders had a major influence on our business in 1994 and, indeed, subsequent years. The interaction between people is still the driving force that makes businesses succeed or otherwise. There have, of course, been some major lenders who have not been able to accept the areas where we add value, or where the personal chemistry has not been inspiring to either side. But, fortunately for us, there have been plenty of times when the personalities and the corporate cultures *have* gelled, which has helped to produce the outstanding new business results we have enjoyed in later years.

In the preceding two years, Britannia had come to dominate our funding. Whenever we had a new idea we put it first to Britannia, and that society normally snapped it up. We had established a strong relationship with Gerald Gregory, Head of Treasury, and with Neil

Rawlinson, the Head of Sales. Even the Finance Director, Trevor Bayley (who never gives much away), had given us a cautious nod of approval. We were therefore a little concerned when Neil Rawlinson announced that he had hired Ian Jeffery as a consultant to look again at Britannia's entire intermediary business.

It turned out that Ian was the perfect choice. With his good strategic brain we knew that he would not hesitate to axe us if he felt that we did not add value, or to build the relationship into something bigger if he thought that we did. After a couple of meetings, where it was not possible to read his intentions, it was eventually announced that all intermediary lending would transfer to the Leek head office under Ian's control, with Ian joining Britannia full time as a manager. We were pleased to learn that we were to feature significantly in Ian's plans, with a new diversion for us immediately agreed.

Ian felt that with some life companies and major brokers we had a better relationship. He therefore proposed a deal where we would have a "sole agency" to promote Britannia standard products as well as those which we had designed. We had always previously shied away from marketing lenders' standard products because a number of so-called packaging companies had launched in competition with us, offering just that service. The fact that we only marketed products which we ourselves designed, and which were exclusive to us, helped to keep a clear distance between us and these packaging operations, who typically had very little capital behind them. Indeed, this possible competition was one of the reasons why in 1994 we increased our paid-up share capital to £50,000, the Plc threshold, to demonstrate our superior size, even though

> The mortgage world is still very much a people business

we preferred to retain the less onerous accounting requirements of a private company. But Ian Jeffery's proposition made sense and we undertook a strategic move that one of our lenders had suggested rather than one we had ourselves devised. In fact, as a back-up to our exclusive product designs, we now market the standard products of quite a number of lenders, so this policy has survived the test of time.

The second person to influence us was Phil Dearing, then of West Bromwich Building Society. We had signed a funding contract with West Bromwich, but had not really found a product that worked. We immediately hit it off with Phil, who recognised the potential fit between our company and his, and we came up with a 4.95 per cent fixed rate for 18 months. This seems a simple concept now, but, in the autumn of 1994, when rates were due to rise again, it captured our distributors' imagination. With a second fixed rate funded exclusively for Scottish Life, we managed to undertake £60m of new business with West Bromwich in a very short space of time – so short that we experienced one of the many lessons in volume management that we had to learn at our Processing Centre until we finally started to get it consistently better (although still not perfect) in 1997. Phil has now become Chief Executive of Market Harborough Building Society, but we still do the odd small piece of business with him, and enjoy his company just as much.

Our Bradford & Bingley relationship was not going anywhere once that society had pulled out of providing the first advance under our 100 per cent product (to be replaced by Britannia, our fourth successive lender in this slot). But Martin Reay had by then come on the scene and we were at last able to get something going. We picked up on the 4.95 per cent fixed rate for 18 months theme with Bradford & Bingley and achieved another £50m of business, running on thereafter with a 3.99 per cent fixed rate as rates softened in 1995. With Martin's influence still strong on intermediary business at Bradford & Bingley, we continue to enjoy a strong relationship with this lender, and currently count them very much in our front line.

The fourth individual to influence our business that year was Richard Brown of Bristol & West Building Society. This concerned another set of funding negotiations which were going nowhere until Richard took over. We did not really see any significant volume with Bristol & West until 1995, but that society's standard products have always been right at the top of the market, and it is a rare day currently when we do not receive at least a dozen Bristol & West standard product applications in addition to the exclusive designs we have with that lender from time to time.

Ian, Phil, Martin and Richard repeated the trend that had started with Nick Deutsch at First Mortgage Securities, and continued with Charles Greenwood at Paribas and Ray Pierce/Barry Meeks at The Mortgage Corporation. The mortgage world is still very much a people business, relying on individuals mutually seeing an opportunity before their companies can be brought together in partnership. We have also learned from experience that, when key people go, it is not always possible to hold onto the relationship in the same way, which is why we task our sales people to keep sufficient simultaneous demand going for a number of lenders.

A MONTH OF MILESTONES

The month of October 1994 represented the 7th anniversary since our launch. In November 1994 I passed a milestone I had been dreading: my 40th birthday. It therefore seemed a good idea to have a joint party, and we invited 200 people to a black tie event at the Langham Hotel in London, with Jimmy Tarbuck providing the cabaret. It is extraordinary to me that, some three years later, people still talk to me about this event. Such large corporate bashes were the norm in the booming 1980s, but not so in the '90s. But this was not a corporate excess on our behalf. Not only had we been saving up for the event for many years, but also I contributed personally so that both I and the company could have a celebration of the type which one would only normally reserve for very special occasions. It was great to see so many people there, including lenders, distributors, competitors, suppliers and faces from the past, including my ex-boss from Citibank.

I do not recommend passing 40. It was – and still is – an unpleasant experience. It marks the threshold when there is almost no context in which you can be described as young. Neither is there any refuge in sport, where – however skilled you were previously – your mind puts your body in the position for a shot several seconds after the ball has gone sailing past you. I will tell my children to try and skip over 40 if at all possible or – if drugs permit by the time they reach that age – defer it indefinitely. But for those of us who were stuck with it, a new year of challenge – 1995 – was waiting.

I met Martin Finegold for the first time at the end of January 1995. Having started Private Label – a business that many have described as a "virtual" mortgage company – it was perhaps inevitable that I would get on with somebody looking to do much the same thing. Martin was ex-Goldman Sachs and was looking to create in the UK the sort of impaired credit market which has some maturity in the United States. The UK market was ripe for this opportunity as there were a number of people who had suffered problems in the recession, but who were upstraight now. Martin was seeking to target those particular borrowers with terms that were profitable and fair to both sides. Whilst I could see the opportunity, my initial reaction was that this was not our end of the market at all. I felt that Martin would be better off seeking other distribution channels. But – shrewdly – Martin felt that to establish his company day one at the top of the market, and to ward off the criticism which might come from the press, he was better off linking with a company like Private Label.

After one false start with a particular funder of Martin's business who subsequently pulled out, the negotiations started in earnest during the summer of 1995 with Nomura International Plc, one of the world's largest investment banks. With initial distribution and pre-offer processing by us, offer issuance and post-offer administration by HML, and with funding via a series of lending vehicles,

Martin's Kensington Mortgage Company was (and is) truly a "virtual" mortgage lender. The specialisation and fragmentation I had talked about in the Citibank strategy paper published nine years previously was truly being exploited by a new lender in a niche market. It was clear to me, however, that the lending terms had to be very precisely drawn if the new venture was not to be knocked off course by bad publicity from day one, and if the intermediary market's eyes were to be opened to this opportunity.

It was from such discussions that LIBOR-linked interest rates, no redemption penalties after three years, controlled commissions which were not at the discretion of the introducer and user-friendly options like free legal fees were born. Rather as Private Label had benefited from the association with an established company, MSL, when it had first launched, I was aware that Kensington Mortgage Company would benefit from its association with Private Label. As an extra precaution I therefore asked for the funding contract to be guaranteed by Nomura. Negotiating a full funding contract via lawyers is always a drawn out and detailed affair. But when it is a tripartite agreement, with three different sets of lawyers, it becomes a little more time-consuming than usual. We had our wobbles on that particular agreement, which we eventually signed on 30 August 1995, but we also had some fun as well.

> We had our wobbles on that particular agreement...but we also had some fun as well

I remember one day when half a dozen mainly Japanese people from Nomura came to visit our Processing Centre. Barry Searle was explaining, in his usual down-to-earth style, how, if "Flo" was taking a call to the effect that the valuation would be carried out next week, for example, and noting this on the computer, another person answering a telephone call on the same application could see that message come on the screen in real time and pass it on to their enquirer. It was obvious from the puzzled expression and body language of one of our Japanese visitors that he had not comprehended this point. I asked Barry to stop and the query came forth: "No understand. What is 'Fro'?" As a football supporter, Barry knows what is meant by a "hospital pass", and I have always thanked him for that one.

We launched Kensington in October 1995, enjoying exclusive distribution rights until the beginning of 1996. We remain Kensington's number one introducer of new business and, in our view, Kensington has remained the market leader for impaired credit lending, even though half a dozen (mainly American) companies have followed Martin's lead into the UK market.

Private Label builds on revival

Private Label Mortgage Services is embarking on a major new campaign to IFAs to take advantage of a forecast upturn in housing-market activity.

The company is offering an exclusive building-society-funded series of products, one of which offers IFAs 0.4 per cent of the loan as a fee if clients take the lender's buildings and contents insurance.

The maximum loan is £150,000 and maximum fee payable will be £600. Executive chairman Stephen Knight says: "We are already hearing evidence of a pick-up in activity at estate agents which should feed through to brokers before long."

The company has also arranged a discount-rate mortgage at 3.25 per cent until January 1995 followed by a discount of 0.5 per cent on the lender's variable rate until January 1996. The loan is available up to 75 per cent of valuation and is offered at an initial rate of 3.95 per cent up to 95 per cent lending.

The company is also offering a 100 per cent mortgage at 7.68 per cent with a maximum loan of £100,000 and the Private Label range also features a 6.95 per cent fixed-rate loan until January 2000.

Money Marketing, 20 January 1994

Barclays opens mortgage house

Barclays Bank is to relaunch mortgage lending through intermediaries later this week.

The bank has set up a subsidiary, The Mortgage House (TMH), which will operate from the Leeds premises of Barclays Direct Mortgage Services (BDMS). BDMS, the previous intermediary lending arm, closed to new business nine months ago.

Barclays spokesman Philip Pashley said full details of the lending products will be announced at the launch. "They will obviously include fixed rates as these are currently best sellers with our direct customers." Unlike BDMS, The Mortgage House will be financed off-balance sheet through securitisations arranged by US investment house Goldman Sachs. TMH is already set to join the panel of Private Label Mortgage Services and is expected to link with some of the former BDMS partners.

Unlike lenders such as National Home Loans and Mortgage Express, which charged existing customers more than market rates after they withdrew from new lending, BDMS charges the same rate as Barclays Bank, currently 7.74%.

Money Week, 19 January 1994

ON THE HOME FRONT

MORTGAGES
100 PER CENT

Private Label has relaunched its 100 per cent product with a lower interest rate and improved terms.

Commenting on the mortgage, Stephen Knight, chairman of Private Label, says, "Our new improved 100 per cent product will enable first-time buyers to get on to the property ladder quickly, or in the case of second-time buyers who have lost their equity, enabling them to move house."

The first loan is provided by a top-ten building society at 6.99 per cent variable (7.3 per cent APR). This represents a discount of 0.75 per cent from that society's new base rate of 7.74 per cent, for the first six months of the loan. The top-up of 25 per cent is provided by the finance subsidiary of a high street bank at 9.75 per cent variable (APR 12.1 per cent). This produces an average rate of 7.68 per cent (average APR 8.51 per cent).

There is no arrangement fee and the package automatically comes with guaranteed accident, sickness and unemployment cover for the first five years.

What Mortgage, February 1994

Private Label sets up admin centre

by Iain Anderson

Private Label Mortgage Services has set up its own mortgage-processing centre to deal with a growing number of unpackaged mortgage applications from introducers.

The move allows Private Label to reduce its reliance on applications from its panel of 20 life companies, which includes GA Life, Friends Provident and Scottish Life, and accept a greater number of applications direct.

Executive chairman Stephen Knight says: "With life offices continuing to close mortgage desks and restructure their approach to lending, Private Label has had to look at a new way of gaining business."

A computer mortgage-processing system designed by Private Label and National Home Loans director Michael Kelly has been created and a phone hotline set up for IFAs.

The centre, based in Guildford, will take business which was handled previously for Private Label by Homeloan Management, the third-party mortgage admin service of Skipton Building Society.

Knight says: "Private Label deliberately did not buy an off-the-shelf application-processing system."

"Our bespoke sales-orientated system, alongside the move towards a total processing and placement service for intermediaries, are the foundation stones for a planned expansion of our business."

Private Label has pledged to process applications to be sent to the lender within 18 working days.

Current Private Label products include a 6.95 per cent fixed-rate loan until 2000 and a 7.62 per cent variable-rate 100 per cent loan.

Money Marketing, 24 March 1994

Private Label withdraws incentive scheme

Private Label has withdrawn its controversial incentive scheme which offered brokers luxury cars and holidays in exchange for large business volumes.

The scheme has been subject to considerable negative press publicity and was investigated in this week's Watchdog TV programme. Chairman Stephen Knight says: "I fully accept the criticism that the structure of the incentive scheme may have drawn greater attention to the prizes rather than the products."

Money Marketing, 5 October 1995

Designer card trick will do for present

FINANCIAL services companies are never slow to exploit an opportunity.

Mortgage design company Private Label is to send out a Christmas card this week to plug its latest offer. It shows a big-boned wife complaining about the £4.75 in coins given to her by her husband. She says: "When I said I wanted 4.75, I meant the mortgage, not my present."

The card then goes on to promote Private Label's 4.75 per cent two-year fixed-rate mortgage.

Inside the card it reads: "Give your clients a Happy Christmas. Fix their rate at 4.75 per cent and their monthly payments should plummet by December 25th."

Forget the cards. We just can't wait for the Christmas parties.

Christmas comes early

Financial Adviser, 12 October 1995

Postcard has the edge on British seaside humour

Summertime special: Private Label's postcard

MORTGAGE design company Private Label is giving IFAs a saucy reminder of its new mortgage.

A traditional-style seaside picture postcard shows a domineering woman telling her frowning husband: "With interest rates at just 4.99 per cent we can afford to stay for two weeks instead of just one!"

Mr Stephen Knight, chairman of Private Label, said: "We did consider other postcard ideas including one with a rather busty young lady but I got over-ruled by our good taste committee."

Indecent can assure readers the hen-pecked man bears no resemblance to Mr Knight who never wears a hankie on his head.

Financial Adviser, 10 August 1995

Private Label hires salesteam

Private Label Mortgage Services is creating a 10 strong regional salesforce to promote the company's product range.

The first four appointments to the salesforce have been recruited from various mortgage lenders including Halifax, Bank of Ireland, Royal Bank of Scotland and HMC.

Six further appointments are expected to be made during the next few months.

Stephen Knight, executive chairman of Private Label, said: "In 1995 we have enjoyed the most successful of our eight years in business, measured by new lending generated and market share of gross advances.

These appointments reflect not only the quality of the people we have within the company, but also the preparations we are making for further substantial growth in 1996."

Private Label has also appointed Simon Knight as sales director.

Knight joined the company in 1990 from UCB Home Loans. Barry Searle who joined the company in 1993 from Homeloan Management has been appointed as operations director.

Judy Lawrence has been appointed as head of Private Label's processing centre. Until 1992 she worked with TMC.

Tony Fisher is appointed as marketing manager. He has been with Private Label since 1988 and previously worked for Citibank.

Investment Week, 22 January 1996

Widows returns to mortgage market

by Clare Conley

Scottish Widows has returned to the mortgage market after an absence of two-and-a-half years in a joint venture with Private Label.

Under the brand Scottish Widows Homeline, the insurer will offer packaged loans from 16 building societies and banks. They include Bradford & Bingley, Britannia, Bristol & West, Bank of Ireland and Kleinwort Benson.

Private Label is also making its full range of 60 products available through the Homeline service.

Widows says it intends to introduce exclusive mortgages, designed by Private Label, within a few months but its initial aim is to re-establish itself in the mortgage market.

Intermediaries will receive a £100 introduction fee paid by Private Label on most of the mortgages. Some loans carry a higher fee while others have no fee.

Brokers will be able to use one standard application form for any of the mortgages. Widows plans to promote the service with a roadshow in the next few weeks.

Mortgages available include a 3.99 per cent fix until March 1998 and the Open Door Mortgage which Widows claims will solve the problem of impaired credit.

Head of marketing David Graham says: "With this important new initiative, we aim to provide IFAs with a comprehensive, user-friendly mortgage service."

Widows pulled out of the mortgage market after it closed the mortgage matching service which it operated from eight regional units.

Money Marketing, 29 February 1996

Private home loans to dispel investor fears

by Julia Clark

PRIVATE Label has responded to concern about deep discount mortgages and redemption penalties by designing two "next generation" mortgage products.

Both mortgages have been funded by major building societies.

The Mortgage of the Century is intended to spread the discounts and cashbacks over a longer period in order to prevent the problem of payment shock for borrowers.

It offers a 2 per cent discount on the current variable rate (6.99 per cent) for the first three-and-a-half years after completion.

In addition, there is a £500 cashback at completion (£1000 for loans over £100,000).

Then just as the next century approaches, the borrower receives another £1000 cashback in December 1999 (£1500 for larger loans).

The mortgage offers a long-term benefits stream which is why there are redemption penalties payable for up to seven years.

The redemption penalties vary from 2 to 4 per cent during that time.

There is an arrangement fee of £295 which is added to the loan. This product has no introducer's fee.

For borrowers who suspect they may want their freedom sooner than the above product will allow, Private Label has created a three-year discount loan with a lower redemption charge.

This product gives a 4.05 per cent discount over three years (1.35 per cent a year). It also allows the borrower to choose another fixed rate mortgage at the end of three years, free.

If the borrower switches to the standard variable rate, the redemption penalty from then on is only one month's interest. This is the equivalent of 0.6 per cent on a £60,000 loan.

The arrangement fee on this mortgage is £195. There is an introducer's fee of £250.

Neither loan carries compulsory general insurance.

Product Adviser, 20 June 1996

One in a millennium

The Mortgage of the Century from Private Label Mortgage Services has been designed for borrowers who will be willing to remain with one lender for a relatively long period.

One of the problems facing the lenders is criticism from some quarters regarding the possible payment shocks that borrowers could receive once a period of reduced interest rates comes to an end. By offering a discount of just 2 per cent a year, but for a longer period, borrowers are still receiving an attractive benefit but with only a small increase in their payments at the end of the discount term, if the variable rate remains at 6.99 per cent.

The two-tier cashback has been introduced for borrowers who do not need an enormous cash sum immediately. The first payment has been designed to be sufficient to repay most of the costs incurred in buying or remortgaging a property while the second amount has been timed to coincide with the end-of-the-century celebrations.

The total benefit to borrowers of both of these incentives is 10 per cent for a mortgage of £50,000.

Money Marketing, 20 June 1996

STEPHEN KNIGHT

David Robertson

Stephen Knight was an 80s icon in the lending market - successful, ambitious and not afraid to splash out on fast cars and nights out at Stringfellows. At least that is what most people thought of him and many still do.

But the founder and executive chairman of mortgage packager and designer Private Label has changed with his business. He says: "I have outgrown all that. If I start dancing now, when I stop, my stomach carries on for several minutes after."

Money Marketing profiled Knight in 1987 just after he had set up Private Label and, nine years on, the business that started with a personal investment of £100,000 is worth over £5m. New applications are worth £70m a month and during March, April and May, lending hit the £100m mark - equivalent to a top-10 building society.

In nine years, a lot has changed for Private Label. From a starting workforce of two, there are now 55 and Knight says the "inevitable cult of the individual" has largely gone as people realise that it is Private Label the company and not Stephen Knight the company.

Knight says: "It isn't just me anymore. I have tremendous respect for the management team and I believe that we have the best salesforce in the industry. Our people go out and each get £50m a year and our top man will get £100m."

Private Label has also changed its way of doing business. It started with a handful of "marzipan-layer insurers" but none of them is now doing business in the UK. Instead, Private Label arranges mortgages for the very biggest insurers and many of the leading building societies.

After the go-go 80s, the executive chairman of Private Label has slowed down but says this makes him a better businessman

Rumours suggest that Private Label struggled through several years of recession but the company has survived and business is booming again. Knight believes this is because the company can offer IFAs innovative products that other lenders just could not afford to put on the market.

He says: "We are like the out-of-town shopping centre. A lot of people used to say 'I will only shop in my high street' but they now drive two miles out of town to a huge and impersonal store where they can get products at two-thirds the price. If you buy in bulk, you get a cheaper price."

"We can go to a lender with a specially designed mortgage with £100m in business which is going to be a huge cost saving to the lender and consequently part of that saving is reinvested in the price."

"Understandably, some IFAs do not like the idea because we all like a bit of personal service. Our challenge is to try as hard as humanly possible to make our service as good as possible. We will never be as personable as the high-street lender but, with good service and cheaper, innovative products, people will make that trip out of town."

In nine years, Private Label has grown and changed significantly but what has not changed is the industry's respect for Knight's achievements. "You have to admire him" and "You have to respect what he has done" seem to be the most common reactions when asked about Knight.

His bullish determination for the company to succeed has not made him universally popular but many judgements on Knight are based on the Stringfellows caricature of nine years ago.

Knight says: "My life has fundamentally changed over the nine years but not necessarily to do with the business. I have two small children and that has changed my life."

"When I started Private Label, I was obsessed with making it a success and it was the most important thing to me."

"Today, the most important things to me are my children and frankly it has made me a better businessman. If you approach decisions from the basis that, whatever happens, it is not the most important thing, you make better decisions."

"I am not working at the pace I used to. I don't work every weekend and I don't work all Saturday. I never miss a parents' evening, school concert or sports day."

Nine years on and Knight has the support of many in the industry and his own expanding team. He expects to continue designing innovative products and may take Private Label to the Stock Exchange in the future.

He says being nine years down the track in an established business means that you do not need to be as pushy.

He says: "One of the most pleasing things of the last nine years is that, every year, the friendships have grown and business becomes more relaxed. My own calming down is because I no longer have to push this idea forward against a sea of resistance."

Money Marketing, 8 August 1996

Private Label has a laugh with launch

PRIVATE Label is planning to win over IFAs with laughter at roadshows staged around the country to launch its pre-election mortgage products.

Private Label, a mortgage designer and distributor, will intersperse the product presentations with two comedy sketches specially written for the company by BBC scriptwriter Mr Terry Morrison.

One of the sketches is in the form of a mock lecture taking brokers through the Council of Mortgage Lenders' Code of Mortgage Lending Practice and how it applies to procuration fees.

Financial advisers will be able to enjoy a send-up of the mortgage credit scoring process as they watch a computer turn down brokers' applications.

Private Label said £60,000 was to be spent on five intermediary presentations.

The roadshows will place in Manchester on 18 March, Solihull on 19 March and Bristol on 20 March. Two shows will be held in London on 25 March.

Mr Stephen Knight, executive chairman, said intermediaries attending the shows would be the first to learn about the firm's "election-beating" mortgage products.

They would also receive free vouchers to local attractions, including a backstage tour of Granada Studios for those IFAs at the Manchester event.

Financial Adviser, 27 February 1997

Our panel of six leading figures from the world of financial services give their instant reactions to the Budget

Brown's Budget splits industry pundits

*Stephen Knight: **Predictable***   *Angela Knight: **broken promises***   *Webb: **creative accounting***   *Kohn: **Reassuring***   *Cameron: **pensioner insecurity***   *Broadberry: **hits healthcare***

Stephen Knight, chairman of Private Label Mortgages, said: "Changes in Miras and stamp duty were predicated on the assumption that house prices are overheating. In fact, in all regions, they are still as much as 26 per cent below the market peak."

"Housing transactions in May 1997 reflected nervousness caused by two rate rises. Transactions are lower than in 1994 or in any of the four years between 1985 and 1988. Further phasing out of Miras and higher stamp duty on house values to which many aspire, will not increase confidence."

"There must also be doubt as to whether enough has been taken out of consumers pockets to prevent another base rate rise."

"Forward dating the Miras reduction to April 1998 may provide some opportunity. Economic confidence may be helped by some of the other measures."

Angela Knight, former Conservative Treasury minister, said: "This is a tax raising Budget and an increased spending Budget. Therefore it breaks the Labour government's pre-election promises only eight weeks after the general election."

"This Budget is good for corporate tax lawyers as they can get their teeth into the complexity of the advance corporation tax changes. But the changes will impact badly on the pension funds of millions of pensioners."

"The chancellor appears to have spent more than he has raised in his windfall tax. The tax raises £4.8bn but he has spent £3.5bn on welfare to work, £1bn on education and another £900m on buildings and the costs of getting lone parents back to work."

"The Miras changes will hit the bottom end of the housing market and stamp duty charges the top end."

Mike Webb, managing director at GT Global, said: "It is far from clear that a Budget expected to introduce fiscal tightening has achieved exactly that. At first sight, it would appear the additional spending plans are not matched by revenue generating initiatives. This must increase the possibility of higher interest rates to keep the economy in check."

"The dramatic reduction in public sector borrowing requirement forecasts looks like wishful thinking resulting from simple reforecasting rather than from any concrete revenue raising initiative."

"The chancellor's plans for corporate tax reforms including ACT has dealt a bitter blow to the pension industry. In addition the Pep industry has been given a finite life which should boost Pep sales over the intervening period before the introduction of the individual savings account."

Roddy Kohn, principal of IFA Kohn Cougar, said: "Overall a reassuring Budget, consistent with electoral statements. No great surprises in the area of ACT, stamp duty and Miras. It was, however, reassuring on personal taxation."

"In the short term these changes will impact particularly on pension funds but most investors understand the long-term nature of these schemes and the programme of long-term investment in industry through lower taxes and increased allowances should act as a counter balance. Bad news was evident, however, for those IFAs who specialise in private healthcare plans."

"Most clients should take comfort from the government's determination to control spending and inflation and to reform and modernise the tax system. If the welfare to work programme results in long-term employment then that must result in an increased demand for pensions."

Steven Cameron, pensions development manager at Scottish Equitable, said: "This was not a good Budget for either pensions or current and future pensioners. By removing tax credits pension funds can reclaim, the chancellor immediately removes any surpluses in final salary schemes and the security these give to active and pensioner members."

"He also reduces the prospects of anyone in a money purchase scheme or personal pension retiring on an adequate pension as their funds will grow by less. Even more reason for IFAs to recommend increased pension contributions."

"The Budget speech suggests that investment growth in individual savings accounts will be taxed less than in pension schemes. This seems perverse. Hopefully the government will now take steps to reaffirm its commitment to private pensions."

Alison Broadberry, financial planning manager at Sun Life, said: "From the new chancellor's speech it seems that the changes will: hinder an already struggling healthcare market by withdrawing the relief for the over-60s on private medical insurance; be neutral for personal financial planning, with no changes to income tax, or capital gains tax; and surprisingly there was no reference to inheritance tax. Advisers may consider this area has been given an extended deadline."

"Advisers should continue to stress the merits of pension contributions, in particular that dividends are not pensionable."

"Corporate financial planning must be carefully considered to determine the best way to distribute profits as the surprising cut in corporation tax rates means there may be more profits to invest, or extract."

Financial Adviser, 3 July 1997

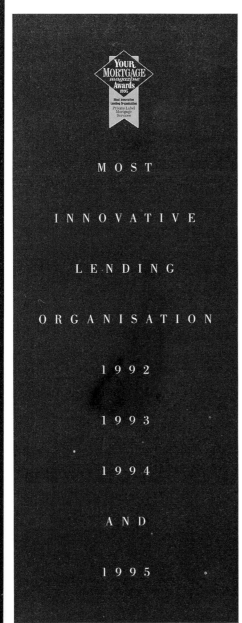

Not bad for a company that doesn't like doing the same thing twice.

YOUR MORTGAGE magazine Awards 1995
Most Innovative Lending Organisation
Private Label Mortgage Services

M O S T

I N N O V A T I V E

L E N D I N G

O R G A N I S A T I O N

1 9 9 2

1 9 9 3

1 9 9 4

A N D

1 9 9 5

Innovation. Everybody's doing it, but what does it mean? To us, it means designing mortgage products which break new ground, producing new and better benefits for borrowers.

It also means delivering those products, via professional advisers, in an efficient manner.

And of course, ultimately it means selling lots of business to ensure that the large building societies and banks we work with will want to continue funding our ideas.

By doing this, we've had a rather successful year in 1995, enjoying our highest ever market share of gross lending. But we're not resting on our laurels.

We have a hatful of new ideas for 1996.

So, although we don't normally like doing the same thing twice, let alone three times, it seems we'll have to make an exception for our fourth successive Your Mortgage award!

Private Label MORTGAGE DESIGN AND DISTRIBUTION

NB. We can only accept enquiries from authorised professional advisers.

Private Label Mortgage Services Ltd., 14 Great Queen Street, London WC2B 5DW. Tel: 0171 404 6966. Fax: 0171 404 6884.

Private Label's entry in the Your Mortgage *Award-winners magazine*

Most Innovative Lending Organisation

Private Label Mortgage Services

Private Label Mortgage Services has won this award in each of the four years that it has been awarded.

As a mortgage packaging and design company, inventing new mortgage deals, finding organisations to fund the loans and then sourcing distribution outlets, Private Label's business is innovation, and its record is second to none. And Private Label's monopoly of the Most Innovative Lending Organisation category provides concrete proof of this.

Examples of products launched in 1995 include Made-to-Measure, where borrowers can select from a menu of options including discounts, cash-backs, etc, to customise their own mortgages; a fixed rate where borrowers can choose their own redemption terms by trading off the initial rate payable; a school fees draw down product where the lender pays each term's school fees direct to the school; and a special second-time buyers' mortgage where the estate agents' fees on the property being sold are paid in full by the lender. In addition to these specific innovations, Private Label has also made available to professional intermediaries a full range of competitive fixed and discounted rate mortgages from a panel of 15 major building societies and banks.

Stephen Knight, executive chairman of Private Label, says: "We estimate that, over the last few years, the market has reduced by 25 per cent at the same time that the product options available to borrowers have increased by 100 per cent. This over-supply means that mortgage products have to be truly innovative, and relevant to customers' needs, to get any attention at all. These market conditions play to our strengths, and in 1995 we enjoyed our highest ever volume of new business."

15

Private Label's 1995 entry in the Your Mortgage *Award-winners magazine*

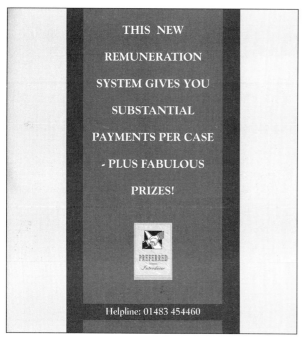

THIS NEW

REMUNERATION

SYSTEM GIVES YOU

SUBSTANTIAL

PAYMENTS PER CASE

- PLUS FABULOUS

PRIZES!

PREFERRED
Introducer

Helpline: 01483 454460

The front cover of the ill-fated Preferred Introducer Remuneration Scheme

NOW, IN ADDITION TO EARNING WITH EVERY CASE, YOU CAN WIN FABULOUS PRIZES!

This exciting new system is exclusive to **Preferred Introducers**. Not only does it pay you a substantial amount for every completion - it also gives you the opportunity to accumulate points leading to fabulous prizes!

It's so simple! When each product launches we will announce both the payment and points allocation relating to that product.

We will reinforce this with regular updates showing £s and points per product, plus this information will always be to hand via our Mortgage Helpline.

MARKETABILITY

The majority of our business is received under our exclusive products - normally found at or near the top of their market sectors.

These exclusive products are supplemented with a wide range of lenders' standard products - which means that our Preferred Introducers have the whole market available to them via one Helpline, and on one application form.

Our aim is to satisfy at least 90% of your mortgage demand, and, by using us on this basis, you will quickly accumulate very large points totals - as well as receiving competitive payments per case!

MORE!

From time to time we will introduce specific products which carry a larger points allocation and/or a higher per completion payment than normal.

This system has therefore been designed to be flexible, exciting, worthwhile, exclusive - and above all to reward those **Preferred Introducers** who use us for most of their mortgage demand.

EVERYONE CAN WIN!

Remember, this is not a 'first past the post' promotion - every **Preferred Introducer** has the opportunity to claim one (or more) prizes.

All you have to do is build up the required points.

MORE!

This points scheme runs for eighteen months from 1 September 1995 or from the date we confirmed your appointment as a **Preferred Introducer** if later, giving you plenty of time to build up points for the prize or prizes you would like. Any **Preferred Introducer** who successfully claims a prize can carry any extra points forward to another prize, or to the next scheme, as required.

Those who do not claim a prize during the eighteen month qualifying period cannot carry points forward into the next scheme.

The full rules of this scheme are printed on the back of this leaflet; please take a moment to read them.

BIG REWARDS!

Look at the fabulous prizes that can be won! These, plus significant payments per case add up to big rewards for our **Preferred Introducers**.

MORTGAGE DESIGN
AND DISTRIBUTION

The inside left page of the Preferred Introducer Remuneration Scheme

THE PRIZES

15,000 POINTS

The Punto was voted European car of the Year 1995. The stylish Cabrio version comes with body coloured bumpers, power steering and electric hood as standard.

Fiat Punto 90 ELX Cabrio

10,000 POINTS

The impressive Ford Fiesta 1.3 LX 5 door manual with distinctive black bumpers and bodyside mouldings. As Ford says, "the small car to catch the eye."

Ford Fiesta 1.3 LX

5,000 POINTS

A luxury weekend in grand style for two couples at Eastnor Castle in Herefordshire, starting at Friday teatime and ending after Sunday lunch. All meals, drinks and accommodation charges are included; attentive staff will look after you and a chauffeured limousine will be at your disposal. A tour on the Saturday, plus one theatre visit, can be arranged and are included within the prize. Your weekend will be customised for you by Venue Solutions, a leading specialist agency at this end of the market.

A Luxury Weekend For Four

The inside right page of the Preferred Introducer Remuneration Scheme

PREFERRED INTRODUCERS' REMUNERATION SYSTEM - RULES

New system

1. This new system supersedes and replaces the previous build-up remuneration scheme with effect from completions on and after 1 July 1995.

Payment per case

2. We will pay an amount per completion for every mortgage you introduce to us. These amounts will normally be paid by the end of the month following the month in which completion takes place, and we will issue a monthly statement with our cheque so that you can reconcile our figures.

3. The normal formula will be £100 per completion for products designed by, and exclusive to, Private Label, and £50 per completion for products which are lenders' standard products. If there is to be any variation to this, we will announce it at the time of the product launch.

4. We intend to introduce products from time to time which carry higher payments per completion. A monthly update will therefore be issued regularly reminding all Preferred Introducers of the exact payment which each product attracts. These details will also be available on request from our Mortgage Helpline.

Points accumulation

5. As well as paying per completion, we will also award points for every completion. Sometimes, when we want to promote a particular product, we will award more than the normal points per completion. Again, this will be announced at the time the product is launched and will be reinforced through the monthly updates and via the Mortgage Helpline.

6. Your new points total will be shown on each monthly statement, taking into account that month's completions. As soon as you have received a statement showing cumulative points equal to or greater than the amount required to claim the prize of your choice, then you should contact the Private Label Manager with whom you normally deal to make arrangements for your prize to be claimed.

Claiming the prizes

7. The prizes illustrated need to be ordered by us. Where the prize involves a specific motor car, any extras are your responsibility; our commitment is to defray the purchase price of the basic model shown plus delivery charge and six months' road fund tax. We accept no liability or responsibility for the performance, availability, delivery time or any other aspect whatsoever relating to the motor car. We will simply order it for you, and pay as above.

8. The same applies where the prize is a form of holiday. We will set it up for you and pay for it, but we cannot accept any liability whatsoever relating to the holiday.

9. Every prize carries an alternative of payment by cheque where 80% of the points convert into pounds sterling. In other words, upon the achievement of 5,000 points, a payment of £4,000 can be claimed instead of the stated prize. For 10,000 points the payment is £8,000 and so on.

Time limits

10. The initial scheme runs for eighteen months from 1 September 1995 <u>or</u> eighteen months from the date we confirmed your appointment as a Preferred Introducer, if later. We expect to introduce new schemes in the future. Points cannot normally be carried over from one scheme to the next. Each new scheme therefore starts with a blank points total.

11. The only exception is for prize winners. If a prize is won and claimed then points accumulated after that win will be carried forward to the next prize or the next scheme, as required. There is nothing to stop more than one prize being claimed during the 18 months qualifying period for the scheme if the correct number of points are achieved. But of course, once points have been put towards any prize, those points are then redeemed.

In the event of a dispute

12. Participation in this scheme is on the strict understanding that the final decision in any dispute rests with the Board of Directors of Private Label Mortgage Services Ltd. If there is some problem regarding a particular prize, including availability or suitability, then there is always the payment by cheque alternative to which the Board may decide to defer at its sole discretion. If your appointment as a Preferred Introducer is terminated for any reason, your participation in the scheme ends and any points accumulated are forfeited. We reserve the right to vary any aspect of the above upon serving notice.

PREFERRED
Introducer

Head Office: Private Label Mortgage Services Ltd, 14 Great Queen Street, London WC2B 5DW Tel: 0171 404 6966 Fax: 0171 404 6884
Private Label Processing Centre, 2 Bell Court, Leapale Lane, Guildford, Surrey GU1 4LY Tel: 01483 454460 Fax: 01483 454468

The back cover of the Preferred Introducer Remuneration Scheme

THE UNIQUE PROGRAMME

MORTGAGE DESIGN
AND DISTRIBUTION

Established in 1987, Private Label Mortgage Services Limited is one of the biggest and longest-established multi-lender programmes, working with a number of major lenders to provide exclusive mortgage products.

Private Label has won awards for an unprecedented 5 years' running, from the Your Mortgage intermediary panel, for innovative mortgage product designs.

Private Label's exclusive products are only available via financial intermediaries; they are not available direct from the lender, nor does it market products to the public direct.

Private Label has arranged for all its lenders to accept one common mortgage application form and pre-offer process, providing interchangeability between lenders, normally without the need for new forms or fees. This is a major added value benefit for the busy financial services professional.

Private Label's size in the market ensures that it can frequently negotiate products that are priced lower than those available from the lender direct, often incorporating an introducer fee as part of the product.

Private Label has a number of lenders' underwriters based at its Processing Centre for speedy case approval and offer issuance - yet another added value benefit.

Private Label constantly has around forty exclusive and standard products available from major lenders. One call to its Mortgage Helpline number accesses all of these products and one application form accesses all lenders.

CALL OUR MORTGAGE HELPLINE ON

01483 72 61 61

All enquiries and applications to the Private Label Processing Centre, Dukes Court, Dukes Street, Woking, Surrey, GU21 5XT.
Tel: 01483 726161; Fax: 01483 726767; DX No. 2950 Woking 1.
Head Office: Private Label Mortgage Services Limited, 14 Great Queen Street, London, WC2B 5DW Tel: 0171 404 6966; Fax: 0171 404 6884

How Private Label presents itself today

Stephen Knight and Godfrey Blight, Winter 1995

Barry Searle, who joined the company in December 1993 from HML,
and is now Operations Director.

Stephen Knight (centre) with his Citibank sales team in 1985. Godfrey Blight is fourth in from the right.

Simon Knight with his Private Label sales team in 1997.

It is interesting how new developments feed off each other. With impaired credit being a relatively new concept for the UK market, we felt it important to have a Kensington underwriter on-site at our Processing Centre so that any queries or grey areas could immediately be resolved. This process worked so well that we subsequently persuaded a number of building societies to put underwriters on-site. With intermediaries rightly concerned about the withdrawal of decision-making from the high street by major lenders, as credit scoring assumes the overriding importance in lenders' assessment of mortgage applications, the positioning of on-site underwriters at processing centres like ours goes some way towards addressing these concerns. We are delighted to have pioneered this concept and hope that we can maintain the daily volumes which warrant this investment on the part of the lenders, and which in turn makes the pre-offer process so much easier for introducers and their clients.

GROWING INTO 1995

Just as 1994 had produced explosive year-on-year new business growth, so that trend was continued in 1995. Our volumes were approaching those of a reasonably sized building society, and we were starting to experience the pains of growth at our Processing Centre. As anybody involved in pre-offer work will tell you, the paperwork and the mechanical functions can always be achieved after a fashion, even in the face of a sharp volume increase. It is the telephone calls that are the real killers.

A survey we had undertaken revealed that, since we launched the Processing Centre, we could not get away from the average of one telephone call per pipeline case per day, plus new business enquiries. It was, of course, the case that some days went by without the introducer, or one of the other professionals in the chain, calling to enquire on the progress of an individual case. But the average was always returned by there being one day when four or five people called on the same case. Moreover, it was clear that, perhaps understandably, we were getting more calls than a lender would have done because we are always the company "in-between".

I asked a favour of Ray Pierce, by then Managing Director of Guardian Direct, the direct telephone arm of Guardian Insurance. Ray took Godfrey and Barry on a tour of his telephone unit so that we could see how a specialist telephone operator handled a high volume of daily telephone calls. Ray recommended a firm of consultants who were also highly thought of by a couple of other people we spoke to. We engaged these consultants to look at our telephone traffic and they concluded that it was impossible for the people processing the work to undertake the telephone calls as well. It was not just the length of each telephone call: we also had to take into account the recovery time after the call had ended for the recipient to regain his or her concentration on the paperwork in hand. We therefore purchased the latest telephone technology and set about hiring a unit of people who would take all the new business calls and update on progress, leaving the back office people to process, as recommended by the consultants.

This revolutionised our ability to handle volumes in 1995, and has made the same sort of contribution to our business for each year since. In 1997 we now regularly take 1500+ telephone calls a day and – although it is sometimes frustrating for callers not to be able to get through to the case manager looking after their particular applications – we have created a situation where everybody can get through to someone who can help them.

The training, monitoring and supervision that go into a telephone unit were brand new skills for us, as was undertaking the first employment interview by telephone. A certain breed of people wish to make their career in telephone work, and it is essential to recruit those with a smiling voice and then teach them the technicalities of the job, rather than to try and make a backroom person a star on the telephone. Having a specialist telephone function has certainly worked for us, and I expand on the processing implications in Chapter 7.

As part of our continuing search for a formula by which we could reward the small panel of intermediaries that comprised our "Preferred Introducers" panel, we decided in the autumn of 1995 to introduce a scheme along the Air Miles principle. Each mortgage achieved would earn a modest £100 introducer fee plus a certain number of bonus points. The points would mount up and, eventually, as with Air Miles, produce a total sufficient to claim a prize.

Ironically, in view of what subsequently happened, one of the main objectives of the scheme was to make less seem more. We refused to pay the very large procuration fees then being introduced by some of our competitors (and, indeed, by some lenders). In order to get our Preferred Introducers to focus on the fact that our designs left more in the product for the customer, and would therefore ultimately earn them more in the long run because they would always sell more of a better customer proposition, we had to devise an interesting and innovative remuneration arrangement to gain their attention.

We devised three long-term prizes involving thousands and thousands of points. The first was a weekend away. The second was a Ford Fiesta. And the third was a Fiat Punto Cabriolet. With 50 points being awarded on most products, and with each point being worth 70p, it is not difficult to work out how many market-leading mortgage products would need to be sold in order to achieve any of the prizes. But it is at the time you launch a new scheme that you need to maximise the publicity. We therefore worked with Britannia to devise a product involving a 2.5 per cent discount for two years plus a "fees free" package. We had to invest some of our earnings in order to obtain this particular deal so we thought – what the hell – we would pay away the rest of our earnings as well, as points under the new Preferred Introducer system, and provide the product at cost. Although 50 points were payable across the product range, this flagship product attracted 500 points, until the limited funds ran out.

The scheme went down very well with our Preferred Introducers. But just one individual within one firm took offence. He did not raise his objections with us and, instead, passed some material to a journalist, who published an article in a consumer magazine, and again in the national press. Like any organisation in the lending market, our product material was marked to the effect that it was not an advertisement complying with the Consumer Credit Act and should not be disclosed to the public. However, the article made it appear that this disclaimer was intended to keep the facts of the scheme away from clients – ironic when you consider our position as a leading campaigner for procuration fee disclosure.

The consumer magazine concerned published a full apology at the behest of our solicitors a couple of issues later. The editor of the national newspaper "noted our comments". But by then the BBC's *Watchdog* programme had received a tip-off and were trying to make something out of the scheme. We have a responsibility to our lenders not to involve them in any kind of adverse publicity – however unfair it is on us – so we reluctantly withdrew the scheme and cut up all the brochures some six days before the *Watchdog* programme went out, and before any new applications were started. Fortunately, our scheme's 30-second mention on the programme put out on 2 October 1995 was overshadowed by the fact that *Watchdog*'s researchers had by then uncovered competitions being run by other organisations on similar lines.

The story, of course, died a death and no lasting damage was done. Although I wish that the matter had been reported more fairly, I nevertheless blame myself for what was probably my biggest corporate blunder since launching with FMS without signing a contract. The result was that Private Label, a company known for being mean on individual introducer fees in order to leave more in the deal for the customer, was portrayed as promoting the very opposite. To the frustration of some of my sales and marketing colleagues, I still to this day veto any initiative that does not favourably pass the test of "What would this look like on *Watchdog*?"

With business now coming at us from the market at large, and with a range of lenders all contributing funding for our product ideas, plus the newly acquired facilities of Kensington Mortgage Company and lenders' standard products, we knew that we were in good shape for 1996. But there was one further change we had to make if we were to fully maximise the opportunities available to us.

Since our launch in 1987 we had stuck faithfully to the account manager concept. It had worked for me at Citibank and for most of Private Label's existence. Whilst almost all other lenders and competitors had split their salesforces regionally, I had always found that one person looking after two or three distributor relationships produced better results, even though it meant that you could have four of your people in Manchester on the same day visiting different contacts. The account structure meant that you could better understand and manage the overall institutional relationship, which had distinct advantages.

I still maintain that the account management concept is correct for major relationships where there is strong control from the centre. The problem is that this type of distributor hardly exists in the mortgage market today. We were delighted to have been chosen to be one of the initial panel of product providers for the newly formed Legal & General Mortgage Club, for example. But even this success story relied on local contact and personal relationships in order to keep a particular product in the forefront of the minds of the various different salesmen working for, and with, L&G.

RECRUITING A REGIONAL SALESFORCE

We therefore decided in the autumn of 1995 that we must set about recruiting a regional salesforce. At first we toyed with the idea of a commission-only structure and, indeed, initially recruited a few people on this basis. But only one survived, and he is now on a full salary. The standard of professionalism and dedication we required just did not sit well with the concept of commission-only people in the field. To sell our products, the regional salesforce had to first sell our concept, and that required salesmanship beyond the norm.

A short advertising campaign, our growing reputation and the fallout from a number of lender mergers, produced ten high-calibre recruits for us from a number of leading organisations. We knew that we had to double virtually every new business indicator in 1996 to make such an investment pay back, taking into account the staff growth at our Processing Centre. We had grown from 23 staff at the end of 1994 through 34 at the end of 1995, to 60 at the end of 1996. This was still tiny by the standards of the major institutions we were serving, but bigger than the "boutique" I had launched in 1987, and a powerful distribution force considering that, in 1996, we handled new applications worth £800m.

> To sell our products, the regional salesforce had to first sell our concept, and that required salesmanship beyond the norm

If we were to achieve the budgets we set ourselves for 1996 our regional salesforce had to hit the ground running. We therefore commissioned a corporate video: not to glorify any success we had enjoyed, but to put across our conceptual sales pitch to local intermediaries who had perhaps not used us before. The total cost, in 1996 money, was around £35,000, but we managed to lay off a third of this by way of sponsorship from four of our lenders. With a professional TV crew the video was written, filmed, edited and produced within a month and was available for our new regional salesforce to use in January 1996. It was certainly an education to have a film crew in the offices over two days, and to learn the techniques used to produce a quality item. For example, the crew spent two hours filming one shot of somebody's hand flicking through a leaflet!

The video, which was yet another example of selectively using marketing money to punch above our weight, worked spectacularly for us on several levels. First, it reassured those who had never dealt with us before that we were a company of substance. Second, it explained what we did. And third, it cut down dramatically on the number of cancelled field appointments all salesforces experience. We would send the video to a new prospect and then write to confirm that we would collect it at the meeting fixed at 2.30pm next Wednesday, for example. Because there was an extra purpose to the meeting (handing back the video), we found that people did actually turn up, having watched the 14-minute pitch about our concept. It meant that we could get straight down to selling the product(s) of the moment, and make better use of the 50 hours of new selling time per day that we were now achieving through the regional sales structure.

We appointed Simon Knight to the Board in January 1996 and, in his new position as Sales Director, he devised with Godfrey a set of sales monitoring rules and techniques which, from what we can see, are still some of the most sophisticated and detailed in use anywhere in mortgages today. Apart from the two days per week that each of them spends out in the field on point of sale coaching, the business generated by each field visit is monitored two, three and four weeks later. These findings are graded by each regional executive in their weekly reports, and statistics are produced at a monthly off-site get-together showing percentage usage of our products by each introducer, highlighting those who only used us once and those who are repeat users. We also analyse what product(s) each introducer has selected. This close attention to detail, on which I expand in Chapter 5, is one of the principal reasons we did, indeed, double virtually every business indicator in 1996 over 1995.

With the regional salesforce able to call on local intermediaries and explain our service, we were able to get more value for money through trade press advertising, and we significantly increased our spend in 1996. In fact, so valuable did we discover a constant presence in the trade press to be, that we booked the back page of *Financial Adviser* for the whole of 1997, save for a few weeks in the summer and over Christmas. We had by then changed the style of our ads to be shorter and totally product-related. Just as the AMG badge confers extra exclusivity and style on the Mercedes car that users know and love, so we now feature the logos of our well-known lenders first and foremost, with our own logo secondary. This confers the same message as the AMG badge – you know the quality institutions supplying the base product: our involvement has simply added some exclusive touches.

It is hard to know which of the new components we introduced to our £300,000 1996 marketing and promotion budget contributed most, since we had also purchased more sophisticated database management software and were undertaking a substantial personalised mailing at least once a month, with personalised faxing at least once a week. But the results spoke for themselves, none more so than our first product with the Halifax, with whom we had signed at last.

THE HALIFAX ON BOARD

After taking over Banque Nationale de Paris (BNP) in 1995, Halifax Building Society took a long hard look at where it wanted to be in the intermediary market. It decided to deal with intermediaries locally via the branches, but to allow its subsidiary, Halifax Mortgage

Services Limited (which included the BNP operation) to service added value schemes like our own. These were basically defined as schemes that provided such defined and mature added value services (for example the common application form, a constant flow of exclusive designs, and so on), that the business would not otherwise come to the society. Thus, in June 1996, after three years of on-and-off negotiation, we launched with Halifax, our first product modestly called "Mortgage of the Century".

The combination of long-term discount with an unusual double cashback (one sum in year one, and another in year three) captured the imagination of our distributors, as well as the preference to deal with a name like Halifax. This product eventually closed out in the spring of 1997 having achieved a record £250m of new business for us. By this time, Halifax Mortgage Services Ltd had joined Bristol & West and Kensington in providing us with an on-site underwriter, thereby further increasing the attraction to our distributors. With £150m having additionally been achieved with Britannia under two versions of a 3+3 product (3 per cent discount + 3 per cent cashback), and a swift £50m towards the end of the year under a 7.95 per cent five-year "General Election Cap" from Bradford & Bingley, we went into 1997 with gross lending that was nudging the equivalent of a top ten building society.

> When your awareness and support are at an all-time high it is important to keep investing

When your awareness and support are at an all-time high it is important to keep investing. You can spiral down in business as quickly as you can spiral up. We therefore kicked off 1997 by announcing a reintroduction of the major set-piece sales conferences in which we had specialised in the late 1980s and early 1990s. But of course, given the progress we had made, these events would need to be larger than we had ever tried before.

With a total promotional spend of £70,000, of which a third was met by sponsorship from three of our lenders, we set about funding some fixed and capped rate deals in January 1997 which would look very attractive once the general election had been announced. The smart money for election day was on 1 May, but, just before our conference invitations were set to go out, there was some press speculation about a switch to 21 March. We had booked two sales conferences for that day, so we moved them to the following week so that our conferences would, if necessary, straddle the election.

In the event, Mr Major stuck to his original date and we were able to announce a number of fixed and capped rate initiatives during a week of sales conferences 18–25 March 1997 that, as in 1992, were praised for their timing. A strong advertising and promotion campaign produced over 1300 registrations for the six conferences, with nearly 1000 intermediaries turning up. We were delighted with this response so near to the end of the tax year and, as always happens following this sort of investment, May 1997 – the second month after the sales conferences – was a new record for us in terms of new business submitted.

A major theme of the conferences was the new Mortgage Code being introduced by lenders as voluntary regulation. Intermediaries were being encouraged to comply with the principles of the Code until a working group could set the ground rules by which they would be formally included. When the Council of Mortgage Lenders (CML) was originally formed we had applied for membership on the grounds that, whilst we were not a lender, we influenced more new business than most of the organisations who *would* be eligible to join. We were pleased to have been accepted on that basis and to have remained the only non-lender, apart from HML, ever to be accepted as a full member of the CML. We played our part by promoting the new Code at the sales conferences, and even hired Terry Morrison again to write and perform a couple of humorous sketches to make some telling points about the new regulation.

One key aspect of this regulation as this book goes to press is procuration fee disclosure. Some argue that the shopkeeper does not have to declare his earnings, so why should the mortgage intermediary? The answer is that the goods you are buying from the shopkeeper are unlikely to have a major affect on your future life, whereas a mortgage will. Every practitioner knows that there is product bias in the market because of the growing trend for large procuration fees. We support transparency so that the customer knows exactly what's going on. I was pleased to be asked by the CML to join its working group dealing with the extension of the Code to cover intermediaries, and I feel sure that a workable and fair system of procuration fee disclosure will emerge.

The vast majority of our products now carry a £150 procuration fee. That is the limit we can stand from our margins without taking something away from the customer proposition. Our philosophy that less per case means more per annum is validated by the fact that we are currently paying out more than £100,000 per month in introducer fees, yet many of our products lead their particular market sectors.

Having achieved £800m of new business in 1996, the obvious target to set ourselves for 1997 was the magic £1 billion. This is gross applications handled rather than net completions, but is nevertheless a substantial figure by anybody's standards. By the halfway stage in 1997 we were ahead of budget. But there is a way to go yet in the weeks leading up to our tenth anniversary, which we are celebrating with another major corporate event. Two hundred guests have been invited to another black tie dinner, to be held this time at Madame Tussaud's.

WRAP-UP

For the first five years or so of our existence, there was no real competitor, or at least no company that came to our attention as such. In the second five years a few more multi-lender programmes have emerged. Many people see us as the leader of this particular sector, although I am still not convinced that we really belong in it. What we do for lenders in terms of research, design, distribution, promotion and the achievement of a 98 per cent offer strike rate is not really comparable with what most of the other multi-lender organisations undertake. Also, we quite clearly act for the lender whereas these other "packaging companies", as they have become known, do not appear to act for anyone but themselves. I am nervous about the ability of some of these competitors to survive financially when mortgage regulation makes insurance companies in particular much more choosy about who their salesmen are allowed to deal with. Nevertheless, on the whole, I do feel that Private Label has been the net beneficiary of this competition rather than the other way around, evidenced by the fact that it is during this period of greater competition that our new business results have exploded.

If you are selling breakfast cereal, you first have to create the demand within your target market for breakfast. You have to establish that it is healthy and slimming to have breakfast and to set yourself up for the day in this fashion. Once demand has been established you then satisfy that need by promoting the fact that your brand of breakfast cereal is the best.

The same structure is necessary if mortgage intermediaries are to be convinced that they do not have to deal with the lenders direct: they can instead access major lenders through the medium of a third party mortgage company. Once you have sold them on that concept you can then sell the benefits of your particular company. For a long time we were virtually the only people in the market trying to promote the multi-lender message. Now there are a couple of dozen such companies helping to create the demand and widen the market, which very often means that intermediaries have previously heard and understood the conceptual message, and are ready to hear about the merits of our particular company which obviously – although I am clearly biased – has the best story to tell in that particular sector. Because of the way in which so much business turns on the interaction of personalities, I am sure that we are similarly involved in some demand creation which is retrieved by our competitors. But, on the whole, whilst I remain nervous about being associated with a sector that does not have our financial resources to withstand a market downturn, I do feel that the competition has been very good for us, and long may it continue.

> ## The cost savings that a lender enjoys...are so significant that the end customer product has to benefit

The ten years have passed quickly. From a small sales and marketing boutique, providing an off-the-shelf mortgage package to small insurance companies, Private Label has grown to be a significant wholesaler of mainly building society products to the intermediary market at large. I see our position versus the bank and building society retailer as that of the out-of-town wholesaler. We cannot offer the local, high street service from people that the customer might also meet in the pub or at the golf club. But the cost savings that a lender enjoys by having us design and distribute mortgages, and process them to pre-offer stage, are so significant that the end customer product has to benefit.

There was a feeling in the market a couple of years ago that subcontracted pre-offer processing was not desirable from anybody's perspective. That position has now fundamentally changed for a variety of reasons. Credit scoring, where an application can be turned down by the computer without a reason being available, makes the prospect of being able to offer the clients an alternative that does not involve the completion of a new form, or the payment of another application fee, much more attractive. On-site underwriters for volume players like Private Label mean that intermediaries can sometimes get closer to a decisive opinion about a particular application via us than they could via some high street branches. And as we continually appraise what we do well, and what produces complaint, we are gradually bringing our service to a level which is giving an increasing number of intermediaries sufficient comfort to give us the next case, and so on.

The coming of our tenth anniversary does, of course, make us pause and reflect: what next? We have commissioned KPMG to undertake a strategic audit of our business, as a result of which will emerge our business plan for the next five years. Already one major project – a leads generation business – is near to launch, with yet further investments and diversifications on the drawing board in commercially sensitive areas that I cannot discuss here. I feel that we are better placed now than at any time in our ten-year history to expand rapidly. In the past few weeks alone we have established a terminal link with one lender, bringing ever closer the direct transfer of data which will speed up underwriting and processing via organisations like us beyond recognition. The seven-day mortgage? Why not?

We can forge new types of distribution relationship, providing even more sophisticated sales and marketing services for lenders, perhaps looking after their complete intermediary strategy. To our distribution market, we offer better and better products through the cost savings we deliver to lenders, backed up by compliance help with the new Mortgage Code.

We also have no fear about the market producing lower front end subsidies on new business. Our business was born at a time when, generally, there were no such subsidies, when product innovation really was at a premium. Reading the market, researching, responding to demand and designing the right exclusive products, has really been the engine room of our success over the last ten years, and this will continue to be our main focus for the foreseeable future. Sophisticated sales techniques to sell those products into the intermediary market, and high-tech processing of applications to pre-offer stage in a responsive way, are by-products of the core product innovation.

There is no doubt that the new Labour Government brings with it a new set of interests and challenges. With a declared inclination to legislate, and with a demonstrated intention to intervene where thought appropriate (e.g. increased stamp duty to help take the froth out of the property market at the top end), those involved in mortgages have a new set of principles and values to contend with at government level. I was pleased to have been invited by *Financial Adviser* to be on its panel of "experts" giving instant reaction to Chancellor Brown's first Budget. Sitting alongside me was Angela Knight (formerly Economic Secretary to the Treasury) and several people involved directly and indirectly in the selling of pensions. The pensions industry came off worse in this first budget, but a MIRAS reduction, and the precedent of increasing stamp duty (to rise again next year?), certainly gave me something to think about as well! Ultimately, any business manager must respect the views and values of the government of the day and work with those sentiments to the maximum advantage of his or her shareholders. Certainly I see nothing in this government's first few months in power to suggest that the mortgage market will not continue to recover, and remain at a volume level sufficient to continue its core importance to the economy.

Businesses go forwards or backwards. They are rarely able to stand still. We have taken an obscure concept – subcontracted mortgage design, distribution and pre-offer processing – and turned it into a substantial business, turning over nearly £8m in 1997, and regularly achieving £100m of new business in a month. We have started a "sector" of multi-lender organisations/packaging companies, and have proved that a focus on quality, integrity and putting the customer first is a winning long-term strategy.

We feel sure that the next ten years will hold many exciting challenges for us. We intend to meet those challenges head on, and prosper from the encounter.

July 1997

PART TWO

The market and how to sell into it

4

PRODUCT RESEARCH AND DESIGN

I t is estimated that today a full status mortgage applicant for an average advance, at an average loan-to-value, would have 4000 mortgage products to choose from. Yes, 4000. When I started my career in the mortgage department at a Halifax building society branch, which was not *that* long ago, there was no such thing as a mortgage product. A mortgage was a mortgage, and you were lucky to get one, let alone worry about different types.

The concept of anything being a "mortgage product" started in the late 1970s in a very small way, with differential pricing depending on the means of repayment, and whether the lending criteria were being relaxed. The wider use of derivatives (swaps, caps and so on) allowed one mortgage to be truly differentiated from another, and I was pleased to have played a small part in that development whilst at Citibank by launching into the UK mortgage market the first interest rate cap in 1986. In the same package we offered LIBOR-linked and fixed rate product offers, calling this new range of products "The Executive Selection". Such an approach seems modest now, but it was new at the time and, I think, helped to reshape the approach to taking a mortgage.

In the late 1980s product differentiation further expanded with cashflow innovation to respond to the high interest rates of the time. The ability to defer interest and have it added to the debt was constrained only by the imagination of the marketing people and the flexibility of the computer department. Michael Kelly would claim, with some justification, to have played a part in inventing in the early 1980s the long-term deferred interest mortgage on the back of some computer wizardry. But deferred products only became a widely sold part of the market during the period of very high interest rates of the late 1980s and early 1990s.

I have been involved in mortgage product design for the best part of 20 years. I introduced differentiated products in my building society days in the late 1970s, to try and mitigate the higher interest rates that a small society had to charge. At Citibank I was at the forefront of mortgage product development on behalf of what was then the largest foreign bank player operating in the UK market. And at Private Label, we have specialised in mortgage product design above all else.

As a concept, mortgage product design can be so much theory. But I am always more attracted by what *has* been done rather than what *might* be achieved. To fully share Private Label's unique experience as a specialist mortgage design company during a roller-coaster ten years of the mortgage market, I have selected 30 of our most interesting products and turned each of them into a case study, discussing how, when and why each product was launched, rating them as to their success.

We have tried most designs. Some have worked spectacularly well, others not so well. One of the company's principal assets is its cumulative experience of specialising in product design. The benefit of that experience is being passed on in this chapter. But first we must consider the role of research.

RESEARCH

No marketeer can operate without research. But it is important to have a healthy cynicism about the process. People often behave in research like the person they want to be, rather than the person they are, in private, when making buying decisions. So attitudinal or generic research should always be viewed against the background of what you know about human nature. Equally, you can't expect other people to innovate on your behalf: you must have the outline of an idea to put before people before you can research it. Having taken these points on board, however, no significant product should be undertaken without some kind of research, even if it is of the desk variety, which can be covered during the course of a business day.

It is important to research a product with those who will be selling it. This sounds straightforward, but I remember being at Citibank in 1986 when we researched "The Executive Selection" in focus groups with members of the public. There seemed to be support for the way we had given products brand names such as "Knightsbridge", "Mayfair" and "Kensington", so this is what we introduced. But the IFAs who were required to sell the product felt very uncomfortable with the brand names and we subsequently dropped them. I learned from this experience, and thereafter always gave mortgage products a descriptive name which simply explained what they did.

There are significant differences in the demand thrown up by various distribution channels which also need to be taken into account. It is my experience that insurance company direct sales-forces respond well to a scripted, structured approach in line with their own training, relating to the sale of investment products. The less money that direct sales people have to collect up front – operating as they often do in customers' homes – the easier the sale, so this can also be an important design factor. Mortgage brokers – and I have found no significant difference between IFAs and ARs in this respect – often respond more to the esoteric idea, although there can be strong regional variations. We sell more cashback than capped rate product in the north of England, for example.

The key point in all this is to decide on the distribution channel for a particular product and then research the idea using the distribution channel who will be selling the product. The technique we use is to establish a dozen or so people whose judgment we trust and to desk research them, simply by telephoning them and gauging their reaction. There is a risk that your idea might leak before it has been fully developed and is ready for launch, but this can be mitigated by choosing carefully the people on your research list.

Always listen to the research. A few interesting ideas I have put out to desk research have had to be abandoned when the intermediaries we approached didn't like them. I felt in some instances that they were wrong, but it is hard enough to get any new product to the top of a pile on an intermediary's desk without trying to overcome the additional hurdle of putting across a concept to which that particular intermediary channel has already demonstrated resistance.

After a product has been researched, it is important not to deviate significantly when putting the final format together, even during the inevitable horse-trading that subsequently takes place with individual lenders, all of whom have their own wish-lists and no-go areas. Desk research rarely enables you to pinpoint specific factors within the product design. Even if this were possible, intermediaries often find it difficult to respond meaningfully to such specifics in what has to be a relatively short telephone conversation. If, at design stage, you are proposing light redemption penalties, for example, it makes no sense to abandon that element, and impose heavy redemption penalties, without returning to the research. Too often we have had to deviate from the initial design of a product, only to find that the amended areas were exactly those that had made the product attractive at research stage. With those areas changed, the final format appeared to be only half the original deal and as a consequence, the product did not sell well.

What I have discussed so far is product-specific research in advance of a launch. However, preceding that research is the normal weekly intelligence-gathering that all active companies should undertake. Our sales team have always been required to submit weekly reports confirming what their key introducers are selling outside of our programme and why. This input from around the country is compared and collated by the marketing function and, if trends develop, we look to take advantage of them. The mortgage market has been over-supplied for the entire time Private Label has been in existence: you only stay ahead by knowing exactly what your competitors are doing, and what is being successful for them.

Research is too often the description invented by marketeers after the event to justify something that they intended to do anyway. "Excuse" would be a better description! There is no substitute for an ongoing, accurate research function and I make no apology for repeating the six golden rules as follows:

1 Factor in the fact that people sometimes behave differently when buying than they indicate in attitudinal and/or generic research;
2 Don't expect those you research to innovate for you;
3 Research a product in the distribution channel through which you intend to sell it;
4 Don't try to educate: if the research is negative, drop the idea;
5 Launch the product you researched – don't tinker;
6 Accept that research is ongoing and daily: always know what's selling outside of your programme and why.

ROLLING VERSUS FIXED END DATE

Before I move on to the case studies, it is important to understand the relative benefits of rolling or fixed end dates when it comes to discounted or fixed-rate products. With fixed and capped rate deals becoming much more common, the biggest headache for any treasurer is managing the expiry dates on the various hedging instruments put in place to support the rate certainty guarantee to the customers. For this reason alone, fixed end dates are increasingly common. There is also another very positive marketing reason for using an end date rather than a rolling period.

A mortgage product launched in January, for example, to a fixed end date of 1 January the following year, will be received as a one-year deal. Yet it will in fact be a seven-month deal in treasury terms. If a lender's financial model, for example, permits it to give away a 3 per cent discount in the first year then, by using an end date of the first of the same month in the year following, a 5.1 per cent discount can be offered – producing a much more exciting headline rate – whilst achieving the same giveaway. A 5.1 per cent discount for seven months equates to a 3 per cent discount for one year, taking into account the build-up of completions. The model below explains this more clearly:

WEIGHTED AVERAGE FUNDING PERIOD
FIRST YEAR ONLY

Month	Commentary	Funding period (Assuming completion mid-month)	Weighted factor
1	Launch	–	–
2	First applications	–	–
3	First packages	–	–
4	First completions	10% @ 8.5 months	0.85
5	Main completions	40% @ 7.5 months	3.00
6	{ Rest of	30% @ 6.5 months	1.95
7	completions	20% @ 5.5 months	1.10
Weighted average funding period first year			6.90

This model covers the period from the month of launch to the first of the same month in the next year, e.g. launch in January to an end date of 1 January the following year.

This deals with the first year period only, because all subsequent periods will be for the full 12 months. For example, a mortgage launched in January to an end date of 1 January two years hence will have a funding period of 18.9 months, whereas it will be received by the market as a two-year deal. There is nothing underhand about this: indeed, those who are able to remortgage quickly will beat the model and obtain maximum benefit. It is a genuine and straight-forward design approach in order to achieve the keenest rate, or to produce surplus in the model which can be used as a "fee-free" package, for example. As the market has become more sophisticated, however, introducers are aware of the advantages and disadvantages of fixed end dates and will very often bring this to the attention of customers when comparing one product with another.

The main disadvantage of a fixed end date is the shelf life it gives to the product. A fixed end date of 1 January has its best marketing period in January and, possibly, the first two weeks of February. Once you get past mid-February the impact starts to diminish. The use of an end date therefore limits the effective marketing period of the product and will have to be adjusted if the initial burst does not produce a sufficient level of applications to use up the money allocated. This is often why a rolling end date can be a better bet.

> It is a genuine and straightforward design approach in order to achieve the keenest rate

If research shows a particular product to have steady, but unspectacular, demand, such that we do not believe we can use up all of the money in a short burst marketing period, then we will design it with a rolling end date which will then give the product "legs". A fixed or discounted rate for a certain number of years from completion gives you a much longer selling period, although you would be faced with competition from products that have rates which look superficially lower, but which aren't cheaper in a financial modelling sense. You then have to be careful about how you sell the benefits of a rolling end date, just in case you scupper your own demand for the next product you come out with, which might have to have a fixed end date! In the case studies that follow, you will see examples of both types of product design.

CASE STUDIES

The rest of this chapter is aimed at providing the reader with practical assistance, rather than theory. As the UK's first specialist mortgage design and distribution company, we have launched an estimated 250+ product designs into the market over the last ten years. Some have been spectacular successes, whilst others have been either failures or moderate achievers only. I have selected some real life products from all three categories and analysed them under a number of different headings.

The analysis follows a consistent format throughout, with each product given a rating based on our actual experience. If the reader is an individual engaged today, or potentially, in mortgage product design, there will hopefully be some valuable lessons to learn from the specialist experience recounted in this chapter. Each product has been rated thus:

1 Sold out spectacularly and overshot the funding;
2 Sold out quickly and well;
3 Sold out, but steadily only;
4 Didn't sell out, but achieved enough business not to be a failure;
5 Failed.

Each case study can be cross-referenced with the illustrations in this chapter which show how the product was marketed at the time, by us or by others. A mixture of marketing styles appears in the illustrations, often reflecting our evolving ideas on product presentation plus our distributors' various advertisements and promotional items.

EYE-CATCHING HEADLINE RATE

CASE STUDY No. 1

Product name: 2.75% Discount 1/95
Lender: Britannia Building Society
Main benefits: Headline rate 5% below the prevailing variable rate, with a discount in year two to dilute payment shock
Timing: Launched January 1994
Rating: 1
Comment: The classic fixed end date approach to make more of the discount. The product featured in all the "best buy" tables and produced a monthly payment on a formal quotation which many customers found unavoidable. Spectacular sellout proving that a market-leading headline rate, producing a low initial outlay, will always have its place in the market.

CASE STUDY No. 2

Product name: 9.95% Fixed 7/02
Lender: Britannia Building Society
Main benefits: Sub-10% fixed rate considered, at the time, to be a "no lose" situation, since the average variable rate over the preceding ten years had been in excess of 12%
Timing: Launched March 1992, just as the general election of that year was being announced
Rating: 1

Comment: A mortgage rate of 15.4% was still very much in people's minds. To achieve the sub-10% rate we had to have an extra 1% for self-certification, an arrangement fee of 0.75% of the advance and compulsory ASU plus buildings and contents insurance. All of these additions blended in to produce a higher effective yield to the lender. Even then it was a tight squeeze over the cost of funds, but we were sure that money market rates would rise in the run-up to the 1992 election and that sub-10% would sell out during that particular period, which proved to be the case.

CASE STUDY No. 3

Product name:	13.75% Fixed 3/91
Lender:	Paribas Lombard Mortgages Ltd
Main benefits:	A fixed rate almost 1.75% below the record high variable rate then being charged by building societies
Timing:	Launched February 1990
Rating:	1

Comment: People had had enough of the 15.4% building society rate, with the press at the time holding out no optimism for an early reduction in rates. Indeed, there was some thought that rates might have to go up again. A fixed rate which shot to the top of the "best buy" tables at the time offered welcome relief and was quickly snapped up. Timing was the key, because we were one of the first to offer the relief that it was possible to achieve off the back of a falling yield curve.

AHEAD OF THEIR TIME

CASE STUDY No. 4

Product name:	Accelerator
Lender:	Leeds & Holbeck Mortgage Corporation
Main benefits:	The facility to pay twice per month in order to reduce the mortgage term
Timing:	Launched April 1993
Rating:	5

Comment: When lenders and the press claim today's new batch of "early payment mortgages" to be ground-breaking and innovative, they forget that we first launched such a product in the UK as long ago as 1993. We developed with the lender a computer programme which enabled mortgage applicants at interview to choose a monthly payment in £50 multiples, so long as this was above the minimum. The software would then immediately predict the new, reduced mortgage term and show how much interest would be saved. We used the Australian idea of twice-monthly payments and combined the product with a fixed rate, which gave it an extra boost. The personal finance editor of the *Sunday Telegraph*, writing on 2 May 1993, described the product as "…the best I have seen for a long time". But borrowers were not ready to pay more in order to reduce their mortgage term in 1993 and, surprisingly, the product did not take off.

CASE STUDY No. 5

Product name: Hedgemaster
Lender: Britannia Building Society
Main benefits: Cap & collar mortgage offering a 1% band above and below the then prevailing variable rate for the best part of five years
Timing: Launched September 1993 with an end date for the cap & collar of 1 January 1998
Rating: 4
Comment: The idea was to design a mortgage which was Utopia from the point of view of customers *and* intermediaries. Customers could hedge their bets in an uncertain interest rate environment by starting at the then prevailing variable rate, but locking into a 1% band either side for the best part of five years. Intermediaries could earn 0.4% of the loan, up to a maximum £1000, by recommending the lender's buildings and contents insurance: the fee being the net present value of five years' commission. The product did not sell because customers (a) wanted a monthly payment on their mortgage quotes which looked small; (b) were not prepared to pay at the standard variable rate even though they were receiving valuable long-term protection; and (c) because intermediaries were just not ready for large introducer fees of the type they are now beginning to get used to and welcoming.

TRIED AND TESTED

CASE STUDY No. 6

Product name: 3+3 "Election Beater"
Lender: Britannia Building Society
Main benefits: The formula that, in 1995/6, was virtually

guaranteed to work, namely a 6% giveaway in the form of a 3% discount and 3% cashback. This product also carried a guaranteed option to switch into a five-year fix within one month of the general election being called – a novel twist.

Timing: Launched March 1996

Rating: 1

Comment: This product had everything: a popular lender, one simple rate structure up to 95% LTV purchase or remortgage (plus fees), a tried and tested combination of discount and cashback plus a unique entitlement to write to the lender, within one month of the general election being called, and be guaranteed a quote for a new five-year fixed rate. When the election came in 1997 about 20% of borrowers took this option and received a generous fixed rate offer from Britannia. When the general year one "giveaway" model was 6%, we tried all types of different formulae (6:0; 1:5; 4:2, and so on), but 3:3, split evenly between discount and cashback, was always the one that worked best.

CASE STUDY No. 7

Product name: General Election Cap

Lender: Bradford & Bingley Building Society

Main benefits: Cap of 7.95% for a full five-year period from completion, with further fixed rate option and low redemption penalties

Timing: Launched December 1996

Rating: 1

Comment: Launching a spectacular rate protection product in the run-up to a general election is tried and tested. We funded this product in November 1996, and launched it in December 1996, which was a time when most other lending organisations were not properly focusing on the forthcoming election. The feeling was that rates might rise, as they traditionally do, after the election, but that the low inflation environment which had prevailed for longer than expected might also produce rate *reductions* in the medium term. A mortgage rate that could only rise by 1% over the then variable rate charged by the lender, but which could drop as low as the market took it, was very attractive, helped by the targeted product name. As with the 3+3 product, we bolted onto an already spectacular deal some benefits which made the product an overwhelming winner. For example, we guaranteed that borrowers would be entitled, at the end of the capped rate period, to apply for any fixed rate which the society was then making available to existing borrowers. Not a massive commitment for the lender, but always a helpful marketing tool. We then persuaded the lender to drop the redemption penalties from six months' interest in the first three years to just one month's interest for the following three years, with no redemption charge thereafter. With the markets not expecting a high interest rate environment in the medium term, the lender was able to secure a cap to hedge this product at a cost which was significantly less than the average cashback then being promoted by the mainstream lenders, so everybody won.

CASE STUDY No. 8

Product name: Fixed & Capped
Lender: Bradford & Bingley Building Society
Main benefits: A fixed rate of 6.99% for two years, followed by a cap at 7.99% for the next three years
Timing: Launched March 1997
Rating: 1
Comment: This product picked up where the General Election Cap left off. Sentiment had moved on during the first quarter of 1997, along the lines that interest rates *would* rise after the election whereas, previously, people were not so certain. The cap clicking in at the end of the fixed rate period gave a nice feel to the product, as it had done every single time we had launched the concept previously. Fixed & Capped is a tried and tested formula for when interest rates are rising in the short term, but predicted to fall in the medium term – a common scenario in the 1980s and 1990s.

CASE STUDY No. 9

Product name: Fixed & Capped
Lender: Branded Home Loans
Main benefits: A fixed rate of 10.95% for the first year of the loan followed by a 11.95/9/95% cap/floor in the following year to July 1993
Timing: Launched June 1991
Rating: 2
Comment: We dust off the fixed & capped idea every few years and it always sells out. To achieve a 10.95% rate, which was 2% below the prevailing variable rate, we had to charge a fee of one month's interest at the outset. We called this the Mortgage Rate Protection fee and brought it right up front in the promotional material. We felt

that nobody would lose out by taking this product, so we charged no redemption penalties, again using the technique of bolting on exciting features to a product which was already pretty spectacular. The view of the money market at the time was ahead of the views being expressed by intermediaries: we were therefore able to fund this product using a zero cost cap and floor (where lenders buy a cap and sell a floor achieving prices that equate to a "no cost" position).

CASE STUDY No. 10

Product name:	Fixed & Capped
Lender:	Paribas Lombard Mortgages Ltd
Main benefits:	A fixed rate of 12.75% for the first year, followed by a cap at the same level for the following year
Timing:	Launched September 1990
Rating:	2
Comment:	It's that same formula again. Relief from a high

interest rate environment (in this example a *circa* 3% reduction on the then prevailing variable rate), followed by a cap giving upside opportunity to the customer if rates subsequently fall.

EXPERIMENTAL DESIGNS

CASE STUDY No. 11

Product name:	10.95% Fixed 8/96
Lender:	Branded Home Loans
Main benefits:	A spectacular 10.95% five-year fixed rate, some 2% below the then variable rate
Timing:	Launched June 1991
Rating:	5
Comment:	We were desperate to achieve a 10.95% five-year

fixed rate at a time when the yield curve was not falling on that sort of gradient. We therefore came up with the idea of a fee equal to six months' interest being capitalised on the loan at outset. Customers would not have to pay this fee out of cashflow: they would only have to pay the interest on it. At the end of five years they would get the six months' interest fee back, and only lose it if they redeemed during the five years. We aimed off the loan-to-value to create room for the fee to always be added. The interest that the lender earned on the fee on a compound basis *during* the five years helped it to achieve an acceptable margin over the cost of funds. We immediately ran into problems, however, when the APR had to assume that the

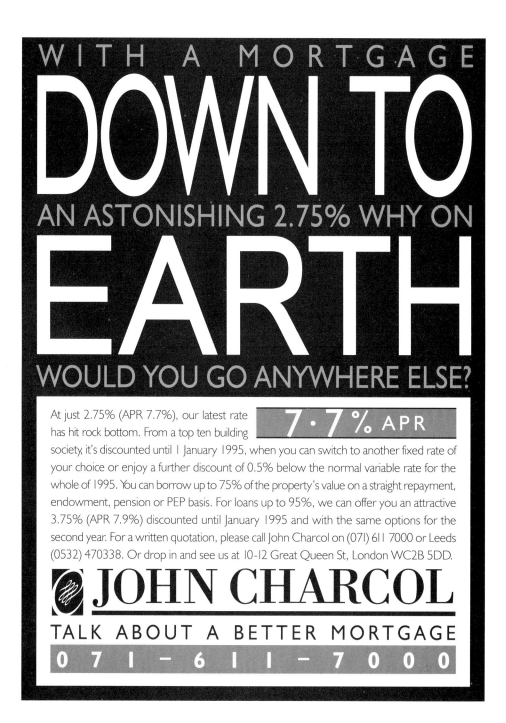

Case Study No. 1

John Charcol's Double Whammy.

A mortgage rate of 9.95% - and it's fixed for ten full years.

12% Typical APR

Over the last ten years, the mortgage rate has averaged out at over 12.5% — and there has not been a single year in which the average has fallen below 11%.*

Yet we can now provide a loan which is guaranteed not to rise above 9.95% (12% APR) at any time in the next ten years. It's fixed right through to July 2002.

And equally important, this unique mortgage is fully portable — so you can take it with you if you move in the future.

In today's uncertain world, we simply cannot see why anyone would choose any other kind of mortgage.

Funds, however, are very limited. To take your place among the small number of members of the Under-10% Club, you must contact us without delay.

For a written quotation, please call us before 8pm on (071) 589 7080. Or write to John Charcol, Mercury House, 195 Knightsbridge, London SW7 1RE.

(FIMBRA MEMBER)

JOHN CHARCOL

Talk about a better mortgage.

0 7 1 – 5 8 9 – 7 0 8 0

Case Study No. 2

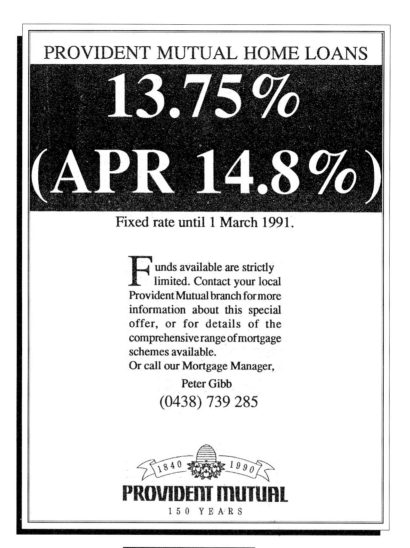

Case Study No. 3

Case Study No. 4

Case Study No. 5

Mortgage of the week

4.49% (APR 4.6%)

■ 3% Discount for 12 months + 3% Cashback to £9000

■ Option to switch free of charge to a five year fixed rate when next General Election is called

FUNDED BY

Britannia

Designed & Distributed Exclusively by

Private Label

MORTGAGE DESIGN
AND DISTRIBUTION

Call now on 01483 454 460

Case Study No. 6

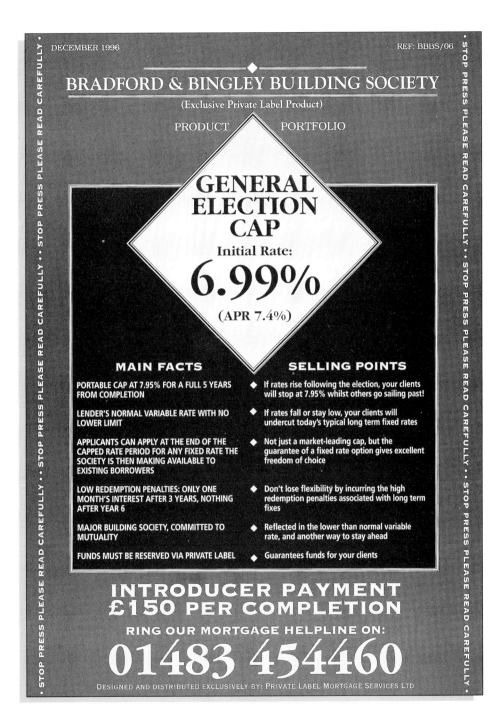

Case Study No. 7

This week's hot property.

£150 introducers' fee

- 5 Year Fixed & Capped
- Fixed at 6.99% to April 1999; then
- Capped at 7.99% to April 2002
- Fixed rate certainty when needed most
- Capped rate flexibility next three years

(APR 7.3%)

Funded by  BRADFORD & BINGLEY BUILDING SOCIETY

Designed & Distributed Exclusively by

Call now on 01483 726 161 MORTGAGE DESIGN AND DISTRIBUTION

Case Study No. 8

Introducing an exceptional new mortgage from MGM.
We've fixed it.
We've capped it.
Now we're plugging it.

In a nutshell, our mortgage is not only fixed and capped but also fully portable and totally free from redemption penalties.

No, it's not April 1st.

To reap the full benefits of this scheme, your clients need only pay a modest fee that amounts to just one month's interest. (We describe this sum more accurately as the Mortgage Rate Protection.)

Once spread over the term of the loan, this becomes insignificant.

For instance, a loan of £50,000 would only require an additional £4.16 interest payment per month.

A small price to pay for the following benefits.

10.95% (13.8% APR) FIXED RATE UNTIL JULY 1992

Nobody quite knows when Mr Major will go to the country.

All we do know is that he'll have to do so before July 1992.

10.95%
FIXED UNTIL JULY 1992

13.8%
TYPICAL APR

Of course, the Government will do its level best to reduce interest rates beforehand.

But just how swiftly this can be achieved is uncertain.

It's not a question, however, which needs to worry your clients.

With our new mortgage, they'll enjoy a fixed interest rate of 10.95% (13.8% APR) until 1st July 1992.

Which is all very worrying for other lenders.

After all, to compete with this figure, they'd almost certainly require Base Rate to average out at 10% (at the very least) over the run-up period to the General Election.

Many economists are currently doubtful that Base Rate can reach 10% before 1st July 1992, let alone average 10%.

Consequently, your clients stand to make a considerable saving by fixing into our fixed rate now.

The good news though, is by no means over.

11.95% CAPPED RATE UNTIL JULY 1993

Following the election of the next Government, it is more than feasible that interest rates could start going up again.

But once again, your clients will have little to worry about.

For a full year from July 1992 to July 1993, our rates are guaranteed not to rise above 11.95%.

Bearing in mind that the average mortgage rate over the last five years has been over 12%, it's not difficult to see how competitive this really is.

Of course, should prevailing rates continue to fall until July 1993, ours will fall with them, down to a minimum of 9.95%.

But what should happen if (and it has to be a very big if) interest rates were to continue to fall below that level?

The answer is simple:

NO REDEMPTION PENALTIES AT ANY TIME

Unlike so many other fixed-rate mortgages, you won't find any small print in ours that penalises clients who redeem their mortgages early.

In other words, should your clients feel they could do better elsewhere, they'd be free to do so without confronting any interest penalties, administration charges or notice requirements.

Since this benefit lasts for the entire mortgage term, it provides the ultimate protection against unforeseen problems.

Needless to say, it also ensures that our rate will always remain as competitive as possible.

Which is precisely why your clients may be very grateful for the fourth and final benefit.

NO PENALTIES IF YOUR CLIENTS MOVE PROPERTY

In the event of moving house prior to 1st July 1993, your clients needn't lose the benefits of the fixed and capped rates.

As long as their new loan is for the same amount as the existing one (or less), all benefits will normally be transferred.

If all this sounds too good to be true, simply call the number below and we'll give you some unusual and convincing evidence, in the form of a video, specifically designed for you to show your clients, which tells the whole story.

It'll leave you in no doubt that as well as fixing, capping and plugging our new mortgage, we've also got it taped.

Available through MGM to Independent Financial Advisers, Appointed Representatives of MGM, including The Corporate Tied Agents Company PLC.

MGM ASSURANCE®

Marine and General Mutual Life Assurance Society

MGM Assurance, MGM House, Heene Road, Worthing, West Sussex, BN11 2DY.

0800 590217

Case Study No. 9

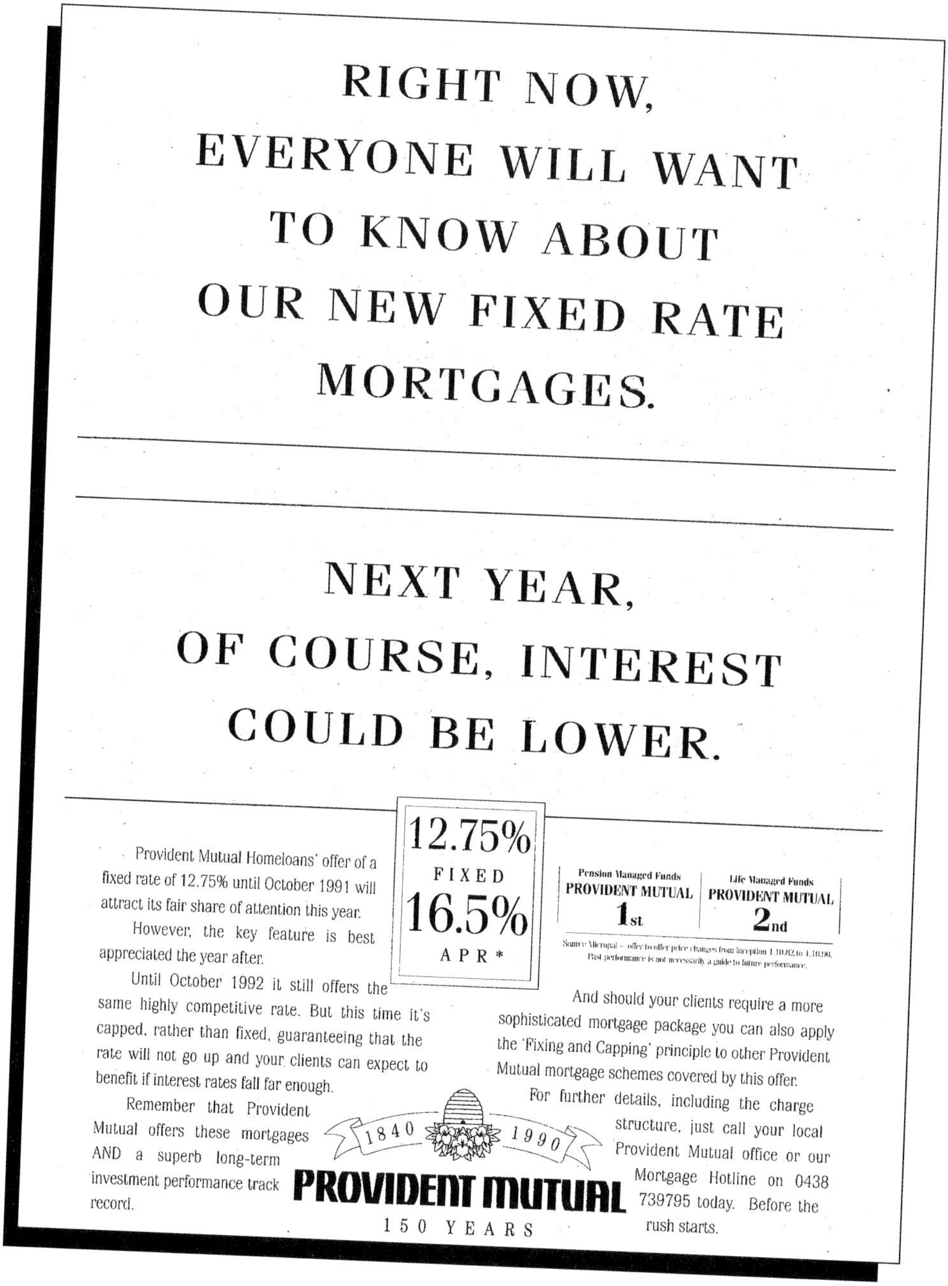

RIGHT NOW, EVERYONE WILL WANT TO KNOW ABOUT OUR NEW FIXED RATE MORTGAGES.

NEXT YEAR, OF COURSE, INTEREST COULD BE LOWER.

12.75%
FIXED
16.5%
APR *

Pension Managed Funds	Life Managed Funds
PROVIDENT MUTUAL	PROVIDENT MUTUAL
1st	**2**nd

Source: Micropal – offer to offer price changes from inception 1.10.82 to 1.10.90.
Past performance is not necessarily a guide to future performance.

Provident Mutual Homeloans' offer of a fixed rate of 12.75% until October 1991 will attract its fair share of attention this year.

However, the key feature is best appreciated the year after.

Until October 1992 it still offers the same highly competitive rate. But this time it's capped, rather than fixed, guaranteeing that the rate will not go up and your clients can expect to benefit if interest rates fall far enough.

Remember that Provident Mutual offers these mortgages AND a superb long-term investment performance track record.

And should your clients require a more sophisticated mortgage package you can also apply the 'Fixing and Capping' principle to other Provident Mutual mortgage schemes covered by this offer.

For further details, including the charge structure, just call your local Provident Mutual office or our Mortgage Hotline on 0438 739795 today. Before the rush starts.

1840 1990

PROVIDENT MUTUAL
150 YEARS

Case Study No. 10

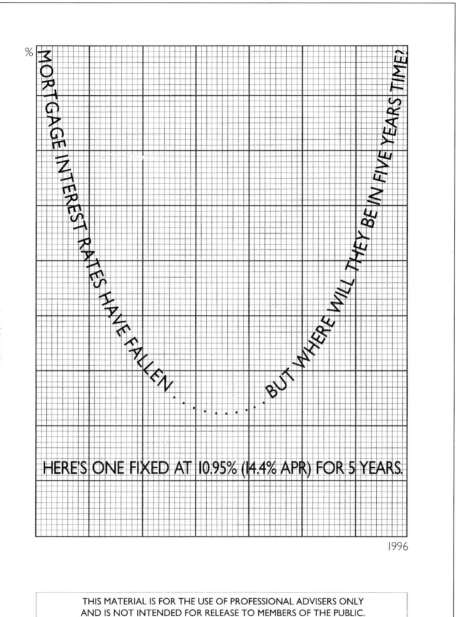

% MORTGAGE INTEREST RATES HAVE FALLEN . . . . . . BUT WHERE WILL THEY BE IN FIVE YEARS TIME?

HERE'S ONE FIXED AT 10.95% (14.4% APR) FOR 5 YEARS.

1996

THIS MATERIAL IS FOR THE USE OF PROFESSIONAL ADVISERS ONLY
AND IS NOT INTENDED FOR RELEASE TO MEMBERS OF THE PUBLIC.
IT IS A SUMMARY ONLY AND THE FULL SCHEME CRITERIA SHOULD BE CONSULTED
FOR A DEFINITIVE DESCRIPTION OF THE LENDING TERMS.

Front cover

Case Study No. 11

**Table 1:
Building
Societies'
Average
Mortgage
Rates
1981-1990**

History shows that whenever mortgage interest rates have fallen, they have have gone up again, sometimes quite sharply, in the following years.

This means that, from time to time, there is a moment in the interest rate cycle when the right course of action is to lock into a low, long-lasting fixed rate.

This is just such a moment: and now there is just such a product available.

Consider the longer-term trends, and you'll appreciate the point. As *Table 1* shows, over the last ten years the average annual Building Society variable rate has been no less than 12.70%°.

Not only that, average annual rates have never fallen below 11%° in the last decade.

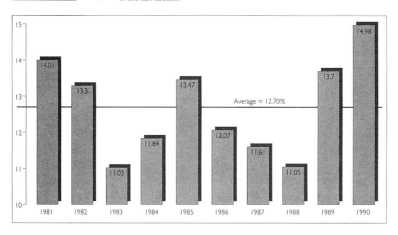

* Source:
Council of Mortgage Lenders
'Housing Finance' May 1991

FIXED AT 10.95% FOR 5 YEARS (14.4% APR)

Just imagine then, how attractive a rate of only 10.95% would be if it was actually fixed for the next five years until 1st August 1996.

It would be an exaggeration to call it a once-in-a-lifetime opportunity: but once-in-five-years would not be stretching a point.

FIVE YEARS OF STABILITY

Another look at the graph will also show you how volatile interest rates have been, and how welcome a period of five years of constant payments (without a penny of deferred interest) would be for your clients.

Inside left page

Case Study No. 11

A SMALL PRICE TO PAY

You might expect that a whole string of special conditions would be attached to this offer.

But in fact, there are only two.

The first is a simple arrangement fee of £395, which will be added to the loan.

The second is a highly ingenious new idea.

It is called a Redemption Bonus, and it involves an additional six months' interest being added automatically to the loan at the outset.

But, at the end of the fixed rate period, this apparent handicap is transformed into a positive advantage. The six months' interest is then repaid in full as a Bonus, either as a cash lump sum or as a deduction from the mortgage balance outstanding.

Of course, the additional six months' interest when added to the loan, does itself attract interest at 10.95% for the first five years.

But, as *Table 2* demonstrates, this would still offer a comfortable saving when compared with average annual Building Society rates over the last ten years.

Indeed, to show just how competitive this mortgage is, the table also includes a comparison with an illustrative 11.99% fixed rate for 5 years.

Table 2:

COMPARATIVE RATE	MONTHLY PAYMENT	TOTAL PAYMENTS OVER FIVE YEARS	SAVING OVER FIVE YEARS
Average Building Society rate over the last ten years @ 12.70%*.	£529	£31,740	£2,880
Illustrative Example: 11.99% fixed for five years	£500	£30,000	£1,140
10.95% fixed for five years, including interest on the Redemption Bonus	£481	£28,860	–

All calculations based on gross interest on a £50,000 loan. These are mathematical comparisons and there can be no guarantees as to how this fixed rate mortgage will compare over the next five years with average variable rate mortgages.

As you can see, the Redemption Bonus is a cost-effective vehicle for five years of interest rate stability. The client then has the option at the end of the fixed rate period of having the Redemption Bonus recredited to the mortgage, or leaving it on the account and taking it in the form of a cash lump sum.

The six months' interest "payment", returnable at the end of the five year period, has been included in the APR calculation as required by law. If this figure is not taken into account, then the equivalent effective annual rate would be 13.6%.

Inside right page

Case Study No. 11

FULL PORTABILITY AND SELF-CERTIFICATION

The benefits under this mortgage are fully portable, and it is only in the event of redemption within the five-year fixed period that the Bonus is sacrificed.

And finally, there is also a self-certification option – which, at an extra 1%, will still prove extremely attractive.

It goes without saying that funds are limited. Demand is expected to be heavy, so apply quickly.

For further information, please respond to:

Key administration points

MINIMUM LOAN	£16,000	MAXIMUM LOAN £235,000
LIFE COVER	110% of loan applied for	
INCOME MULTIPLES	2.75 x primary plus 1 x secondary or 2.25 x joint	

LOAN SIZE	MAXIMUM LOAN-TO-VALUE
£16,000 – £150,000	90%
£150,001 – £200,000	85%
£200,001 – £235,000	80%

The six months' interest Redemption Bonus will be automatically added beyond the income multiples and loan-to-values shown.
The lender is Branded Home Loans, which is a trading style of The Mortgage Corporation Ltd. The products and interest rates available from Branded Home Loans are SEPARATE and DIFFERENT from those available via The Mortgage Corporation Ltd in its mainstream lending. Branded Home Loans' registered office is Victoria Plaza, 111, Buckingham Palace Road, London SW1W 0SR.

Typical example

Example Loan: £50,000. Six months interest added to loan, amount £2737.50. Monthly payment fixed at 10.95% APR 14.4% until 1st August 1996. Current Standard Variable rate 12.95% APR 13.9%. APRs include 6 months interest, arrangement fee £395, and estimated legal and valuation fee. Initial monthly interest payments of £481.23 (Gross). Monthly average endowment premium £73.84 may be payable (assuming a single man aged 29 years). THIS IS NOT AN ILLUSTRATION AND THE ENDOWMENT PREMIUM MENTIONED MAY DIFFER FROM THE PREMIUM ACTUALLY QUOTED. Total Amount Payable £218,895 Gross, (300 monthly payments). Loan repayable at the end of the term. A life assurance policy may also be required. A Mortgage Guarantee Policy may also be required. Max loan to value 90%. Minimum Age 20. Written Quotation available. Subject to status and valuation.

Back cover

Case Study No. 11

It's 50-50 whether mortgage rates will rise or fall.
So here's a 50-50 mortgage.

Right now, times aren't easy for mortgage advisers.

The market is flat, and you'll no doubt be feeling the competition from high street institutions.

So wouldn't you have a better chance of competing if you could tell your clients about a completely new kind of mortgage? One that's <u>not</u> available in the high street. One that's tailor-made to today's economic climate. And one that's <u>only</u> available from mortgage advisers.

Something different to tell your clients

Some clients ask, "If I choose to take out a variable rate loan, what happens if interest rates start to rise again?" Meanwhile, others say, "If I take out a fixed rate loan, what happens if interest rates continue to fall?"

If only there was a mortgage that could give them the best of both worlds. Well now there is.

We call it the '50-50', because it's 50% fixed and 50% variable.

It allows clients to take half of their mortgage at a highly competitive variable rate, with the remaining half at an equally attractive fixed rate.

In other words, clients can hedge their options, while at the same time minimising some of the worst pitfalls of old-fashioned variable or fixed rate loans.

"So much for the simple theory," you're saying, "but how will such a mortgage work?" Surprisingly enough, the answer is simpler than you would imagine.

A fixed and variable rate of 9.99% (11.9% APR)

Both halves of this entirely new mortgage will initially be set at 9.99% (11.9% APR).

The average annual building society mortgage rate over the last ten years has been 12.6%, so it's not difficult to see just how competitive this rate really is.

The fixed element will remain in place until 1st September 1995. And its variable counterpart – which represents a discount of 0.71% from the lender's current variable rate until 31st January 1993 – will move in line with building society rates generally.

From inception of the loan, your clients have just one standing order. It's as simple as that.

The nitty-gritty

In addition to these highly unusual benefits, we can offer up to 95% LTV for purchases and 90% LTV for remortgages (as long as the uplift on the remortgage does not exceed £20,000 or 15%—whichever is lower).

The minimum loan is £40,000 and the maximum is £200,000. You'll also find the income multiples on the generous side at 3.25 times single, or 2.5 times joint income. The arrangement fee is just £295 (which can <u>always</u> be added to the loan if required).

And unlike some mortgages we could mention, the redemption penalty associated with this loan only amounts to a single month's interest, during the fixed rate period.

But the real icing on the cake is that this loan comes from a major building society, alongside a cast-iron customer security guarantee designed to help advisers like you.

<u>So don't waste a second. For more details, please call Laura Marlow on 0494 466124.</u>

50% FIXED RATE 9.99% (11.9% APR)

50% VARIABLE RATE 9.99% (11.9% APR)

EQUITY & LAW
AN AXA *INTERNATIONAL COMPANY*

Case Study No. 12

133

Introducing the Cap and Garter Mortgage.

(It's like a collar, but is too low to be shown in public)

10.95%

8.99%
(10.7%)
APR VARIABLE

5.95%

3 Years' Protection -
to 1st September, 1995

The problem with most cap and collar mortgages has been that the band between the maximum and minimum rates is too narrow.

Until now, that is. Our new Cap and Garter mortgage is different.

Its rate can fall to as low as 5.95% during the period from completion to 1st September, 1995, yet remain protected under a very competitive 10.95% cap.

That widens the band to a huge 5% differential, a benefit bound to appeal to customers.

Launch Rate 8.99% (10.7% APR Variable)

Another problem with most cap and collar mortgages has been a launch rate at the same level as the cap. So one is never quite sure whether the full benefit of rate reductions will be applied as and when they occur.

Until now, that is. Again, our new Cap and Garter mortgage is different.

We're launching *this* cap and collar at 8.99% (10.7% APR variable) – almost 2% below the level of the cap.

This reflects a 1% discount on the lender's normal base rate, and it's guaranteed for the first six months following completion, *whenever completion takes place.*

Competitive Arrangement Fee

Yet another problem with most cap and collar mortgages has been a large loading on the arrangement fee to cover the cost of the cap.

Until now, that is. Once more, our new Cap and Garter mortgage is different.

Its arrangement fee is just £245 and, like the indemnity premium, can always be added to the loan if required.

Cap and Garter Summary of Benefits

Even now, we haven't revealed all the benefits. Here's the full list:

- 10.95% cap and 5.95% collar to 1.9.95
- 8.99% launch rate (10.7% APR variable)
- 1% discount from lender's normal base rate for first 6 months
- Arrangement fee, only £245, may be added to loan
- Income multiples 3.25 + 1 or 2.5 x joint up to £75k; 3 + 1 above £75k
- Lender's ASU *or* buildings and contents during the period of the cap and collar only
- Min loan £20k; max loan £150k
- Only three months' redemption interest prior to 1.9.95; normal terms thereafter
- Max 95% LTV purchase; 90% LTV remortgage
- Full portability
- No cross-selling guarantee
- Top 20 Building society lender.

How to Apply

Funds are limited and will be allocated on a first come, first served basis. They must be booked in advance and accompanied by a reservation fee of £35.

But don't delay, and apply soon for our new mortgage.

You'll find that like any good garter, it won't let you down.

For further details, an application form or a written quotation, please contact one of the companies listed below.

Typical Example: An interest only mortgage of £50,000 on a property valued at £75,000, repaid over 25 years, assuming completion 15/12/92. Gross repayments of £399.68 in each of the first six months with interest at 8.99% (10.7% APR), followed by gross repayments of £441.38 at a current variable rate of 9.99% (10.7% APR) in each of the next 26 months, followed by 268 gross repayments of £416.30 at a current variable rate of 9.99% (10.7% APR). Gross repayments include £29.08 in respect of the premium for the compulsory buildings and contents insurance during the capped period from completion to 1/9/95. Total cost of credit £126,292.62 calculated to include £245 arrangement fee, non-refundable £35 reservation fee, £200 legal fees, £150 valuation fee, £222.76 accrued interest and and £117.50 redemption fee. A suitable policy may be required. Loans subject to status, type and value of property. Written quotations are available on request. Security will be required. Limited funds available.

Case Study No. 13

APRIL.1995   REF: CMS/WB/05

PRODUCT
PORTFOLIO

WEST BROMWICH BUILDING SOCIETY

ZEROLOAN WITH MIGP ADDED
5.55% (APR 5.7%)

KEY FACTS	KEY SELLING POINTS
• NO ARRANGEMENT FEE, <u>FREE</u> VALUATION AND £350 CASHBACK.	• Zero cost of entry for most borrowers - ideal for first time, next time and remortgage borrowers alike.
• MIGP ALWAYS ADDED (WITHIN INCOME), EVEN AT 95% LTV.	• No cash outlay required for MIG premium either.
• 3% DISCOUNT TO 1/1/97 UPTO 95% LTV PURCHASE OR REMORTGAGE.	• Simple sale - one rate for everybody (no need to worry about down-valuations).
• NO COMPULSORY BUILDINGS AND CONTENTS INSURANCE.	• Applicants, and their advisers, are free to choose their own buildings and contents insurance arrangements.
• LENDER'S LOAN PROTECTION INSURANCE REQUIRED OVER 90% LTV.	• Valuable (and topical) cover for high LTV borrowers.
• RESERVATION FEE OF £95 TO ACCOMPANY <u>ALL</u> APPLICATIONS, REFUNDED AT COMPLETION OR IF CASE FAILS INITIAL ASSESSMENT.	• Another zero cost for those who complete or who fail the criteria day one.

EXCLUSIVE PRIVATE LABEL PRODUCT, NOT AVAILABLE FROM THE LENDER DIRECT. SEE OVERLEAF FOR IMPORTANT CRITERIA AND ADDTIONAL INFORMATION.

RING OUR MORTGAGE
HELPLINE ON:
01483 · 454460

Designed and distributed exclusively by: Private Label Mortgage Services Ltd

Case Study No. 14

FIXED PAYMENT MORTGAGE
Set your mortgage repayment according to your budget

House Sales & Mortgages

At a time when interest rates are higher than they have been for many a year the amount you set aside for your mortgage repayment each month has never been so important. It looks likely that the current high interest rates are here to stay for a while. So we have developed a mortgage scheme that allows you, within reason, to set your mortgage payment according to your budget. This mortgage is available through Stuart Wyse Ogilvie under our own 'Prestige' scheme.

HOW DOES IT WORK?

The Fixed Payment Mortgage allows you to make a payment each month equivalent to an interest rate of as little as 9.99% p.a. (typical APR 12.5%). It is available for new mortgages or, if you already have a mortgage, to replace your existing loan. You can set your payment at a fixed rate for either two or three years, depending on the amount you want to borrow and the value of your property.

HOW MUCH CAN YOU BORROW?

You may be able to borrow more than you thought and perhaps buy a better house than you expected. This is because we are able to offer higher multiples of your income on this scheme than for ordinary mortgages. The multiples are up to 3.5 times the main salary (plus a second applicants salary, if applicable) or, for joint borrowers, up to 2.75 times your joint salaries.

CAN THE PAYMENTS BE CHANGED?

This mortgage is virtually as flexible as you want it to be. The payment you make each month for the first two or three years (depending on which option you select) can stay the same; that is at a rate as low as 9.99% p.a. (typical APR 12.5%). However, if you decide to set your payments higher; you can change your mind by simply giving one month's notice in writing to our administrators. You can do this as often as you like, but you must always make a payment that is at least at the minimum rate of 9.99% p.a. (typical APR 12.5%).

WHAT HAPPENS AT THE END OF THE FIRST TWO (OR THREE) YEARS?

The mortgage then becomes an ordinary variable rate mortgage. If you have made a payment throughout the first two or three years (according to your selected option) at a rate less than the prevailing charge rate, there may be an increase in the amount you owe on your mortgage. This is because the lender will add any shortfall between the payment you are making and the full charge rate, to your mortgage account. However, the charge rate is variable, so if interest rates come down the amount to be added will reduce accordingly.

WHAT ABOUT TAX RELIEF?

Although you are free to set your repayment where you like at any rate from 9.99% upwards, tax relief will be granted at the prevailing charge rate so the net cost of your mortgage will be reduced further.

ARE THERE ANY FEES INVOLVED?

There is an administration charge and there may also be an Indemnity Guarantee premium, depending on the percentage of the value of your property your new mortgage amounts to. However, irrespective of your income, or the amount of the loan when compared to the value, these fees will always be added to the loan. This will reduce your costs at the outset.

HOW DO YOU APPLY FOR A FIXED PAYMENT MORTGAGE?

You will need to satisfy the basic conditions for the Fixed Payment mortgage. The mortgage consultant at your local branch of Stuart Wyse Ogilvie will be able to help you and will be able to tell you if you qualify for a Fixed Payment mortgage. You must be at least 21 years of age (or 23 if you wish to obtain the joint multiple) and be in permanent employment. Additionally, the maximum mortgage you can obtain is 75% of value for the two year option or 70% of value for the three year option.

WHAT IS THE BENEFIT OF THE FIXED PAYMENT MORTGAGE?

At a time of unusually high interest rates the amount you have to pay each month for your mortgage is usually crucial to you. It can be of great comfort to know that your mortgage payments are fixed and need not change for a given period of time. The usual answer to this problem is to take a 'fixed interest' mortgage. However, it seems likely that interest rates may not rise much higher, so taking a fixed interest mortgage at present may not pay in the long run. The alternative is the Fixed Payment mortgage from Stuart Wyse Ogilvie. You still have the advantage of being able to budget for a regular mortgage payment for a set period, but with the flexibility of changing the payment if you wish.

Licensed credit brokers.
Mortgages subject to status.
Full written details available on request.

Stuart Wyse Ogilvie are appointed representatives of
GA Life Assurance and Pensions
A member of Lautro
Stuart Wyse Ogilvie are Licensed Credit Brokers

Case Study No. 15

DESIGN A MORTGAGE FROM A TOP TEN BUILDING SOCIETY.

Private Label

Made to Measure Mortgage

And get £400 per case for your skill.

Front cover

Case Study No. 16

Funded by

Britannia

Designed and distributed exclusively by

Who else gives you the opportunity to sit down with each client and say "What would <u>you</u> like from your mortgage?"

Our Made-to-Measure Mortgage has already been acclaimed in the trade press (see back page comments). We are pleased to announce that it is now available to you.

Each mortgage can be designed according to individual needs, and is funded by Britannia Building Society exclusively for Private Label. It is not available from Britannia direct.

Each mortgage is based around a normal variable rate loan with no compulsory general insurances.

The idea works as simply as this: your clients can choose between a range of benefits (see table opposite) to the maximum value of 8 points. You tick the appropriate boxes, and your clients get a Made-to-Measure Mortgage.

Let's take the example of a first-time buyer. A 1% discount, free valuation and reservation and a £600 cashback would use the 8 points to maximum effect. A remortgage customer might wish to transfer to a 1% discount with a £1,000 cashback covering costs plus a cash sum on top. Others might be tempted by free ASU for up to two years, free MIG or a substantial contribution to legal costs. The choice is <u>yours</u>!

We appreciate that this product requires extra skill and attention on your part. It is no more than your clients deserve, but we feel you should be rewarded for it. In addition to the substantial customer benefits, therefore, we will be paying you **£400** per completion. No clawback. No fuss nor paperwork. Just a cheque from us to you within a few weeks of completion.

If you have any queries, call our Mortgage Helpline on 01483 454460.

Inside left page

Case Study No. 16

Using the Made-to-Measure Points Scheme could not be easier. One selection can be made from each of the seven categories up to a maximum of 8 points. The selections should then be entered in the options boxes and sent to us with the application form. You can photocopy the matrix printed below or ask us for a loose leaf supply:

Made-to-Measure Mortgage

Categories 1-7	Points System	Selection (max one from each category)	Enter Your Points in Box
1. DISCOUNTS		(Tick box)	
■ 1% discount for 12 months	= 3 points		
■ 2% discount for 12 months	= 6 points		points
2. Free MIG	= 5 points		points
3. Valuation and reservation fees refunded (up to a maximum £250)	= 2 points		points
4. Legal costs contribution (up to £600)	= 3 points		points
5. Reservation fee refunded	= 1 point		points
6. CASHBACKS			
■ £200 cashback	= 1 point		
■ £400 cashback	= 2 points		
■ £600 cashback	= 3 points		
■ £1,000 cashback	= 5 points		points
7. FREE ASU (employed applicants only)			
■ Free ASU for 6 months	= 1 point		
■ Free ASU for 12 months	= 2 points		
■ Free ASU for 24 months	= 4 points		points
		Enter total (maximum 8)	points

■ If the Free MIG option is not selected, and the application is for a 95% LTV loan, then the MIG charge can be added within income so long as we are notified at reservation stage. There is only a limited sub tranche of "MIG added" funds, and applications without the special reservation number will not enjoy the "MIG added" offer condition. So do specify "MIG added," if required, when submitting the application.

■ With 1 above the lender will specify in the offer.

■ With 2 and 7 above the lender will not charge.

■ With 4 above, applicants send the legal bill to the lender for reimbursement post completion.

■ With 6 above, applicants apply to the lender for reimbursement post completion.

■ With 3 and 5 above, we will refund to the introducer post completion.

If you have any queries, call our Mortgage Helpline on 01483 454460.

Inside right page

Case Study No. 16

What the papers say.

"Private Label Mortgage Services seems to have hit on a winner."
Financial Product Review, 9 March 1995.

"Designer mortgage from Private Label meets client needs."
Product Adviser, 2 March 1995.

"Private Label, the specialist mortgage design and distribution company, has launched a mortgage which will enable intermediaries to design and customise mortgages according to their clients' circumstances."
What Mortgage, April 1995.

"You cannot have any greater input than being able to design every new mortgage differently, according to each customer's needs."
Mortgage Marketing Digest, April 1995.

"Private Label to tailor mortgages for brokers."
Money Marketing, 2 March 1995.

Other Key Points

- Income multiples — 3+1 or 2.5 x joint.
- Loan size — £15.5K-£3m.
- Repayment method — Repayment or interest only.
- Term — 10-30 years.
- Loan purpose — Purchase or remortgage.
- Age — Minimum 18. Maximum 70.
- Redemption — 120 days in the first three years; 20 days in years four and five.
- Solicitors — Applicant's if known to Society.
- Rate — Society's standard base variable rate (less discounts if requested).
- Arrangement Fee — £150 (on completion only).

ALL ENQUIRIES TO PRIVATE LABEL PROCESSING CENTRE, 2 BELL COURT, LEAPALE LANE, GUILDFORD, SURREY GU1 4LY. TELEPHONE: 01483 454460; FAX: 01483 454468.

The material in this brochure is for the use of professional advisers only and must not be handed to clients or used to promote or advertise the product.

Back cover

Case Study No. 16

The Chancellor hopes for interest rate cuts over the next six years.

We guarantee them.

If we offered you a fixed rate loan at 9.99% (11.6% APR) from completion until 1 November 1995, you'd think it was a good deal.

If we then guaranteed that the fixed rate would reduce to 9.49% (11.6% APR) for the following two years until 1 November 1997, you'd think it was a very good deal.

But if we further guaranteed that, in the final year to 1 November 1998, the fixed rate would reduce again to 8.99% (11.6% APR), you'd probably bite our arm off.

Which is why we've already started to shorten our sleeve!

Because those are exactly the terms of our exciting new mortgage offer, giving welcome mortgage rate certainty whatever happens politically or economically over the medium term.

SPECIAL IN-HOUSE FAST-TRACK REMORTGAGE DEAL

We expect that quite a few clients will wish to remortgage into this exciting new offer. So we've made it as easy as possible to achieve this quickly and inexpensively.

The speed comes from the lender's rapid remortgage insurance policy (free to the customer), which allows remortgages to complete without the need for most of the normal time-consuming legal work.

The inexpensive element arises from a very special offer that the lender's legal department is making to all remortgage applicants. If applicants choose to instruct the lender's legal department to complete the remortgage formalities, a charge of just £90 inclusive of VAT (plus disbursements) will be made. An astonishing bargain on top of a mortgage offer which already justified that description!

GENEROUS TERMS AVAILABLE

Loans are available from £15,500 to £250,000 within criteria, and above that figure by negotiation. Up to 95% of valuation can be considered for purchase or remortgage, with no interest rate loading for remortgages.

Income multiples are 3 + 1 or 2.5 x joint and this fully portable loan is available on a capital and interest or interest only basis. A reservation fee of £35 is payable, and the (normally added) arrangement fee is just £395. In the unlikely event that clients wish to redeem early, the redemption charge is six months' interest during the fixed rate period. The lender also requires its accident, sickness and unemployment, and buildings and contents cover to be taken.

CUSTOMER SECURITY FROM A TOP TEN BUILDING SOCIETY

If you like the beginning and middle parts of this product, then you'll love the ending! Because not only is the lender a top ten building society, making this offer via mortgage advisers only, but there's also a cast iron customer security guarantee in place that there will be no cross-selling of life or pension products.

Sounds like Utopia? You bet! But Utopia is only achieved by a privileged few. In this case the privileged few who book funds very quickly before they run out. So don't waste a second.

Book funds today and fix a low – and lower – rate future for your clients.

For further details, an application form or a written quotation, please contact one of the companies listed below.

LOW - AND LOWER - FIXED RATES FOR THE NEXT 6 YEARS

9.99%*   9.49%*   8.99%*

YEARS 1-3   4,5   6

(*11.6% APR)

Legal & General
Legal & General House
Kingswood, Tadworth
Surrey KT20 6EU

THE LIFE ASSOCIATION OF SCOTLAND
113 Dundas Street
Edinburgh EH3 5EB
Tel: 031 550 5574

SCOTTISH PROVIDENT
6 St Andrew Square
Edinburgh EH2 2YA

Prolific FINANCIAL MANAGEMENT
Bridge Mills, Stramongate
Kendal LA9 4UB
Tel: 0539 733733

MGM assurance
MGM House, Heene Road
Worthing, Sussex BN11 2DY
Tel: 0903 204631

Britannia Life
190 West George Street
Glasgow G2 2PA
Tel: 041 332 6462

LAURENTIAN FINANCIAL GROUP
Home Loan Service
Laurentian House, Barnwood
Gloucester GL4 7RZ
Tel: 0452 612939

AXA EQUITY & LAW
Amersham Road
High Wycombe, Bucks HP13 5AL
Tel: 0494 466745

WITH AN INITIAL SAVING OF

3 PER CENT

HERE'S ONE FIXED RATE MORTGAGE YOU CAN'T

DISCOUNT

You'd be impressed if our latest mortgage simply fixed your rate at 8.99% (9.4% APR) until May 1998. But it's even better than that: in fact, the rate is just 5.99% until August this year, and then it rises by 0.5% every quarter until it reaches its fixed level of 8.99% in November 1994.

Since funds are limited, it's first come first served. For a written quotation, please call John Charcol Limited now on 071-611 7000 or write to us at 10-12 Great Queen Street, London WC2B 5DD.

FIMBRA MEMBER

JOHN CHARCOL

TALK ABOUT A BETTER MORTGAGE

0 7 1 - 6 1 1 - 7 0 0 0

ALSO AT LEEDS 0532 - 470338

Case Study No. 18

BANK OF IRELAND
ONE YEAR DISCOUNTED FIXED RATE

4.99% (APR 8.1%)

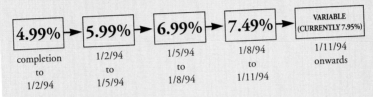

4.99%	5.99%	6.99%	7.49%	VARIABLE (CURRENTLY 7.95%)
completion to 1/2/94	1/2/94 to 1/5/94	1/5/94 to 1/8/94	1/8/94 to 1/11/94	1/11/94 onwards

- EXCLUSIVE OFFER - only available to the selected few, and that includes you!

- Acceptance fee only £195 (on completion)

- Acceptance fee and MIG premium <u>always</u> added

- No compulsory insurances

- Max. 93% LTV purhcase; max 85% LTV remortgage

- Income multiples - 3.25 + 1 or 2.75 x joint

- See overleaf for key criteria points

All enquiries/applications via:
PRIVATE LABEL PACKAGING CENTRE
FLAGSHIP HOUSE
READING ROAD NORTH
FLEET, HANTS, GU13 8YA
Tel: 0252 811000
Fax: 0252 811054

Case Study No. 19

Mortgage spotlight.

£150 introducers' fee

● Rate reductions *guaranteed* each year until 1999 - 6.99%/5.99%/4.99% Step-Down Fixed Rate

● The money markets are still predicting rate rises through 1999; this product sends rates in the opposite direction

● Lender's underwriter based at our Processing Centre for speedy case approval and offer issuance

(APR 7.1%)

Funded by

BRISTOL & WEST
Bristol & West Building Society

Designed & Distributed Exclusively by

Private Label

MORTGAGE DESIGN
AND DISTRIBUTION

Call now on 01483 454 460

Case Study No. 20

JUNE 1996

REF: WB/06

WEST BROMWICH BUILDING SOCIETY

(Exclusive Private Label Product)

THREE YEAR DISCOUNT WITH LOW REDEMPTION CHARGE

MAIN FACTS

DISCOUNT OF 1.35% FROM SOCIETY'S STANDARD VARIABLE RATE FOR THE FIRST THREE YEARS OF THE LOAN

APPLICANTS WILL BE OFFERED A FREE SWITCH INTO A FIXED RATE AT THE END OF THE DISCOUNT PERIOD

APPLICANTS CHOOSING TO SWITCH TO THE SOCIETY'S STANDARD VARIABLE RATE MAY REDEEM AT ANY TIME THEREAFTER AT A REDEMPTION CHARGE OF JUST ONE MONTH'S INTEREST

ONE RATE TO 90% LTV PURCHASE AND REMORTGAGE: MIG CHARGE ALWAYS ADDED WITHIN INCOME

NO COMPULSORY GENERAL INSURANCES

SELLING POINTS

◆ Generous discount for a full three years amounting to a 4.05% benefit

◆ Take the discount when rates are low, and flip into a fix when some say rates will be rising

◆ Exceptionally low redemption charge representing just 0.6% of a typical £60k loan at current rates, in return for a 4.05% benefit!

◆ Simple rate structure avoids disappointment with down-valuations

◆ No extras subsidising the rate

INTRODUCER PAYMENT £250 PER COMPLETION

RING OUR MORTGAGE HELPLINE ON:

01483 454460

DESIGNED AND DISTRIBUTED EXCLUSIVELY BY: PRIVATE LABEL MORTGAGE SERVICES LTD

• STOP PRESS PLEASE READ CAREFULLY •

Case Study No. 21

Dear John

I gather you now offer a low fixed-rate mortgage with no penalties if I then repay some of the capital early.

In case I get a bonus in the future, could you tell me more?

yours optimistically

Ben Thompson

The fact is that with most fixed-rate and discount mortgages, there are penalties if you subsequently want to make early repayments. That's bad news if you anticipate company bonuses, or other lump sums, which would enable you to pay off some of the capital. But not with the latest exclusive fixed and discount rate mortgages from John Charcol. You can enjoy a two year fixed rate of just 5.95% (APR 6.2%), for example - and then, each year, you can pay off up to half the outstanding balance with no penalties at all. For full details, call (0171) 611 7000, or Leeds (0113) 2470338 or our new Cambridge office on (01223) 464146. Or, drop in and see us at 10-12 Great Queen Street, London, WC2B 5DD.

5.95% / 6.2% APR

JOHN CHARCOL

TALK ABOUT A BETTER MORTGAGE

0171 - 611 - 7000

Case Study No. 22

Most capped rate mortgages have a redemption penalty. Here's one with a redemption bonus.

Can you be sure that the advice you offer clients will keep them happy for very long?

Variable mortgage rates have been so volatile that you naturally look for ways of protecting your clients against future uncertainties.

You might recommend a fixed rate – only to find that clients tear their hair out when, as in 1987/88, variable rates fall by 5 percentage points in eight months. In these unfortunate circumstances, redemption penalties could lock them into an unfavourable rate.

You might try a capped rate – only to hide under your desk when the capped period ends, the variable rate turns out to be somewhat less than competitive, and your clients *(now balding)* are locked in once again by redemption penalties.

So what is the alternative to this far from perfect state of affairs?

INTRODUCING THE REDEMPTION BONUS.

You will already be very familiar with the typical redemption penalty that requires your clients to pay 3 to 6 months interest to get out of a fixed or capped rate.

However, you won't be familiar with our redemption bonus – which is exactly the same principle, in reverse! If you're intrigued, read on.

£250 GUARANTEE.

Should our variable rate between 1st July 1992 and 1st January 1994 exceed the average rates charged by the top five building societies° we will actually give your clients a cash bonus of £250 towards their remortgage costs at redemption.

Which, as far as we're concerned, is a powerful motivation to make sure that our rates stay competitive.

But the good news doesn't end here.

EXIT FREE AT ANY TIME.

In addition to this highly unusual benefit, comes yet another. Namely, an exit free guarantee.

In other words, should your clients wish, at any time, to move their mortgage away, they can do so without facing any redemption penalties, notice requirements or administration charges.

They can walk away, free, gratis and for nothing.

But to attract their initial interest, we can also offer a front end cap.

A CAPPED RATE UNTIL 1ST JULY 1992.

Your clients will enjoy a very competitive rate that is capped at 9.8% (12.2% APR) until July 1st 1992, which is beyond the date of the next General Election.

Since this rate is capped, your clients will obviously benefit if Mr Lamont managed to engineer some reductions to base rate on the run-up to the election.

SO WHAT'S THE CATCH?

There isn't one.

The whole purpose of this mortgage is to remove the small print catches normally associated with fixed or capped rate mortgages.

And the initial charge for all this amounts to a remarkably modest £395 arrangement fee *(normally added to the loan)*.

For this sum, your clients will enjoy all the major benefits outlined above, as well as confidence and peace of mind in a highly volatile market.

And that's something that can only be described as a very special bonus.

XYZ Home Loans

A mortgage fixed at just 11.75% until August 1993.

And read my lips: no redemption penalties.

14.8%
Typical APR.

It's a heads—you—win—tails—you—can't—lose mortgage. Funds are extremely limited, so find out more without delay.

For written details, call John Charcol on (071) 589 7080. Or write to us at Mercury House, 195 Knightsbridge, London SW7 1RE.

JOHN CHARCOL

Talk about a better mortgage.
0 7 1 — 5 8 9 — 7 0 8 0

Case Study No. 24

Simply the best.

Read about the best long-term fixed rate mortgage with early exit options on the market today.

We all think rates will rise, but how high? Then they'll fall, but how low? Given the uncertainty, we've designed a new fixed rate with exit options.

At 7.49% (APR 7.8%) until April 2002, our fixed rate is well below today's building society variable rate.

If that's not exciting enough, the early repayment charge on this mortgage reduces by 1% each year, starting at 5% in the first year and ending at 1% in year 5, with nothing to pay after 5 years.

So, if rates fall below the level of the fix, your clients aren't locked in by massive charges.

It gets better. There are no compulsory insurances, so your clients won't be paying a hidden extra 0.25% or so through that route.

And we don't restrict it. These terms are available, up to 95% LTV (plus add-ons) for purchase or remortgage.

But hurry, before demand takes **your** options away.

Funded by

£150 introducer fee.

Designed & Distributed Exclusively by

Call now on 01483 72 61 61

Case Study No. 25

100% Mortgages available with no deductions.

And it's not even April 1st.

Our new 100% mortgage is anything but an April fool's joke. In fact, we're deadly serious that it's the right product at the right time to get your clients, and the market, on the move.

There's no arrangement fee and loans are available from £25,000 to £80,000. 100% of purchase price is guaranteed, because the competitive 8% indemnity premium is *always* added, never deducted. And the prudent lending terms will ensure that only suitable applicants will qualify.

The product is open to second as well as to first time buyers. So if you have clients who have lost their equity, they'll be equally as welcome as first time buyers looking to exploit today's property bargains.

The package is funded by two lenders, but there's only one application form to complete, one life policy to write and both offers of advance will come out in the same envelope. So it's simple as well as effective.

The major part of the package up to 75% LTV is from a top ten building society at the normal 7.99% variable rate (APR 8.4%) - note that there is *no* loading. The top-up portion of 25% LTV is funded by a bank at 13.99% variable (APR 17.3%). The illustrative average rate on a 75/25 split is 9.49% (illustrative APR 10.6%), and it wasn't so long ago that this rate was considered an outstanding rate on *any* loan, let alone a 100% mortgage.

100% OF PURCHASE PRICE GUARANTEED

(SUBJECT TO VALUATION)

The first loan is available on a repayment or interest only basis; the top-up loan must be repayment with the lender's payment protection policy taken. Funds are limited and have to be reserved, but otherwise it's as simple as that.

A 100% mortgage launched in 1993, designed for 1993's market conditions and just waiting for you to galvanise your clients into action. What's more it's only available via financial advisers; it can't be accessed by the customer direct. With house prices where they are today, what better motivation to write business could there be?

For further details, an application form or a written quotation, please contact one of the companies shown below.

TYPICAL EXAMPLE:

First Loan: An interest only mortgage of £37,500 on a property valued at £50,000 repaid over 25 years assuming completion on 15.03.93. 300 gross monthly repayments of £249.69 with interest at 7.99% variable (8.4% APR). Total cost of credit £112,981.30 calculated to include £250.00 legal fees, £127.00 valuation fee, £149.82 accrued interest, and £50 non refundable reservation fee; Second Loan: A capital repayment and interest mortgage of £12,500, plus a Mortgage Indemnity Guarantee Premium of £1,000, on a property valued at £50,000 repaid over 25 years assuming completion on 15.03.93. 300 gross monthly repayments of £170.52 with interest at 13.99% (17.3% APR variable). Gross repayments include compulsory payment protection cover at 5% of the monthly capital and interest repayment. The interest rate will be reset on the second loan at the beginning of each calendar quarter at 8% over the 90 day London Interbank Offered Rate as published in the Financial Times on the last working day of the previous calendar quarter. Total amount payable £51,156; Both Loans: Security will be required. Loans subject to status, type and value of property. Purchases and employed applicants only. Written quotations available on request. The first 75% of valuation @ 7.99% (8.4% APR) and the remaining 25% of valuation @ 13.99% (17.3% APR) produces an illustrative average rate of 9.49% (illustrative APR 10.6%). Limited funds available.

Legal & General

Legal & General House
Kingswood, Tadworth
Surrey KT20 6EU

M G M
a s s u r a n c e

MGM House, Heene Road
Worthing, Sussex BN11 2DY
0345 222220

Britannia Life

Britannia Court
50 Bothwell Street
Glasgow G2 6HR

AXA EQUITY & LAW

Amersham Road
High Wycombe, Bucks HP13 5AL

Case Study No. 26

STERLING BANK & TRUST LTD
INDEMNITY BEATER

- Up to 85% second charge

- (90% in some northern areas)

- £2,000 - £25,000

- Repayment or Int. only

- 13.5% APR; no MIG premium, no arrangement fee and no legal and valuation fees

- The ideal further advance substitute; leaves the existing mortgage untouched

- Up to 25 year term, employees only, payslips required with application

- Raise new funds quickly for any purpose

All enquiries/applications via:
PRIVATE LABEL PACKAGING CENTRE
FLAGSHIP HOUSE
READING ROAD NORTH
FLEET, HANTS, GU13 8YA
Tel: 0252 811000
Fax: 0252 811054

Case Study No. 27

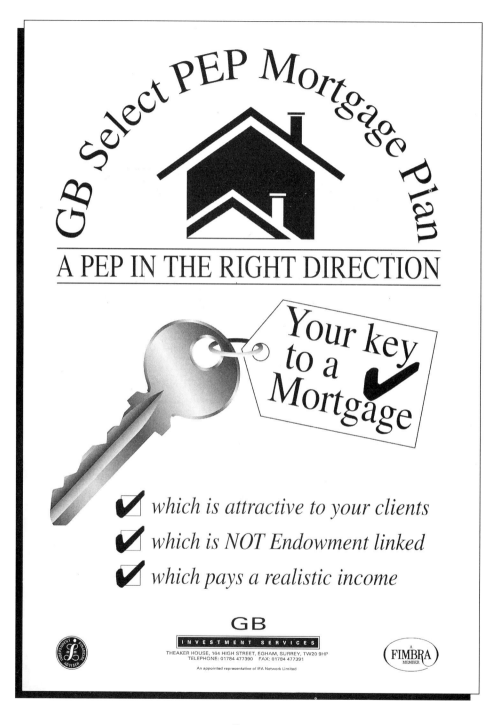

Front cover

Case Study No. 28

A new concept in mortgage lending

GB Investment Services have developed a totally new concept in mortgage lending and offer it as an alternative to the traditional (fast fading) endowment mortgage.

When giving mortgage advice, one of the problems we face as IFAs, is that whilst a PEP with some form of term insurance, may be more suitable advice than an endowment, it does not satisfactorily reimburse us for the work we put in.

The **GB Select PEP Mortgage Plan** has overcome this problem by building in a remuneration package which will be attractive to IFAs who wish to combine sound advice to their clients with a fair initial reward for the work done. In fact over the long term it pays substantially more than an endowment.

How does the GB Select PEP Mortgage Plan work?

It is an interest only loan with a PEP, instead of the traditional endowment, used to repay the capital sum. More than one lending source may be available but a common application form and central administration of the mortgage ensures continuity. Details of the current lender's criteria are enclosed.

Within 28 days of completion of the loan the lender will make a rebate, equivalent to 1% of the loan, direct into your clients bank account. This is to be invested by your client into their PEP. Because of Inland Revenue rules the payment must be made by your client and a form is enclosed to facilitate this. A regular contribution is paid into the PEP which has been calculated using a 10% growth assumption. The effect of compound growth on the single contribution is considerable and reduces the regular contribution required from your client, thereby making it far more competitive than an endowment premium.

Your client may choose a PEP from M&G, Scottish Equitable or Perpetual (names which speak for themselves) whose details are enclosed.

An introductory fee, equivalent to 0.5% of the loan, is paid to the introducing IFA with **NO CLAWBACK**. This fee will normally be paid within 6 weeks of the end of the month of completion.

You will benefit from receiving all the initial commission from the PEP (including the single contribution) and also Fund Based Renewal Commission (FBRC) of 0.5% per annum. The FBRC has a significant effect on your earnings over the term of the loan and adds considerable value to your business.

In addition to the above you have complete independence to arrange whatever life and/or critical illness cover is appropriate to your clients needs. On the Illustration we have left space for you to include Life Cover and Total Monthly Cost.

Inside left page

Case Study No. 28

Earnings Comparison

GB Select PEP Mortgage Plan v Endowment mortgage

The tables below illustrate how your income is paid over the term of the mortgage. Although the endowment (fig 1) shows a slightly higher income in the first year this is soon outweighed by the FBRC in figs 2 & 3 and, as you can see, the cumulative earnings soon overtake the endowment. Also by year 5 the annual income has almost doubled. At the end of the term the cumulative income from the **GB Select PEP Mortgage Plan** is more than twice that of the endowment. The effect of the PEP commissions and the FBRC is to add inherent value to your business.

Endowment commision Initial and renewal		
Year	Annual Income	Cumulative Income
1	£845.88	£845.88
5	£22.80	£868.68
10	£22.80	£982.68
15	£22.80	£1,096.68
20	£22.80	£1,210.68
25	£22.80	£1,324.68

fig 1

IFA Fee+Term commission+PEP commission+PEP FBRC based on 10% growth		
Year	Annual Income	Cumulative Income
1	£533.97	£533.97
5	£42.40	£670.88
10	£70.44	£962.44
15	£112.60	£1,434.27
20	£176.00	£2,177.16
25	£217.33	£3,327.63

fig 2

IFA Fee+Term commission+PEP commission+PEP FBRC based on 12% growth		
Year	Annual Income	Cumulative Income
1	£534.04	£534.04
5	£43.64	£673.68
10	£76.40	£983.66
15	£130.38	£1,516.87
20	£219.30	£2,417.85
25	£365.80	£3,924.71

fig 3

Figs 4 & 5 below graphically illustrate how your income from the **GB Select PEP Mortgage Plan** increases over the years, thereby effectively indexing your earnings. Fig 4 compares your annual income from the **GB Select PEP Mortgage Plan** with an endowment and fig 5 shows the cumulative effect.

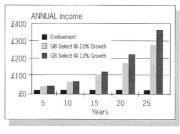

fig 4

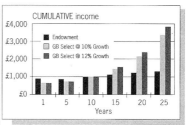

fig 5

Inside right page

Case Study No. 28

Monthly Cost Comparison

GB Select PEP Mortgage Plan
versus
Endowment mortgage and Repayment mortgage

You will see from the table below the savings that can be achieved for your client by recommending the GB Select PEP Mortgage Plan. It is most important to remember that a PEP can be cashed in at any time and on this basis, should the fund grow at the higher LAUTRO growth rate of 12% the mortgage could be paid off after 22 years and 1month, saving interest payments of £8822.92.

	GB Select	Endowment	Repayment
PEP contribution	£48.33		
Term / Endowment premium	£13.09	£76.00	£13.09
Net payment to lender	£221.83	£221.83	£297.24
Total monthly cost	**£283.25**	**£297.83**	**£310.33**

Summary

Main problems with endowment mortgages
- Possible clawback of commission
- Adverse media coverage
- Internal taxation within life funds
- Poor (if any) surrender value in the early years
- Penal charging structure
- Hard disclosure of commissions

Main benefits of the GB Select PEP Mortgage Plan
- A single contribution of 1% of the loan is paid into your client's PEP
- Lower monthly outgoings for your client
- A sum equal to 0.5% of the loan is paid to you as an introduction fee
- In addition to the fee, you will receive 3% initial and 0.5% FBRC on the PEP throughout the life of the contract
- NO CLAWBACK of the fee or any commission from the PEP
- High PEP surrender values, even in the first year
- You share in an increasing fund thereby effectively indexing your income and adding value to your business
- All proceeds of the PEP are completely tax free

The following criteria have been used in this publication and every effort has been made to ensure the content is accurate and up to date at the time of going to press.
Clients: Male aged 35 nb; Female aged 33 nb; Introduction fee: £250.00; Mortgage: £50,000 over 25 years at 6.05%; Term Assurance: £13.09 p.m. taken from "The Exchange", being the most competitive shown for joint life 1st death; Endowment: £76.00 p.m., using a 7.8% growth assumption; Regular PEP contribution: £48.33 p.m. calculated on a 10% growth assumption; Commissions shown are calculated at 140% of LAUTRO.
This material is intended for use by authorised intermediaries and professional finance advisers only. It is not intended as an advertisement complying with the Consumer Credit Act and as such must not be given or distributed to potential borrowers or otherwise used to promote or advertise the products referred to.

Back cover

Case Study No. 28

JUNE 1996

REF: H1

PRODUCT PORTFOLIO

FUNDED BY

HALIFAX
MORTGAGE
SERVICES
LIMITED

DESIGNED AND DISTRIBUTED EXCLUSIVELY BY

Private Label

MORTGAGE DESIGN AND DISTRIBUTION

MORTGAGE OF THE CENTURY

MAIN FACTS

AN INCREDIBLE PACKAGE OF BENEFITS, WORTH 10% ON A TYPICAL £50K MORTGAGE

BENEFIT NO. 1 IS A 2% DISCOUNT FOR THE FIRST 3½ YEARS OF THE LOAN

BENEFIT NO. 2 IS AN INITIAL £500 CASHBACK (£1,000 FOR LOANS £100K+)

BENEFIT NO. 3 IS £1,000 CASHBACK (£1,500 FOR LOANS £100K+) PAID IN DECEMBER 1999

A SPECIAL BOOKING AND VALUATION FEE MUST ACCOMPANY EACH APPLICATION (SEE OVERLEAF FOR DETAILS)

ONE RATE STRUCTURE TO 95% LTV PURCHASE AND REMORTGAGE WITH NO COMPULSORY GENERAL INSURANCES

SELLING POINTS

◆ Worthy of the description MORTGAGE OF THE CENTURY

◆ The equivalent of a 7% benefit that continues into the next century

◆ A further 1% benefit on a typical £50k loan, effectively refunding our up front costs

◆ Another average 2% benefit to pay for the Millennium celebrations!

◆ Guarantees a place for your clients, with these costs also refunded by us if the case fails our initial assessment

◆ All the ingredients you would expect from the MORTGAGE OF THE CENTURY

RING OUR MORTGAGE HELPLINE ON:

01483 454460

Case Study No. 29

Case Study No. 30

customer kept the mortgage for 25 years but didn't get the six months' interest back (a situation that couldn't happen, but such was the complexity of the Consumer Credit Act advertising rules). A fixed rate of 10.95% with an APR of 14.4% rather spoiled the headline rate, whilst intermediaries and customers found the design just too esoteric. The idea failed.

CASE STUDY No. 12

Product name:	The 50-50 Mortgage
Lender:	Leeds & Holbeck Mortgage Corporation
Main benefits:	A combination fixed and variable rate mortgage
Timing:	Launched May 1992 (just after the general election)
Rating:	4
Comment:	Once the Conservatives had won their surprise

victory in 1992, nobody knew where interest rates were going. We therefore thought it would be smart to put half of the mortgage onto a fixed rate, and the other half onto a variable rate. To simplify the presentation, the initial rate was 9.99% on both elements: the discount on the variable rate element being sufficient to achieve that net rate. The fixed rate was to September 1995, with a low one month's interest redemption penalty during the fixed rate period. The product had everything going for it, but it proved to be too complicated and neither "fish nor fowl". We have not launched a combination fixed and variable rate product since.

GIMMICKY NAMES

CASE STUDY No. 13

Product name:	Cap & Garter
Lender:	Leeds & Holbeck Mortgage Corporation
Main benefits:	Wide band cap and floor
Timing:	Launched October 1992
Rating:	4
Comment:	This was essentially a three-year cap in conjunction

with a six-month discount. The prevailing standard variable rate was 9.99%, so our lead rate was 8.99%. The customer cap was at 10.95% until September 1995, to which we added a floor at 5.95%. The lender could not sell a floor at this level, so the 5.95% minimum was simply a marketing device to indicate to customers that we believed that interest rates might go that low, thereby requiring a low minimum. Caps normally sell best when the initial charge rate is also the level of the cap, so we tried everything to make this product seem different and eye-catching, including the use of the word "garter" instead of "floor" or "collar". Although the product had too many benefits to be a complete failure, we did not regard it as a success and felt that, with hindsight, the gimmicky name almost certainly detracted from the value of the product. We have not repeated the experiment of a wide band between a cap and floor, and a cap at the same level as the initial rate is the tried and tested formula for success with this type of product.

CASE STUDY No. 14

Product name:	Zeroloan
Lender:	West Bromwich Building Society
Main benefits:	A substantial discount with cashback and fee-free package
Timing:	Launched April 1995
Rating:	3

Comment: The typical giveaway package for discounts and cashbacks at the time was 5.5%–6%. Rather than launch a "me-too" product of this type, we applied only part of the product design model to the discount (although the choice of a 1 January 1997 end date meant that it had a two-year "feel", whereas it was only for 16 months in reality). A free valuation and fixed sum cashback was added alongside a refundable reservation fee. Only a few lenders at that stage had started to add the MIG charge (the MIG companies had banned this during the recession), so we brought that benefit into the headline as well. This was a steady product which eventually achieved full utilisation, but – as with the Cap & Garter – we felt that the gimmicky Zeroloan name ended up detracting from the product rather than assisting it.

FLEXIBLE

CASE STUDY No. 15

Product name:	Fixed Payment Stabiliser
Lender:	Paribas Lombard Mortgages Ltd
Main benefits:	The facility to fix the mortgage payment on a variable rate loan at 9.99% for the first two or three years, increasing the repayment level when required
Rating:	3
Timing:	Launched September 1989

Comment: With interest rates well into double figures, and the recession really starting to bite, this was one of the more esoteric of the genre of deferred interest products. The entry level loan-to-value determined whether the customer could take a two- or three-year fixed payment stabiliser. The pay rate then became 9.99%, almost 3% below the then building society variable rate, thereby allowing higher income multiples to be offered (because borrowers had easier cashflow). Customers could serve one month's notice in writing of an increase in payment, with tax relief available at the *full charge rate* being added to the loan, thereby producing an even lower net outlay. It was sold as the alternative to a fixed rate in a potentially falling rate environment and was one of the more responsible and sophisticated deferred interest mortgages, although it still left the borrowers with an increased debt against a reducing property value, which unfortunately turned out to be the case with all deferred interest products of the period.

CASE STUDY No. 16

Product name: Made-to-Measure
Lender: Britannia Building Society
Main benefits: A product through which customers designed their own benefits package
Timing: Launched February 1995
Rating: 3
Comment: The first of the "menu"-type mortgages, this product was originally designed for the builder market, where different regions within building firms had different approaches to mortgage promotions, let alone the fierce competition between firms of builders themselves. The basic model was built around a 4% giveaway calculated on a £50,000 loan giving a sum to work with of £2000. A maximum of ten points was therefore allocated, each worth £200. For the broker market, two of those points were allocated to a £400 introducer payment, thereby leaving eight points for the customer to use in a variety of ways, choosing between discounts, cashbacks, legal costs contribution, free ASU, and so on. The fixed sum benefits package was exposed to misuse, and a small section of our distributor base targeted particularly low loan sizes, where the total benefits package represented a large total percentage giveaway. The product was another innovation "first", and spawned many lookalike deals over the ensuing years.

CASE STUDY No. 17

Product name: Step-Down Fix
Lender: Britannia Building Society
Main benefits: Guaranteed rate reductions over six years
Timing: Launched July 1992
Rating: 2
Comment: This was our second Britannia product after the spectacular sellout of the ten-year fix. There was a feeling that interest rates would reduce under the newly elected Conservative government: we capitalised on this mood by saying that "The Chancellor hopes for interest rate cuts over the next six years. We guarantee them". We were lucky enough to have this product advertised in all three trade press publications of the time on "White Wednesday", when interest rates rose by 5% on the day and we exited the ERM. The lender's in-house legal department, underworked in the recession, offered to act for customers on remortgage advances for a fee of just £90 (much less than the norm), which was an excellent feature on top of a spectacular deal: a design approach with which the reader will now be more familiar in connection with Private Label products. Essentially, this particular fixed rate rode the yield curve, but in a way which was slightly ahead of intermediaries' and customers' thinking at the time in terms of how fast interest rates would reduce; both were therefore keen to snap up guaranteed rate reductions.

CASE STUDY No. 18

Product name: Discounted Fix
Lender: Britannia Building Society
Main benefits: An initial 5.99% fixed rate which then stepped up by 0.5% every quarter until November 1994 when the maximum rate of 8.99% was reached. The product stayed fixed at 8.99% until May 1998
Timing: Launched March 1993
Rating: 4
Comment: The average five-year fixed rate we could offer at the time was not particularly attractive. The basic design of this product was therefore an initial eye-catching rate of 5.99%, with a step-up arrangement, followed by a period at 8.99%, which achieved an average near to the norm of a five-year fix. To mask the fact that this was a stepped fix in the opposite direction to the one that customers would wish, we positioned the initial deal as a "discount on a fixed

rate", which had never previously been offered. However good the packaging, though, intermediaries and customers saw that this was an increasing rate, albeit one offering five years of protection. The product was not a success, particularly as the eventual rate of 8.99% was slightly higher than the then typical building society variable rate of 8.55%: the yield curve by then having levelled up a bit.

CASE STUDY No. 19

Product name:	One Year Discounted Fixed Rate
Lender:	Bank of Ireland
Main benefits:	Very low initial fixed rate
Timing:	Launched July 1993
Rating:	5
Comment:	The typical variable rate was then 7.95% and we

wanted a lead rate which was 3% lower, to achieve a headline eye-catching rate and a consequential low initial monthly outlay on the customer quote. This meant stepping up the fix at irregular intervals in order to get to a weighted average which was greater than the cost of funds. Again, the step-up nature of the fixed rate was masked by referring to it as a discount, and the product was launched on a semi-exclusive basis to our recently formed panel of Preferred Introducers. This was our second and final experiment with a step-up fix, our conclusion being that this sort of structure does not work.

CASE STUDY No. 20

Product name:	Step-Down Fix
Lender:	Bristol & West Building Society
Main benefits:	Two years of guaranteed rate reductions
Timing:	Launched July 1996
Rating:	3
Comment:	With one year to go to the election we thought a

good design would be one that fixed the initial rate at the then typical building society variable rate of 6.99%. With many commentators predicting rate rises at the time of the election, we positioned the product as guaranteeing rate *reductions*. This did capture the imagination and the product sold well. The interesting aspect of this design was that it was adapted from a standard two-year fix which the lender had available at the time. We took that particular model apart and put it back together again, showing that the same average fixed rate would be achieved over the same period as the lender was achieving on its standard product. It is often advantageous to prove to a lender that your idea boxes back to a standard product they are themselves marketing at the time. This works particularly well with a fixed rate which might not be selling spectacularly for the lender at the time (thereby encouraging them to give you a slice of the funding to give your design a try). If you think rates will increase it will allow your guaranteed tranche to look very competitive in an interest rate environment where the lender's standard version might have long since sold out. This is essentially what happened with this Step-Down Fix.

REDEMPTION THEME

CASE STUDY No. 21

Product name: Three-Year Discount with Low Redemption Charge
Lender: West Bromwich Building Society
Main benefits: A three-year discount with a "fixed or variable" choice when the discount ended, accompanied by a low charge exit option
Timing: Launched June 1996
Rating: 4
Comment: By the summer of 1996, intermediaries and the press were complaining about the long, high redemption charges which lenders had to impose in order to make the large discount and cashback giveaways make sense. Our proposal with this product was therefore to reduce the total giveaway a little whilst reducing the redemption penalty a lot. The discount was still a total benefit of 4.05%, albeit spread at 1.35% over the first three years. At the end of the discount period borrowers would be guaranteed a free switch into a fixed rate. If they didn't like the fixed rate on offer then they could exit for just one month's interest, which we demonstrated was just 0.6% of a typical loan, *in return for a 4.05% benefit.* A decent introducer payment was added to the product in order to gain attention, but the product shows how fickle customers and intermediaries are. It was not a great success because what was really demanded was a continuation of the massive giveaways with lower redemption charges. If there had to be a trade-off then the massive giveaway would win every time.

CASE STUDY No. 22

Product name: Fixed rate with partial redemption concession
Lender: Bristol & West Building Society
Main benefits: 50% of the loan could be repaid penalty-free after the fixed rate term had expired
Timing: Launched November 1995
Rating: 2
Comment: This product was designed to appeal to the increasing number of mortgage applicants whose income is made up of a significant performance-related element. Such applicants always believe at the beginning of the year that their bonuses will be larger than they actually turn out to be. They also believe that they will apply these bonuses to paying down their mortgage. In practice, the bonus often turns out to be less than originally anticipated, and is used to purchase consumer goods. We found with this product that applicants were prepared to pay a little more on the fixed rate in order to have a partial redemption concession. We therefore took a 5.75% two-year fixed rate Bristol & West standard product of the time and loaded it by 0.2% per annum in order to create the additional income necessary to allow us to promote the product as an exclusive and pay our distributors. We also included the innovative feature of allowing one penalty-free partial redemption, up to a maximum of 50% of the loan, in each financial year in lieu of the rate loading. If there was a second redemption transaction (full or partial) during the same financial year then the full redemption penalties applied to both redemption transactions. An active lender with alternatives to offer a borrower with itchy feet should back itself to retain a disproportionate number of them, even with easy exit terms like these. We found that this product was not for the mass market, but it did attract significant interest in the City of London from dealers and brokers.

CASE STUDY No. 23

Product name: Cap with Redemption Bonus
Lender: Branded Home Loans
Main benefits: A competitively priced short-term cap followed by a two-year interest rate guarantee, backed up by a "reverse redemption penalty"
Timing: Launched September 1991
Rating: 4
Comment: Designed as the flagship product for our autumn 1991 sales conference, it turned out to be the last exclusive deal we

did with Branded Home Loans. TMC, the ultimate funder, had become very cautious about its lending and the best we could achieve was an unhedged nine-month cap, albeit at nearly 2% below the then variable rate. Interest rates were very volatile at this time in the run-up to the 1992 election, and the only redeeming feature about the cap was that it had an end date which expired after the next election, thereby providing some rate protection during the really volatile period. To persuade people that their rate would remain competitive when they transferred to the variable rate, we offered a reverse redemption penalty, which we called a redemption bonus. If the variable rate should exceed the average charged by the top five building societies during the period from July 1992 to January 1994 there would not only be no redemption charge, but the lender would pay the customer to go. By and large, however, people were not persuaded by this argument, and the product was not a success, although it did achieve some volume.

CASE STUDY No. 24

Product name: Fixed Rate with no Redemption Penalties
Lender: Leeds & Holbeck Mortgage Corporation
Main benefits: A fixed rate substantially below the prevailing variable rate, with no redemption penalties of any description
Timing: Launched April 1991
Rating: 2
Comment: The yield curve was pointing to reduced interest rates and this product was secured at a margin over the cost of funds. Intermediaries and customers had not yet tuned into the prospect of reducing rates and were keen to take this fix, even though it was not the leading rate available at the time. We reckoned that nobody would actually want to redeem during the fixed rate period because the rate being offered would still undercut what was predicted as the typical variable rate, with the opportunity taken by the lender towards the end of the fix to transfer the customers onto another deal. The product was running at the time of the American presidential election, when George Bush spoke those famous words: "Read my lips, no new taxes". John Charcol picked up on this theme with an advertisement saying, "Read my lips: no redemption penalties". This product proved to us that no redemption penalties whatsoever *is* a clear formula that works.

CASE STUDY No. 25

Product name: Fixed 4/02 with reducing redemption charge
Lender: Halifax Mortgage Services Ltd
Main benefits: A competitive long-term fixed rate with redemption charge presented as an early exit option
Timing: Originally launched March 1997, but relaunched May 1997
Rating: 3
Comment: The original product was launched at rates of 7.74% and 7.79% for above and below £60,000 advances respectively with a £500 cashback. This was a variation on a 7.75% standard fixed rate product which Halifax Building Society had available via its branches. The typical variable rate at the time was 7.25% and it had traditionally been difficult trying to persuade borrowers to buy a fixed rate – even one offering long-term benefits – when the lead rate is above the prevailing variable, and so it proved with the first version of this product. We therefore relaunched it, taking the cashback away from both rates and reinvesting it in the lead rate, bringing the latter down to 7.49%. By then the prevailing variable rate had increased to 7.6%, positioning the product much better. With the relaunched version we brought the generous 54321 reducing percentage of loan redemption penalties more to the fore, and the entire package then started to bite. However, generous redemption terms only succeed when offered as a feature on a product where the rate is already very competitive. Our experience is that generous redemption terms do not of themselves motivate a purchase of a fixed rate which is not already amongst the leaders in the market of the time.

SECOND CHARGES

CASE STUDY No. 26

Product name: 100%
Lender: A total of five first lenders and four second charge providers
Main benefits: A coordinated first loan/top-up loan arrangement producing an attractive average rate
Timing: Available within our programme almost non-stop between 1989 and 1997
Rating: 3
Comment: During and immediately after the recession, 100% mortgages were rare indeed. When they were available the rate was

heavily loaded. Our initial foray into this market involved a 90% first advance from a mainstream lender and a 10% top-up. Pressure from MIG insurers reduced this to a 75/25% combination, but we were subsequently able to return to a 90/10% split. The version illustrated in this chapter was offered during the period when the first advance was up to 75% LTV, but with no rate loading. The top-up rate was LIBOR-linked to give some rate protection, and the integrated nature of the product allowed us to offer an average rate of the two loans which was always very competitive with the loaded rates competitors were offering. There was no arrangement fee or MIG charge on the first loan, and the top-up lender was prepared to capitalise its charges on the second loan, resulting in no deductions and 100% of purchase price always available – another major selling point. Only one application form had to be completed and we arranged for both offers of advance to go out in the same envelope, to avoid the traditional problems of a split loan arrangement where, for example, the first lender offers but the second lender doesn't. Under our scheme, if either lender rejected then this was simply presented by us as a reject without explaining who had actually turned the case down. Eventually, market conditions permitted us to revert to offering new business discounts on the first loan. The top-up loan by that time was down to 4% over LIBOR, meaning that, although competitors were now making 100% products available with no loading, and even marginal discounts, we were still able to undercut them with our spectacular average rates, achieved by the loan split. The 100% product is the only time we have made a second charge work within our programme.

CASE STUDY No. 27

Product name:	Indemnity Beater
Lender:	Sterling Bank & Trust
Main benefits:	A second charge alternative to get round the further advance problems then being caused by the MIG insurers
Timing:	Launched January 1993
Rating:	5
Comment:	We had identified a niche problem with further

advances in 1992/3. Borrowers whose status was acceptable to lenders when the loan completed were finding that the same status was no longer acceptable to lenders in the harsher credit policy regime forced by the recession. This sometimes prevented such borrowers from being able to obtain further advances. Much of this new credit policy had been imposed by the MIG insurers. Moreover, falling property values could easily have turned an initial 75% loan-to-value advance into, for example, a 90% loan-to-value deal once the further advance was added. This produced the farcical situation where the MIG premium charged on the further advance could take away as much as 50% of that advance. Second charge lenders were much more flexible in their status assessment and did not charge MIG premiums. Instead of applying for a further advance, we therefore suggested that intermediaries sometimes (where appropriate) advised customers to take out a second charge product where the funds could be made available quickly and where a generous introducer payment could be made. The theory was sound, but our experience is that finance brokers do not sell first mortgages, and mortgage brokers do not sell second mortgages. This is one of those strange distribution quirks that we all have to live with, and we eventually quietly dropped Indemnity Beater as a failed idea.

PEP MORTGAGE

CASE STUDY No. 28

Product name: GB Select PEP Mortgage Plan
Lender: Bank of Ireland
Main benefits: A PEP-linked mortgage with a capital injection into the PEP and substantial intermediary commission
Timing: Launched April 1995
Rating: 5
Comment: We were approached by GB Investment Services, a member of the IFA Network, with an idea that they had failed to get off the ground with a number of lenders. They wanted a normal discounted variable rate mortgage where part of the front end giveaway, which would otherwise be available to the customer, could be channelled by way of an injection into a PEP plus a payment to the introducer which, when added to the PEP commission, would equate to the sort of remuneration intermediaries would expect on an endowment mortgage. As this product was eventually launched at the same time as a report criticising endowment mortgages, the timing could not have been better. However, we ran into several problems.

First, there was the question of the net benefits available to the customer once the other product benefits, and the various parties involved, had been paid. Initially signed off in December 1994, the product was so complex that we could not bring it to the market until

April 1995. The 2% discount to January 1996 was therefore not by then thought to be competitive enough. It was the maximum we could give to the customer because a further 1% of the loan was being injected into the PEP day one, in accordance with GB's specification, to give it an extra boost. There was then 0.5% of the loan going to the introducing broker, with a payment on top of that to GB. It is how the product had to be structured, but there were too many mouths to feed.

Second, in order to make a capital injection into the PEP, the lender had to effectively pay a cashback into the customer's bank account. The PEP providers then had to debit the amount out again in order to take it into the PEP, so as to provide a direct route from customer to PEP provider and thereby preserve the tax relief. Putting these processes into place caused the delay in the first quarter of 1995 and subsequently were thought to be too complex by the introducing brokers.

Third, the limit of just three PEP providers did not find favour in some sections of the press. Fourth, brokers were twitchy about sending applications to another broker (GB Investments), who would then pass them onto us, who would then pass them onto the lender.

This was a good example of a great idea, which could not be criticised at design stage, but that ended up being too complex for its own good.

DESIGNED FOR THE BALANCE SHEET

CASE STUDY No. 29

Product name: Mortgage of the Century
Lender: Halifax Mortgage Services Ltd
Main benefits: A long-term discount with double cashback
Timing: Launched June 1996
Rating: 1
Comment: HMSL is the intermediary lending arm of Halifax Building Society specialising in major schemes. Formed following the takeover of BNP Mortgages Ltd, there had been a long period of reflection by Halifax before they decided to launch into this market. They wanted to achieve a spectacular relaunch, but had the challenge of a lending policy by which initial cashbacks were not amortised, as other lenders were doing.

Halifax took the hit in year one of all up-front benefits, which was of course the more prudent approach. A product was therefore designed which spread the benefits over three years. In addition to the long-term discount, we structured a relatively modest initial cashback (sufficient only to refund most of the fees), with a second cashback paid in December 1999. The lender could therefore recognise the second cashback in profitability terms when it was actually paid away, with this unusual structure also creating an interesting sales script. When a benefits package is part percentage of loan, and part absolute sums, it is necessary to convert it into one currency for ease of communication: we therefore expressed the total discount and cashback benefits as 10% of a typical £50,000 loan. As the standard giveaway of the time was 6%, this looked spectacularly competitive and went immediately to number one on the Mortgage 2000 mortgage-sourcing system which – unlike its competitors – assessed loans as to the total benefits package over the first five years. Ours was, of course, a total benefits package over several years to which, in truth, a net present value calculation had to be applied for a true comparison with a year one giveaway.

We gave the product our biggest ever marketing spend and modestly called it "Mortgage of the Century". With £250m of new business generated in the nine months we were marketing the product, it became our best-selling product ever. The original design had been structured to meet the balance sheet need, although this necessity spawned a spectacular customer package unequalled before or since. A further study into how we sold this record-breaking product appears in Chapter 5.

THE ONE THAT GOT AWAY

CASE STUDY No. 30

Product name: Index-linked Mortgage
Lender: Didn't find one
Main benefits: A mortgage rate linked to inflation
Timing: Spring 1993
Rating: We never found out
Comment: I was approached by the capital markets division of a major clearing bank who had a counterparty with significant funds earning an income stream linked to the Retail Price Index (RPI). Their request was for me to design an index-linked mortgage funded by one of our lenders, so that a variable rate income could be swapped into an index-linked one. The design looked feasible and, given a modest spread, an RPI-linked mortgage rate would, with hindsight, have beaten the normal variable rate structures over the ensuing years. The problem was that the RPI is an historic index, in

that it plots the RPI in a particular month versus the same month the previous year, and reflects the difference. This structure could push the resultant mortgage rate up in a month when interest rates might be softening. Moreover, to even out the rate adjustments in order to make the product easy to understand to the borrower, and to cover everybody's interests, required a spread over RPI which did not create sufficient opportunity to justify the "risk" of taking this new type of mortgage when such generous discounts and cashbacks were still available from competitors. If inflation continues to stay low, and today's generous front end giveaways eventually start to recede, we might well see the return to the market of "the one that got away".

WRAP-UP

The object of these 30 case studies has been to share with the reader our successes and failures with a number of different designs, hopefully imparting along the way the various skills and techniques used to bring the products about. Mortgage design is, like fashion, a cyclical business, where core designs come round again, but with a contemporary twist. The products I have illustrated were used (or intended to be used as in no. 30) within the mass market, via the intermediary channel. There is a great deal more innovation which can be applied to niche markets, but the volumes are not there and, by and large, I have ignored the many innovations seen in those areas from different lenders over the years. I hope that our experience has been of some use to the reader.

5

SELLING THROUGH THE INTERMEDIARY MARKET

Included in our logo is the strapline "Mortgage Design and Distribution". The compliments (and occasional awards) that we have received for our mortgage design skills are most welcome. But the "and Distribution" element deserves as much profile. Without the ability to sell our products on to our customers – the intermediary market – we would never have got our business off the ground, let alone steadily increased the volumes to their current level, on a run rate set to exceed £1 billion of new applications in 1997.

In this chapter I break down the various component parts of the sales process. It will be of interest to those who operate in the inter-mediary sector of the mortgage market, which currently accounts for more than 50 per cent of new business. I will share my own, and Private Label's, experiences and general approach on the basis not necessarily that they are the right methods, but that they are the methods that have worked for us with reasonable success over a long period of time as a specialist "Distribution" company.

Very few school, college or university leavers express a wish to become salesmen. Yet there are very few career opportunities available to those who cannot promote themselves and influence others. This is all that selling entails. Look at any successful businessman and you will see a good salesman. There are some extra skills relevant to the mortgage market, but, for the most part, the approach set out in this chapter could be successfully applied to almost all selling situations. I have used the male gender throughout for convenience only.

SELLING THROUGH OSMOSIS

Promoting mortgages through the intermediary market means that you are at least once removed from the end customer. If you are selling to an IFA life office, for example, you could be thrice removed, since the life inspector will have to relay your ideas to his supporting brokers who will, in turn, have to relay them to the customer. In this process you have to build up a level of demand within the person you are selling to, that is strong enough to push itself through to others, and which I describe as "osmosis".

In a hectic, over-supplied market, too few salesmen take maximum advantage of the limited time and audiences available. We often take our place amongst a number of lenders, each of whom have a ten-minute slot to sell their wares at an insurance company seminar, for example. We are amazed at how often these valuable opportunities are missed by lenders' representatives stating the lending criteria or the income multiples: facts which are or should be available in easy-to-read form. What you actually need to do in those situations is to create scripts and to make yourself memorable. The former demonstrates to your audience that you are adding value by showing them how to use a product's best features in order to create demand; the latter ensures that the intermediaries remember you when you follow up the meeting.

It is, of course, essential to have attractive product fact sheets available for intermediaries to refer to. I expand on this aspect in some detail in Chapter 6. But mortgage intermediaries do not want lenders to spout facts at them. They want new ideas, new angles, fresh approaches and ways in which you can demonstrate added value. It is often said of Private Label that there is never a shortage of new ideas for the intermediary to try out. Never is this more important than when selling to someone who is himself once removed from the customer. *Selling through osmosis.*

The mortgage intermediary is bombarded by new product detail every day. Yet few intermediaries can honestly claim to be actively selling more than half a dozen mortgage products at any one time. You must aim to get your product amongst the six. Unless it happens to get there on its own by being an out-and-out market leader, you will need to sell it into that slot. This means demonstrating how the product can be sold on to the client, and why it will generate more sales for the intermediary than something that might appear to be a better rate.

Know your products, know your markets. It is classic sales training contained in the hundreds of sales videos and textbooks available on the subject of selling. But it works. If you cannot immediately come back on a sales objection by pointing out the areas in which the product you are promoting scores over the competitor deal the objector has raised, then you are most unlikely to succeed in getting your product onto that all-important agenda. It is a marketing function within our organisation to critique new competitor products as they come out, giving our sales team the ammunition with which to argue against the competition. But this information must be absorbed and be immediately retrievable by the salesmen if they are going to win the moment. We follow up at our monthly sales meetings by having random tests, asking our sales team to argue against two or three competitor products, chosen because the feedback is that those deals are selling well.

Listening to what is being said is another one of those straight-forward textbook theories that we have probably all read. But how many of us actually put it into practice? We tend to go one stage further, asking our sales team to canvass general opinions when fixing up a sales call in the first place. If the answer comes back that the intermediary you are going to see is selling only fixed rates at the moment, because he feels that base rate is going to rise again, don't turn up trying to sell him a variable rate, unless that's all you've got. Go with the momentum, and convince the intermediaries that your particular fixed rate will create more selling opportunities. I will expand on this later when analysing the sales cycle. But adding value and being memorable are the fundamental skills involved in selling by osmosis. After that introduction, however, we need to examine the profile of the good salesman, and what training he will need, before we review the sales cycle.

WHAT MAKES A GOOD SALESMAN?

Someone who gets business for you. There is no other measure. People often kid themselves about their effectiveness.

> First salesman: *"I made many valuable contacts today."*
> Second salesman: *"I didn't get any orders either."*

The analogy I always use is the person on the street corner selling shoes out of a suitcase. If he doesn't sell any shoes then he takes home no money to feed his wife and children. One day he's got blue slip-on shoes to sell, and that's it. If people ask for brown, he has to say they're out of fashion. If they ask for buckles he has to say that there's a metal shortage. If they want lace-ups, he has to say that they're dangerous. What choice does he have? He can't pay "valuable contacts" or "positive feedback" into his bank account. He has to sell. The only measure of his effectiveness in feeding his family is how much money he brings home.

Of course, nobody selling mortgages is in that desperate a position. Moreover, a mortgage is the sort of long-term commitment that can only be sold professionally and responsibly. But my stark example of "starve or sell" is often necessary to bring our sales team up with a start. There is only one measure of whether a sequence of field visits has been successful, and that is whether any business resulted. Similarly, after the appropriate period of training, we remind our people that it is the numbers they chalk up each day in terms of new applications which will ultimately judge their success in the job. I have met many people in our market who can talk a good story, but I reserve my respect for those who consistently deliver the required levels of business.

When we recruit salesmen we are looking for no particular profile or track record. Selling on behalf of an unusual company like Private Label is different from representing a big institution. To us, the right attitude is the key element. We look for someone with a good personality, who communicates clearly and who will be remembered by intermediaries. But the will to succeed is paramount. If you go forward in business on the assumption that "no" is a "deferred yes", then you are more likely to always achieve your business objectives. We like to see a well-presented, written application for employment and the ability to survive at least three different interviews with three different executive directors. It is a long-winded time-consuming business, but the costs of recruitment and training are not to be allocated lightly. It will cost you more in the long run by rushing the appointment of a new salesman than it will to go through the right selection techniques. For every hundred CVs we receive, we call about 15 for first interview, six for second interview, and two or three for final interview, in order to get one new appointment.

> We look for someone with a good personality who communicates clearly and will be remembered

It is equally important for the new recruits to be "sold" on you. Tell them about your business and show them as much of it as possible. Expose them to the culture, to their potential colleagues and to the realities of the job. In our particular case, we often have to sell mortgage intermediaries on the idea of using a company like us in the first place before we can even begin to talk about our products. Although our volumes are ever increasing, we are still a tiny part of the market. Most intermediaries still deal with the lenders directly and see no reason to break that chain by placing us in-between. The ability to paint an exciting picture, persuading intermediaries to make that leap, is an essential part of the job of salesman. So we major on that difficulty in recruitment interview situations, hoping to exclude those who will not be able to deal with the objections and knock-backs, or those who cannot describe our concept in a few, short sentences.

The final selection criterion we use is: "Is this a good career move for the interviewee?" Our entire philosophy towards business partnerships is to ensure that dealing with each other makes sense. Unless a proposal passes that test, it is unlikely to last in the long term, and all of the business relationships we seek are long term. This applies equally to new recruits. We do not want people realising that they have made a mistake a few weeks or months after joining us. It is therefore important to discuss with new recruits where this particular move fits into their career strategy.

We have found there to be no identikit for the good salesman. They come in different colours, sexes and sizes. Personality, determination, communication ability and a culture fit are all on the initial checklist. How much business they deliver is the only subsequent measure. Some organisations are heavily dependent on psychometric testing and role-playing during the interview phase. Our size permits the three executive directors to become personally involved and to use their own judgment. But if we had a hundred people on the road a more production-line like process would have to prevail.

SALES TRAINING

How many times are we all aware of new sales recruits in the mortgage market being given product literature, a contact list and a shiny new car to go out and see people in, all within their first week of joining? This does both the organisation and the individual more harm than good, and breeds dissatisfaction, a lack of confidence and high staff turnover. New recruits cannot be expected to promote your company, or its products, to any standard of professionalism until they have undertaken at least six weeks of training. Our new recruits are greeted on their first day with a hectic programme mapped out for their first six weeks.

All key managers within the business are required to commit between one and three training sessions during this schedule in order to explain their area of the business. At the same time, there is product information to absorb, together with technical background. The new recruits must learn all aspects of the business which might impact their sales life, preferably carrying out some of the functions if possible. New sales recruits in our organisation will always, for example, spend at least half a day in our call centre taking supervised calls from our customers on a wide range of topics.

Whilst all of these new experiences, and new information, are being absorbed it is necessary to fully expose the new recruit to the culture of the company and its general policies. You can't have a new sales recruit committing that the company will do X when this is strictly against policy. Any organisation worth its salt would wish to compensate the intermediary in those circumstances, and this can be costly. Learning what cannot be done is as important during an induction programme as learning what is available. And there's no point in assuming that the information fired at the new recruits will automatically be learnt and be available for retrieval in a sales situation. There must be formal testing, and we impose two such tests before a new recruit is able to represent the company in the field.

Product, criteria and procedures are tested in written papers designed to catch the new recruits out. This may seem harsh, but it is better to surface any misconceptions or previously undiscovered shortcomings in a private one-on-one situation than for such deficiencies to be exposed by a demanding mortgage intermediary, with the company's reputation on the line. And, yes, we do terminate new recruits if they fundamentally fail the tests, although I am pleased to say that our selection techniques have been sufficiently good that this has only happened once in the last five years.

A crucial part of the initial training is for new recruits to accompany members of the existing sales team on their day's calls. We try to achieve four different days out with four different salesmen, chosen for their contrasting styles. Whilst we look for consistent personal traits in salesmen, we feel it is important to give them the necessary space to run their particular patch with a high degree of individuality. We therefore have members of our sales team who are highly analytical, with a relatively few number of key contacts, and others who are much more personality-driven. Yet others use telesales much more than our recommended minimum, whilst some prefer regular mailshots. We like to expose new recruits to all of these different styles so that they can work out which is the best formula for them. We impose some core disciplines which are common to all of our sales team, such as call planning and preparation. But the ultimate judge of success will be what works for them as individuals, which brings us back to those all-important sales results.

Having passed out of the induction course, the supervised training does not, of course, stop there. On at least two days each week for the first few weeks the new recruit will be accompanied by one of our directors, assessing, revising and helping. We send our people on external courses and devote at least 50 per cent of our monthly off-site sales meetings to training in the form of videos, external speakers, role play, group workshops and, always, a monthly test.

> Mortgage intermediaries are busy professionals with their own priorities. They need to be approached properly and followed up accordingly

In our experience, new recruits will always suffer the "J-curve". This means that they will hit the road initially all fired up, and thereby attain a degree of success. They will then start to encounter sales objections and realise that promoting a company like Private Label is not the same as representing a large institution, even though the products are often better. Confidence will then start to slip and business will, therefore, begin to follow the shape of the letter "J". Once it hits the bottom, however, it needs to plateau for only a short while before the individual who is going to ultimately be successful will get angry. That will push results up the long side of the "J" until, hopefully, they soar to the top. We try to prepare all of our new sales recruits for the inevitable "J-curve", with varying degrees of success. It always happens, however, and always needs to be addressed.

It takes at least six months after passing the induction course for a salesman to become really effective. For the less flexible, more earnest individual it might take a year. So long as you the employer are confident that the individual concerned has the right personality traits and level of intelligence, then you should always persevere with them. You have played a significant role in persuading that individual to make a career change, so you have to bear most of the responsibility if things do not turn out successful in the short term. Many of our top salesmen did not take off like a rocket in their first six months so, whilst our judgment is always harsh if, ultimately, acceptable sales figures do not materialise, our period of nurturing and support is longer than most. We feel that this approach has contributed to the fact that we have only lost one salesman to another company through resignation in our ten-year history.

I have never met a successful salesman who did not have a disciplined approach. An ad hoc "scattergun" approach will achieve nothing. Mortgage intermediaries are busy professionals with their own priorities. They need to be approached properly and followed up accordingly. We give this discipline a structure by calling it the sales cycle, starting with appointment-making, illustrated below:

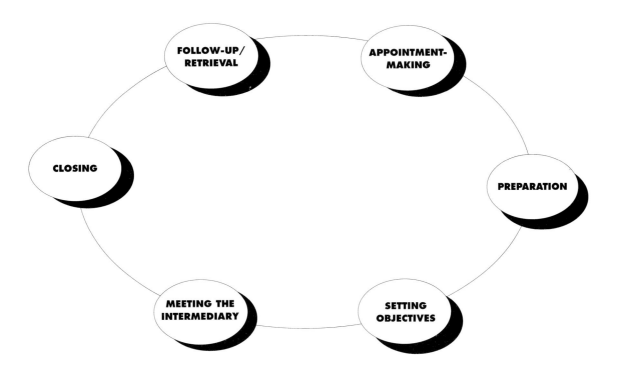

APPOINTMENT-MAKING

At the start of the cycle, appointment-making is a simple process, but is often an area that sales people find difficult. You need to set aside sensible, specific times in the working week (not Friday afternoons, for example) and then be disciplined enough to stick to those times. Diaries need to be booked with appointments at least 10–12 days in advance (but not much farther than that). With that sort of advance notice you should get in to see the right people, because those who aren't busy probably won't have much business for you. There is also the added benefit of having your name in their diary for a couple of weeks before you see them – often a subliminal sale.

There is a great temptation for sales people to continually chase new connections. But that isn't necessarily where the most business is. It is often said to be six times more expensive to attract a new customer than to sell again to an existing customer. Previous users are the ultimate warm lead because they have found you once. It should then be an easier job to ensure that they find you again, and we ask our sales team to spend at least 70 per cent of their time with existing users, developing the relationships.

To support this process, we make available to our sales team by the end of each working day a list of all applications received that day. This has the added benefit of showing each salesman how colleagues are doing, but the main point of this exercise is to highlight who is sending us business. If it is a new user in a particular region then the opportunity is created for a sales call to thank them for the business and to make an appointment for a visit. By submitting an application, that intermediary will be entered on our database, and our marketing department additionally makes available per sales region a report of all new entrants to the database each month. If there is anybody that the salesman has missed, he can follow up based on that list. In today's market, where mortgage sourcing systems are used more and more, and where a high profile advertising campaign of the type we use can create demand across the market from those who have never dealt with you before, it is essential to follow up on new or previous users as a priority over and above new prospects.

> **80 per cent of your business will come from 20 per cent of your contacts**

It is important to pre-qualify a source before charging off to see them. Find out, tactfully, how much business they are doing. You may have received the only mortgage application they have placed in that month. You can then take the opportunity to thank them for the business, but it probably isn't worth committing your time to make a visit. Occasional users can still be satisfactorily serviced by telephone.

The 80/20 list is the famous old sales standby: 80 per cent of your business will come from 20 per cent of your contacts. It might be so old as to be a cliché, but very rarely is it miles out. We ask our sales team to compile an 80/20 list by strict reference to the business they have achieved in the preceding month, and not subjectively according to who they feel "should" be supporting them. It is then part of our sales management process to ensure that appointments are made during the month with the 20 per cent who have produced 80 per cent of the business in the preceding month, to ensure that the regular and demonstrable users are being followed up.

"Activity breeds activity" is another famous old saying. It is, of course, true, although effectiveness cannot always be measured by the number of sales calls made each day. We look for an average of four to five, but the main focus has to be on the quality of the contact rather than the quantity. Working rigidly to a minimum call level each day can result in the priority becoming the number of people you see, rather than what is discussed when you get there. Well planned, quality time is the most successful formula for maximising sales. This means that more than lipservice has to be paid to geography and logistics. For example, if you decide to be in the office to catch up on your paperwork, be there for a full day. Don't pop in and out because you'll just waste time. Similarly, if you are out for the day, don't plan to spend long hours in the car: ensure that your visits are well placed and geographically viable.

We tend to encourage a day's field activity that is built around at least two "core" appointments with major sources. These two appointments are then built on with other, possibly less important, calls. If one of the core appointments postpones it is worth considering whether this changes the effectiveness of the whole day. If it does then it might be worth rearranging the lot and spending a day teleselling. As a salesman, your time is the most precious commodity you have.

Appointments should be made directly with the person that you need to see. A clear communication should then take place as to why you want to see them: *"I want to come and see you to discuss our new five-year fixed rate which I feel will be ideal for your market"*. Cold calling, or "popping in", is not recommended because such field activity will be treated less seriously. It is preferable to confirm in writing and to prepare well, which is the next step round the cycle. But appointment-making, like any other task in life, will produce benefits in line with the effort and commitment put in. We sometimes send our corporate video when confirming appointments with new prospects: it sells our concept in advance and gives a reason for the meeting not to be cancelled (i.e. they have to give the video back!).

PREPARATION

Preparation is vital. A brief meeting in an over-supplied market, where others will come in after you and dilute your message, is a very small window in which to get your message across. It is important not to spoil that by lack of preparation. The start point is as simple as thinking about what you will need for the meeting, i.e. a business card, marketing literature for the product(s) you intend to promote, application forms and sales aids. We prefer our people to carry A4 leather workstations rather than briefcases, because there is nothing more likely to stem your flow, and lose your customer's attention, than the sight of you rummaging around in a briefcase for papers that have become lodged underneath your sandwiches. The minimum paper requirements for the meeting should be in correct, chronological order, easily to hand within one folder.

Most salesmen promoting mortgages to intermediaries have a wide range of products from which to select. But selling too many products is as useless as not turning up in the first place. Your pre-qualifying call should have established what an intermediary is currently attracted to. Keep your product selection to a minimum of two, and then major on one. You can always follow up later with other products if the position changes. Having selected the product(s), get your script sorted out. The intermediary does not want you to read out all of the criteria. He wants you to explain clearly, in short sentences, and preferably backed up by visual aids, why this product should go onto his agenda and knock one of the others off. You need to capture his imagination with the appropriate script, including ideas as to how he can promote the product to his clients.

The final aspects of the physical preparation for a field-based meeting are a smart appearance and being ready to talk business. If the appointment is your first of the day, it may well be that you have spoken only a few words, if any, before leaving home. Try, therefore, to get to your appointment early, so that you can clear your vocal cords in the car park before going into the meeting. If it is your second or third appointment of the day, with the previous meeting having turned out to be difficult, find some time to compose yourself and ensure that you are positive, friendly and relaxed for the next call. Don't take baggage into one meeting that belongs in a previous one. If you are well prepared physically, and with your support material in place, you are giving yourself the best chance of succeeding. But there is one further step around the sales cycle before the meeting can actually take place, namely setting your objectives.

SETTING OBJECTIVES

A business meeting without objectives will drift aimlessly and lead to disappointment. Any piece of communication should have an objective, and this should preferably be written down. By knowing where you want the meeting to go, you are more likely to be able to control it. Do you need a specific piece of business to arise from this meeting, or is the objective to calm the customer down following an unfortunate processing experience? Is there a particular marketing initiative (a mailing to his client database, for example) you want to emerge from the contact? Or is it a meeting with a branch manager of an insurance company leading, hopefully, to an invitation to address the inspectors at a branch meeting? How can you decide whether the meeting has been successful if you have not previously set the objectives? Once you are clear on what is to be achieved you are ready to step round the cycle again.

MEETING THE INTERMEDIARY

Without being rude, try and keep "small talk" to a minimum. Too much chat about the weather, your journey or last weekend's football match all use up valuable time. You must be professional, focused and prepared. You are there to achieve business, so be hungry and deliver your pitch.

You are not there to listen to the sound of your own voice. You are there to add value to your customers' business. You should therefore always be prepared to talk about new marketing initiatives, customised sales aids, mailers that we would be prepared to draft, advertising campaigns that we would be prepared to help with creatively, posters to get walk-by customers to look in the window and so on. *"How can we add value to your business?"* is something that needs to be asked during every intermediary meeting.

Tactical or closed questioning is the other major technique when operating face-to-face. *"What are you selling currently?"* or *"Is it fixed or discounted rates that your clients are currently going for?"* It is a core skill to listen attentively and to observe reactions. "Buying signals" are obvious to the well-trained salesman. If the intermediary has picked up on an aspect of the product which he likes then work with that, rather than trying to convert your customer to the point you had in mind to promote. If your customer likes the product and expresses an intention to use it, shut up and move swiftly round to the next stage of the sales cycle and close. Too many times I have seen salesmen win the intermediary over with a particular product and then, feeling themselves to be on a roll, start diluting the original message by selling something else from the range which is in a completely different market. If your objective is to get the mortgage intermediary to start using you, and that objective has clearly been achieved, then don't muddy the water.

> You are there to achieve business, so be hungry and deliver your pitch

Before closing, however, you need to be sure that you have overcome all objections. The first thing for a salesman to do is to ensure that there are no issues in his own mind about a particular product. In order to get spectacular market-leading rate structures and benefits packages, we sometimes have to invest part of our earnings. In order to recover some of these, we sometimes have to charge a higher up-front fee payable by the customer. We only do this when the product benefits are self-evident, but it is sometimes necessary to role play with the sales team before they hit the road to promote a particular product in order to overcome *their* objections.

In the early days of our business we had more than one product where the initial fee amounted to as much as one month's interest. Mostly this was necessary to achieve a spectacular rate, and it all went to the lender. Rather than hide the initial fee, or come to it last in the sales meeting with the intermediary, we brought it right up front in all promotional material and in the sales scripts:

> *"The first thing you'll notice about this product is a high up front payment of one month's interest. That is much larger than the norm. There would have to be some pretty spectacular benefits accruing before your customers could be persuaded to part with that sort of money. So let's examine what those benefits are to see if they justify this sort of payment".*

This type of script promotes confidence and can often turn a negative into a positive.

Objections received at point of sale are sometimes generalised. Without being aggressive, you need to turn these into specific trans-action-based objections, or eliminate them. No salesman can deal properly with the criticism *"Your administration is bad"*. In order for the criticism to be constructive you need it to be related to a specific example, such as the case of Smith, which is the transaction that has caused that intermediary to raise an objection. To this end, our sales team have access to a laptop with a built-in modem. The laptop can dial into the computer system at our Processing Centre, and the case of Smith can then be looked up, with the progress screen revealed for all to see. You have to be confident that, nine times out of ten, your company's processing will have turned out under scrutiny to have been efficient. But by turning generalised objections into specific ones you can hopefully turn a negative round into a positive, showing that there was a mismatch between perception and reality rather than bad administration. Once the real issue is identified, it can be isolated and overcome, allowing the sale to continue.

Product objections can only be dealt with using a broad knowledge of the market, which I have already covered. If there are aspects to the product you are promoting which are negative (e.g. great rate, but high redemption penalties) have your script prepared in order to overcome that objection. Explain that, with a rate this good, the redemption penalties are academic, because the customers won't want to redeem. Knowing a product inside out, and knowing its position versus competitors, is the key to winning the moment.

CLOSING

You made the appointment, prepared for it, set your objectives, met the intermediary, overcame all objections and surfaced a buying signal. Now is the time to "close", which is the most important part of the sales process. Put simply, ask for the business. Don't be aggressive or desperate, but make sure you ask in a confident and positive way:

> *"You like the product – will you use it?"*
> *"When will you be submitting an application?"*
> *"Is the two-year fix or the cashback product the one you will be recommending to your clients?"*
> *"Do you have any cases you would like to discuss now?"*

There is no better way to close than to discuss a specific case. Our sales team have to have detailed knowledge of each lender's criteria and are therefore well placed to give an indication of whether an application will fit. The first application is the big hurdle to overcome with a new prospect. Once that goes through smoothly, selling the next deal should be easier. It is the ultimate closing opportunity for the intermediary you have called on to be so impressed with your product that he selects it for an application currently in hand. But whether there is a specific case to discuss or not, no "closing" has taken place without an agreed action point. That is the stage at which you need to summarise what has been discussed, ensure that the next action point is the last word left with your customer and then get out of there and move on to the next appointment.

FOLLOW-UP/RETRIEVAL

It is felt by some that the sales cycle ends when the sale has been "closed". But that is not our experience. The market is so over-supplied that an intermediary may express a genuine buying intention, and then become sidetracked by subsequent promotional visits from other lending organisations. There are also those customers who feel that it is more polite to tell you that they are going to buy when, actually, they have no intention of doing so. The final step in our sales cycle is therefore "follow up/retrieval". Our people often say towards the end of a face-to-face meeting: "I'll give

WEEKLY REPORT				
NAME:			**DATE:**	
	APPOINTMENT - contact, firm and location	DATA BASE CODE/NEW ENTRY	PI ✓	RESULT
MON	1.			
	2.			
	3.			
	4.			
	5.			
	6.			
TUE	1.			
	2.			
	3.			
	4.			
	5.			
	6.			
WED	1.			
	2.			
	3.			
	4.			
	5.			
	6.			
THUR	1.			
	2.			
	3.			
	4.			
	5.			
	6.			
FRI	1.			
	2.			
	3.			
	4.			
	5.			
	6.			

Comments on week's activity:

Requirements:

Number of confirmed appointments for next week; summary overleaf:

RESULT KEY: 1. No Good, 2. Warm, 3. Good Prospects,
4. Using us, 5. Strong Supporter, 6. Business Secured.

NB: Can be more than one category.

Signed .... Reviewed GB/STK ....

Page 1 of the Weekly Report used by the sales team

CALL PLAN

NAME .... REGION ....

WEEK COMMENCING 1997

MONDAY	TUESDAY	WEDNESDAY	THURSDAY	FRIDAY
am	am	am	am	am
pm	pm	pm	pm	pm

Page 2 of the Weekly Report used by the sales team

MONTHLY REPORT FORM - REGION............

NAME:
DATE:
REPORT FOR 1997

A   Business transacted in month

	APPS to Processing centre	
	Minimum Volume Target	
	Variance	

Comments:

B   Month's Performance - Highs and Lows - Your comments on your region.

C   Activity in month with Preferred Introducers and your comments

D   Detail any PIs in the region not seen this month and why?

Page 1 of the Monthly Report used by the sales team

E	Hot Prospects for business you have identified; indicate potential Pls
1.	
2.	
3.	
4.	

F	Marketing or other support requirements?

G	Competitors - which products most affect you and why?

H	Activity planned for next month and specific objectives

I	Summary and Conclusions

Signed .... Date ....

*A copy of my 80/20 list is enclosed.

Page 2 of the Monthly Report used by the sales team

189

Front page of Product Portfolio guide

Mailing postcard

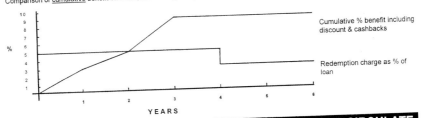

HALIFAX MSL/PRIVATE LABEL MORTGAGE OF A LIFETIME

The graph below shows that, after 2 years, the redemption penalties on this product never seek to reclaim from the borrowers the benefits package they have received. The <u>net benefit</u>, i.e. the gap between the two lines, amounts to 4% in the customer's favour when the redemption charge is at its highest. It is a generous 6% benefit <u>net</u> of the redemption charge after year 4, explaining why this product is **THE MORTGAGE OF A LIFETIME**.

Comparison of <u>cumulative</u> benefit on a £50,000 loan against potential redemption charges if the loan is redeemed early.

Cumulative % benefit including discount & cashbacks

Redemption charge as % of loan

YEARS

URGENT SALES NEWS FROM PRIVATE LABEL - PLEASE CIRCULATE
HELPLINE:01483 726161

This material is for the use of professional advisors only.
It is not intended as an advertisement with the Consumer Credit Act and must not be handed to clients or used to promote or advertise the product

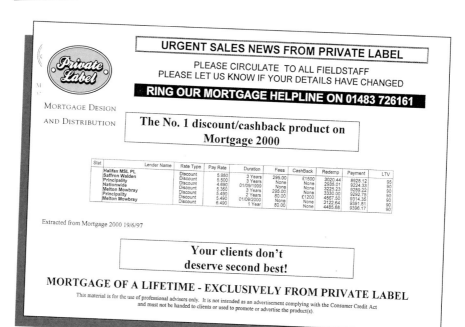

URGENT SALES NEWS FROM PRIVATE LABEL

PLEASE CIRCULATE TO ALL FIELDSTAFF
PLEASE LET US KNOW IF YOUR DETAILS HAVE CHANGED

RING OUR MORTGAGE HELPLINE ON 01483 726161

MORTGAGE DESIGN
AND DISTRIBUTION

The No. 1 discount/cashback product on Mortgage 2000

Stat Lender Name	Rate Type	Pay Rate	Duration	Fees	CashBack	Redemp	Payment	LTV
Halifax MSL PL	Discount	5.950	3 Years	295.00	£1500	3020.44	8928.12	
Saffron Walden	Discount	5.500	3 Years	None	None	2935.01	9224.33	95
Principality	Discount	4.690	01/09/1999	None	None	3225.23	9289.22	90
Nationwide	Discount	5.350	3 Years	295.00	None	3330.00	9292.75	90
Melton Mowbray	Discount	5.490	2 Years	80.00	£1200	4567.50	9314.35	90
Principality	Discount	5.490	01/09/2000	None	None	3122.64	9391.81	90
Melton Mowbray	Discount	6.490	1 Year	80.00	None	4485.68	9396.17	90

Extracted from Mortgage 2000 19/6/97

Your clients don't deserve second best!

MORTGAGE OF A LIFETIME - EXCLUSIVELY FROM PRIVATE LABEL

This material is for the use of professional advisers only. It is not intended as an advertisement complying with the Consumer Credit Act and must not be handed to clients or used to promote or advertise the product(s).

Sales fax/sales aids

For the typical £50k borrower, a <u>total</u> of:

3% Cashback
+
6% Discount

- Two cashbacks, worth £1500   (3%)

- 2% discount for the first three years (6%)

- To 98% LTV purchase or remortgage (including add-ons)

- The No. 1 discount/cashback product on Mortgage 2000

- Your clients don't deserve second best!

Funded by

Designed & Distributed Exclusively by

Call now on 01483 726 161

Trade press advertisement

you a call next week to see how you got on with that client". Once the sales meeting has taken place with the intermediary a diary note is then made for the salesman to call that intermediary at an appropriate time to follow up. Too often we are able to show to our sales team that the meetings they thought would produce business didn't, whereas the perceived lukewarm contacts did. Sometimes a customer appears lukewarm because he or she is busy and focused on the job in hand. That is the sort of business professional that can often produce high volumes of business.

You can't pay "positive feedback" and "friendly vibes" into the bank account. There is only one measure of whether a sales visit was successful, and that is if new business arose. But you always stand more chance of obtaining that business if you embrace the discipline of following up each meeting with a telephone call aimed at ensuring that the intermediary remembers you, and what was agreed.

THE SALES MIX

The sales cycle is the engine room by which existing customers get serviced, and new customers are added. The sales mix describes the various techniques that a salesman can use to influence business. We encourage our sales team to try out all aspects of the sales mix to see which ones work best for them. We ask those who have found one particular technique to have worked well for them to share this experience at the monthly off-site sales meeting. It is not cost-effective in my experience to have significant numbers of salesmen working small geographic patches. Much better to have a smaller number of professional, higher-paid individuals working smarter in larger patches – smarter meaning supplementing the one-on-one sales call with a range of other techniques within the sales mix.

Telesales is key. With the right preparation, it should be possible to have 30–40 quality conversations in a day as opposed to the four or five that would normally be possible on a day out in the field. Such sessions deliver major value when they follow up on a mailer or product launch and, on average, we would expect to launch at least 12 new products each year, with at least another half a dozen full database mailings on top of that. There is therefore normally a mailshot to follow up on at most times.

Each member of our sales team is issued monthly with an updated version of his or her database. This contains all of the important contact details. Before a telesales session, the salesman must highlight on a working copy of that list who is to be contacted, and what single topic is to be discussed. The proposed script should be written out and then summarised. The point of the exercise is a "smash-and-grab" raid on the database to get a single point across and then move on. We do not believe that customers can be satisfactorily serviced by telesales alone, but we do see our best results deriving from those salesmen who devote at least one day a week in the office to contacting 30–40 of their best connections.

If you cannot get through to the right person, don't leave a message. Just flag that particular contact up for a call back later in the day, if possible. It is important to work methodically and in a disciplined manner through the list using an office-based telephone (not a mobile). For members of our sales team who do not have reasonable access to head office or our Woking Processing Centre, we provide the necessary equipment for their home offices. As with the face-to-face meetings, we encourage only a minimum of "small talk". There will be a single topic to discuss and, whilst you want the encounter to be pleasant and memorable, everyone will ultimately benefit from brevity. This way, the intermediary will be more inclined to accept your call next time around.

To supplement the individual telesales sessions that we expect all of our salesmen to undertake each week, our sales management team will arrange *group* telesales sessions every six weeks or so on a major topic. There is a certain buzz and excitement in getting the entire sales team into one room with a bank of telephones to promote one topic, for example, "Base rates have risen again, so this is a major push on our five-year fix". There is much satisfaction to be gained from achieving a group target of telephone contacts to be made in a day and, hopefully, some good camaraderie and banter in the process. Telesales – individual and group – is probably the most important part of the sales mix after face-to-face calling.

> Telesales is the key. With the right preparation, it should be possible to have 30–40... conversations a day

We also budget for each member of our sales team to undertake a certain number of personalised mailings to their particular database over the course of the year. This is coordinated with the marketing department and a single topic/product is chosen. The salesman is encouraged to write the first draft of the mailing, which we adhere to as far as possible within the normal grammatical and regulatory constraints. Our sales regions are quite large and some salesmen have a database in excess of 1000 entries. But the norm is less than this and, so long as they are appropriately coordinated, we are usually able to handle one mailing every few weeks or so. These are in addition to the full database mailings that the marketing department undertakes.

There is no doubt that mortgage intermediaries get over-mailed. However, you can reach many more people with a mailing than you can with either face-to-face calling or telesales. At the same time you can get a longer message across and enclose a sales aid or some product literature. However, it is important to ration the number of mailings because of the law of diminishing returns. It is also true to say that not all members of our sales team find this to be a useful part of the sales mix on anything more than an occasional basis (whereas they all conduct weekly telesales). But the job is to generate new business and I believe that no stone should be left unturned towards that end.

Individual marketing initiatives are yet another part of the sales mix, encouraging intermediaries to advertise a particular product, or undertake a mailing to their client database. We are happy to draft such initiatives (subject always to the intermediaries obtaining for themselves the appropriate legal and regulatory advice), and to show how the maximum benefit could be obtained from promoting a product in one particular way. Persuading your customers to undertake regular marketing initiatives with you is a key goal for all of our sales team.

Because we started out in business providing branded mortgage schemes for insurance companies, we still obtain a significant proportion of our new business from that sector. Working with insurance companies opens up another element of the sales mix,

> The point of the exercise is a "smash-and-grab" raid...to get a single point across

namely the seminar or "round table" session with *their* brokers, whether they are IFAs or ARs. We know some lenders that refuse to participate in these sessions because normally a contribution of a few hundred pounds is required to cover the catering and venue costs. But we nearly always participate, not least because we are trying to cover a lot of ground via a relatively small sales team. There will normally be at least three or four lenders or lending organisations represented, with the insurance companies able to promote their particular products. In a seminar situation, the insurance company makes its pitch and then each lender has about ten minutes to present. In the round table set-up, each lender "sets up camp" at a table, and delegates move from table to table every ten minutes or so. These sessions can normally be arranged at no cost to the insurance company branch concerned, but they can represent a good opportunity to get in front of 50 or so intermediaries to talk about the topic of the day.

To take advantage of this opportunity means that your sales team must be good on their feet in front of a large group of people. This is a basic requirement for all of our sales team, and we practise such techniques in role plays and by way of formal presentations at our monthly off-site sales meetings. To be a good salesman you have to be memorable, which means that, at set-piece presentations, you must be using the latest technology. Anybody that turns up with overhead slides typed out that morning, and full of thumbprints, will be remembered, but for the wrong reason. Our laptops link with an easily transportable projector. We can produce interesting graphics, and play extracts from our corporate video, through equipment that one person can easily transport from car to office and vice versa. We also have the normal mobile presentation stand so that we can participate in the exhibition-type of meeting which the direct sales life companies often set up for their salesmen. The group presentation is another important part of the sales mix when dealing with insurance companies, and we often encourage the branches we visit to set them up, even if they had not previously thought of doing so.

SALES REPORTING

There are no prizes in our business for long, flowery sales reports. We ask our sales team to complete just two reports in a pre-set format. The weekly report covers that week's activities and, on the reverse, shows the call plan for the following week. These reports must reach the Sales Director by nine o'clock each Monday morning by fax. Both pages of this two-sided report appear in the illustrations with this chapter (pp. 186–7), from which it can be seen that each week's calls must be graded as to result. There is room for a short comment on the week's activity (which would include a note of any competitor deals we were coming up against, for example) plus any requirements as to product material, sales or marketing help. Those intermediaries who wish to enter into a volume arrangement with us can obtain Preferred Introducer (PI) status, and this report has a specific column for PIs since our sales team are required to call on all of the PIs in their patch at least once a month.

The weekly report is particularly important, because it is fed into our analysis system. We track the business generated by the contacts called on over the following two, three and four weeks and give this report back to the sales team. It obviously involves company names and cannot be repeated in this book. But at the monthly sales meetings, we use the same report to demonstrate to each individual salesman their particular strike rate. It is immediately apparent from such an analysis as to who is closing, and who is not, with the appropriate action then being taken.

The actual strike rate analysis for April 1997 appears below to show what we mean. The "dashes" in regions 7 and 9 respectively for the month of January indicate that the salesmen for these regions were in training during that particular month.

STRIKE RATE REPORT

Region	Jan	Feb	Mar	Apr
1	44%	51%	56%	52%
2	44%	50%	28%	46%
3	51%	54%	52%	63%
4	16%	24%	51%	43%
5	41%	53%	30%	49%
6	27%	30%	48%	43%
7	–	33%	23%	37%
8	34%	44%	61%	55%
9	–	31%	29%	38%
10	45%	42%	46%	53%

The second side of the weekly report is the call plan. This again is fed into our analysis system so that activity can be assessed. We look for a minimum of four appointments per day and are able to demonstrate at each monthly sales meeting who is falling behind that average. Again, an extract from our April 1997 reporting pack appears below to illustrate this point.

CALL PLAN – APPOINTMENTS MADE EACH DAY

Region	Jan	Feb	Mar	Apr
1	3.5	4.6	3.9	3.9
2	3.6	4.0	4.4	5.4
3	3.3	4.1	3.8	4.3
4	3.0	4.5	4.3	5.7
5	3.4	3.7	3.4	4.7
6	3.2	5.1	4.3	5.2
7	–	5.0	4.9	5.0
8	5.0	5.2	5.4	5.6
9	–	4.8	4.8	4.8
10	4.3	4.5	5.1	4.9

But the analysis does not stop there. In line with our philosophy that all communication should serve a purpose, the weekly sales reports are used to provide yet more information to enable the individual salesman to analyse his business, and to enable our sales management team to expose training needs or under-performance. For example, we have already discussed the importance of repeat usage. It is easier to get somebody who has used you successfully on one occasion to repeat that experience, than it is to start a new contact from cold. So we analyse for the benefit of our sales team the number of users in any one month who also sent in an application in the previous month. Sticking for consistency with our April 1997 reporting pack, the report for this month follows:

REPEAT USAGE

Region	No. of users in March	No. of users in March, using us again in April	%	March over February
1	69	51	74%	52%
2	101	54	53%	48%
3	69	49	71%	51%
4	55	42	76%	49%
5	86	58	67%	47%
6	77	55	71%	44%
7	48	41	85%	46%
8	86	52	60%	48%
9	54	40	74%	46%
10	84	51	60%	43%
Nominal average			69%	47%

The only other report that we ask our sales team to complete is the two-sided monthly report, also illustrated in this chapter (pp. 188–9). The importance of this document is to ensure that each salesman is forced through the loop of analysing his piece of the business, demonstrating that they are thinking about the job in hand and planning for the next month. Attached to the monthly report is the 80/20 list previously mentioned, as prepared from the new application statistics for the preceding month, which we always get to the sales team by fax on the second working day of the next month.

No sales team does exactly what it is required to do every month without a little help. So we also analyse how successful they were at following up on their 80/20 list as illustrated by the following final extract from our April 1997 reporting pack:

80/20 LIST – ACTIVITY

Region	Feb	Mar	Apr
1	81%	60%	78%
2	38%	17%	64%
3	71%	40%	77%
4	60%	66%	64%
5	26%	28%	50%
6	100%	50%	53%
7	66%	67%	67%
8	86%	75%	79%
9	100%	60%	75%
10	71%	68%	56%

A salesman is rarely able to achieve 100 per cent contact with the key members of the 80/20 list during the following month, because holidays and diaries will get in the way. But the table shows that, in the early part of this year, some of our sales team were just calling on the wrong people. We got everybody to or above 50 per cent in April and have built on those figures since. This method of reporting is relatively new to us, having been introduced at the beginning of 1997. As this book is prepared in the summer of 1997, I feel that the mid-point between introduction and relative maturity, e.g. April 1997, is the most honest point to illustrate how the reporting techniques work.

Too often in my experience salesmen are asked to produce long reports that are subjective, do not always get read and on which there is no feedback by the sales management. We do not believe that this is an effective way to maximise new business. Reports should be kept brief and with a specific objective in mind. They should be closely read by the sales management, with feedback given in the form of analysis and discussion at the monthly sales meeting. This is the professional way to use sales reporting to maximum effect.

SALES MANAGEMENT

You cannot manage a sales team by monitoring alone, producing statistics that then get thrown at the individual salesmen without analysis. But good, timely and accurate reporting gives you the basic tools for the job so that there is a firm base from which to develop the key coaching and development role. In sales, as in business generally, he who possesses the detail wins the day. We have a rather unusual set-up in that we have a Sales Director, to whom all of the sales team report, but have the added resource of Godfrey Blight, our Managing Director, who is always focused on sales. Godfrey and I have always worked as a partnership, largely splitting the roles with me producing the bullets and him firing them. Godfrey has been able to replicate a similar, successful partnership between himself and Simon Knight, our Sales Director, with the result that the two of them quite happily split the various sales management functions between them in a way that works.

An important point is to talk to all salesmen each day. Sales can be a lonely job, and you need to keep each person feeling part of the team. Communication lines should be readily open, with the opportunity being taken to "catch somebody doing something right", as well as correcting things that might be going wrong. Daily contact can also be valuable when a particular individual might be feeling down about something, the opportunity being there to counsel and motivate them.

Godfrey and Simon impose on themselves the discipline of each spending one day in the field every week. This often involves a lot of travelling, creating pressure on other day-to-day responsibilities, which then have to be undertaken out of hours. But we are essentially a sales and marketing company and, if we do not sell mortgages, we don't eat. One day out each week with the sales team focuses everybody's minds on the fact that new business is the only judge of whether we are doing well. Whilst out in the field Godfrey and Simon can assess and coach, helping to develop the presentations that work best, and staying in very close touch with what the market is selling and why. This, in turn, means that the cross-referencing and analysis which goes on at the monthly sales meetings run jointly by Godfrey and Simon is relevant and up to the minute.

There are two types of field visit undertaken by Godfrey and Simon. The most commonly used technique is the pre-planned day, where the salesman in question is asked to produce a day of visits which includes servicing previous users plus a couple of new prospects. There may even be a regular user that wishes to be considered for appointment to Preferred Introducer status. These days can also be used as an opportunity for the executive directors to say thank you to top users, and perhaps to discuss whether there is anything more we could do to build that intermediary's business. Equally, the days are useful to slot in a call to a dissatisfied customer, who obviously crops up now and again in any high volume environment.

The other type of day out is where Godfrey or Simon turn up unannounced on the first appointment of the day for a particular salesman. This is more of a check on performance and is not commonly used. Nevertheless, it is a valid technique to use in respect of those salesmen who might not be getting the best out of their regions, and the fact that there are no clues as to when it might happen keeps everybody on their toes.

The individual days out have to be balanced with the fact that new recruits require a disproportionate amount of time, but the result is that everybody on the sales team has at least a few days out with the Sales Director and the Managing Director each year – a valuable communication process on several levels. Even top sales people can always improve, and no sales management team should ever stop investing in their people or coaching them. However, this does involve occasionally "biting your lip" so that the senior person does not end up taking over the sales call. It must always be remembered that the purpose of attendance is to monitor, help, coach and listen, unless of course it was pre-agreed that one particular call would be managed by the senior person to demonstrate how a point should be put across.

Two out of every three monthly off-site sales meetings are undertaken at our Processing Centre, so that the sales team mingle with the processing staff. Every other one of those meetings links with a buffet into the evening for socialising. It is a key ingredient of the sales management process to ensure that sales staff do not believe themselves to be more important than processing staff, or vice versa. It is one team and everybody needs to work together. Those relationships are best achieved when all sides know each other, having spent some time together in a social environment. Keeping the sales and processing teams apart is a mistake, in our view.

Once every calendar quarter the off-site sales meeting is held at a good quality hotel, with sporting facilities, located in a different part of the country each time so that everybody, wherever they are based, has their "fair share" of travelling. Arrival is on the late afternoon preceding the sales meeting, with the opportunity to engage in various sporting activities from five-a-side football to golf, swimming and use of the gym. We have a dinner in the evening at which there is a presentation and discussion, and then start bright and early the next morning with the sales meeting. Just as it is important for the sales team to have good relations with those who process the applications, so it is important for sales colleagues to meet with each other in a social environment and "compare notes". These are important aspects to the management of a sales team and those who regard them as simply domestic or peripheral will not be maximising the performance of those who work on the sales side of their business. The agenda for these meetings is tightly prepared, with the accent on variety. The core part of the meeting is always the same, however, in terms of analysing how well we have done in the preceding month, and how much better we intend to do the following month.

Before we launch a product we spend some time trying to get to the script that presents it in its best light. Through the feedback systems inherent in the reporting mechanisms and monthly meetings, we adjust that script in order to take into account the sales objections. I thought it would be helpful to illustrate one product and show some examples of that approach in practice. This section could have just as easily been covered in Chapter 6, but as it relates to sales scripts that we evolve in response to objections, I have decided to cover it here.

THE PRODUCT

The "Mortgage of a Lifetime" product, funded for us by Halifax Mortgage Services Ltd, was the successor to the "Mortgage of the Century", which is discussed as case study no. 29 in Chapter 4. The new product retained many of the characteristics of its predecessor and we gave it the same sort of immodest title. The front page of the product portfolio guide is shown on p. 190: we also made some regulatory changes and had some large posters printed, which we gave to brokers and estate agents for display in their windows. We even dedicated the product to our "summer postcard" – a humorous attempt at a different intermediary communication medium that we use most years, an illustration of which appears on p. 191. The thinking behind the postcard idea is discussed in more depth in Chapter 6.

The "Mortgage of a Lifetime" product offered a 2 per cent discount for three years with two cashbacks. The basic script for the product was therefore the long-term nature of the discount, the fact that the first cashback made it a low cost of entry product, with the final cashback probably coming as a surprise to the applicants in December 1999, creating further sales and relationship-building opportunities for the intermediary. When interest rates started to rise we promoted the fact that they would have to increase quite a bit further before a 2 per cent discount for three years would disadvantage borrowers versus the long-term fixes then available.

REDEMPTION CHARGE PROBLEM

All this worked well enough, but queries started to arise about the redemption penalties, which lasted for the first six years of the loan. This was necessary because the discount and cashback benefits were similarly spread out. But it was clear that we needed to overcome the objection of six-year redemption penalties in order to maximise the volume. We therefore produced the redemption graph, which appears on p. 192.

NEW REDEMPTION CHARGE SCRIPT

In this sales aid we showed graphically the cumulative percentage benefits experienced by the borrowers by virtue of the discounts and cashbacks. We then overlaid this onto the redemption penalties, which were 5 per cent of the loan during the first four years, and 2 per cent during years five and six. Through this device we were clearly able to show that, after the first two years, the lender was not seeking to reclaim from the borrower the full benefits package they had by then received. We went further and introduced the concept of net benefit, i.e. the difference between the discounts and cashbacks received and the redemption penalty due. We were able to show that the structure of the benefits package required the unusual approach to redemption penalties, with borrowers much better off than they would be by taking a straightforward cashback where, typically, the full amount received would be repayable in the event of early redemption. This one sales aid, faxed to our database, and used by our sales team at point of sale, eliminated this particular problem. Our script had changed to meet the objection.

THE PROBLEM OF SPREADING THE BENEFITS

The next problem to arise concerned the fact that the benefits of this product were so spread out. Some competitor deals, although not offering the customer as much in total as "Mortgage of a Lifetime", were nevertheless promoting more immediate benefits. Intermediaries could see the advantages of "Mortgage of a Lifetime", but needed help in getting across to customers the fact that, if they waited for all the benefits to come through, they would get more in the end.

NEW BENEFITS SCRIPT

To address this problem we were aided by the fact that Mortgage 2000 was not only growing strongly as a popular product sourcing system used by intermediaries, but also had programmed its system to calculate the total benefits of a product by reference to giveaways less charges over the first five years. A printout of the Mortgage 2000 data in the discount/cashback section clearly showed our product to be number one. We therefore turned this into a sales fax, and a sales aid, and the message could not have been better put across. Intermediaries were able to show to customers that this was the number one discount and cashback product, albeit that it had to be accessed over a five-year period for its merits to be fully appreciated. This item is illustrated on p. 192, and represents yet another script adjustment.

COMPETING WITH STRAIGHT PERCENTAGE DEALS

The next issue to address was the launch by a number of high profile lenders of large cashbacks, all expressed in percentage terms. Often these products were accompanied by a loading above the standard variable rate. The customers tended to see the large percentage figures and be attracted to them. In practice, our "Mortgage of a Lifetime" product offered better benefits with no rate loading, but we needed to give those intermediaries suffering from this competition the opportunity to hit back.

NEW PERCENTAGE PRESENTATION

Our product mixed "currencies" in that there was a percentage discount and cashbacks expressed in pounds. We therefore needed to find a loan size at which they could be converted into one percentage figure, and we chose £50,000. We then ran an advertising campaign showing that, at this loan size, the £1500 cashback represented 3 per cent of the loan plus the 6 per cent discount. This advertisement – which was also available to our regional salesforce as a sales aid – is the final illustration in this chapter (see p. 192).

ADJUSTING THE TILLER

It sounds as though there were never-ending problems with our "Mortgage of a Lifetime" product, which is not the case. Like its predecessor, "Mortgage of a Lifetime" has sold outstandingly well. But it has achieved these results because we were prepared to amend the original scripts and deal with the competitor problems which arose. This is just one case study, but hopefully it demonstrates the need to be responsive to market problems as they develop and to "adjust the tiller" accordingly.

WRAP-UP

As a company, Private Label performs three functions – mortgage design, distribution and pre-offer processing. Our mortgage designs are high profile and are often attributed as the main reason we achieve the volumes we do. In fact we would not be half as successful if we had not developed well thought-out and highly disciplined distribution techniques. Our customers are the mortgage intermediaries who promote our products and much of the sales theory and practice included within this chapter is only relevant to that sector. But we hope that the honest and frank sharing of views, procedures and skills will help different readers in different ways.

6

THE ROLES OF ADVERTISING, PUBLIC RELATIONS AND DIRECT MAIL IN THE MARKETING OF MORTGAGES

W hen I started my career, advertising, public relations and direct mail had no role to play in the marketing of mortgages. In fact, there was no marketing of mortgages. Applicants were expected to visit a branch of a building society and, when they asked how they stood for a mortgage, the clichéd response was "You don't stand, you grovel".

An excess of supply over demand has changed that. Mortgage products are promoted as strongly, if not more strongly, than investment products. For example, according to DMB&B Financial, a leading advertising agency, there were 156 mortgage advertisements during April 1997 in just four titles (the *Daily Telegraph*, the *Guardian*, the *Independent* and *The Times*) representing 11.3 per cent of all financial advertisements. This is from a standing start of virtually nil not so long ago. Consumers and mortgage intermediaries are also bombarded by direct mail about mortgages, with the result that "no post today" is a distant memory.

In this chapter I examine the emerging and evolving role that advertising, public relations and direct mail have played in the development of Private Label's business, sharing the lessons learned as our strategies have developed. I also incorporate the views of some leading players in this field to develop a wider perspective on the advertising and direct mail theme. As with every chapter in this book, the aim is to give readers information and experiences which will hopefully be of interest and value to their business lives.

THE EARLY YEARS AT PRIVATE LABEL

Our original concept was to provide insurance companies with mortgage products that they then promoted to the market under their own brand. We would encourage the insurance companies to undertake (and pay for) these advertising campaigns by putting forward drafts under the dummy style of XYZ Homeloans. An example of this approach appears as case study no. 23 in Chapter 4. Occasionally the insurance companies responded, examples being case studies 3, 9, 10 and 12. This was at a time when the insurance companies' wish to build mortgage business was broadly in line with our own. However, when the housing market recession really started to bite, the insurance companies' priorities started to change.

We therefore revised our strategy, and started to fund and place advertisements ourselves, but still in a "private labelling" way, by arranging the logos of a group of insurance companies at the foot of the advertisement. Examples of this form of advertising are case studies 13, 17 and 26. This seemed to work for a while, but the insurance companies were not able to provide us with much in the way of statistics regarding enquiries generated. It was at this juncture – five years after launch – that we therefore started to have a major rethink about how Private Label – designed to be a behind-the-scenes company promoting the brands of others – could take more control of its life by advertising in its own name. A good example of the identity crisis we were going through at the time is the illustration which appears in this chapter (p. 220) under the heading: "At last, we reveal the people behind five years of mortgage innovation". This was the advertisement we placed in the awards magazine of what was then *Which Mortgage* when we won the first of our prizes for "Most Innovative Lending Organisation". It reflected our dilemma about how much profile we could or should take for ourselves.

when the housing market recession really started to bite, the insurance companies' priorities started to change

Up until then, we had had no choice about who should retrieve the enquiries resulting from the advertising, because we had no pre-offer processing capability. The insurance companies received the applications and processed them to pre-offer stage, and we did not accept mortgage applications other than via the insurance companies. But in 1992 we had started processing applications via the "packaging centre" that we set up with HML. So we began to review whether we should be advertising in our own name. Today, Private Label is a well-known company within the intermediary sector, and has been advertising in its own name for many years. With hindsight, it looks less obvious as to why the decision to go it alone should have been so significant. But the whole concept of the company up until that point had been to promote the brands of others, and we had even chosen a name – Private Label – which described that principal purpose. It was therefore not a straightforward decision.

I have already covered briefly (in Chapter 3) how a new marketing agency had approached us just as we were pondering this problem, offering to undertake research as to how we were perceived by mortgage intermediaries at the time. This was considered essential before making a leap in the dark. Not surprisingly, the research revealed that we were perceived as a lender. Our name had very much been associated with the contemporary-style lender organisations which had launched with such high profile in the period 1985–7. The advice we received from the marketing agency was that we would have to address this popular misconception if we were to stand a chance of generating mortgage enquiries directly. It was thus that our "Popular Misconceptions" campaign was born.

> We developed the strapline "For exclusive designs from major lenders, look for the Private Label"

There is no doubt that the campaign was clever. The initial advertisements appeared in four consecutive pages within such trade press publications as *Money Marketing* and *Financial Adviser*. The first two pages would catch the attention of the reader with some obscure misconceptions such as "The tomato is a vegetable", "Touching toads causes warts", with the oval of our logo subliminally featured. The third advertisement, picking up the same style, would deal with the misconception that we were a lender. The fourth advertisement would then be for the product. Examples of various different advertisements in this style are illustrated on pp. 221–8.

If we had been able to afford a budget of, say, £50,000 to support this campaign over several months I believe it might have worked for us, although we still had the problem of countering a negative instead of promoting a positive. But we could only afford a short burst campaign, and the new business results at the time did not suggest that the campaign had been a great success. We were therefore back to the drawing board.

Using another agency, we decided to play on the fact that our company name was unusual, and perhaps not the best choice for a company that was now seeking to attract new business from the intermediary market at large. We therefore developed an advertising campaign where each product was featured on a differently shaped label. We developed the strapline "For exclusive designs from major lenders, look for the Private Label". We were trying to strike some kind of "atmosphere" connection with designer labels in the fashion industry, which fitted well with our concept of exclusive products (not available for the clients to buy direct from the lender) and designer products (giving the intermediary something different, and more forward-thinking, to explain to clients). As with the "Popular Misconceptions" campaign this was a clever and well thought-out campaign by the advertising agency. Unfortunately, however, it was no more successful.

After our second attempt at trying to promote ourselves in the forefront, we decided that intermediaries didn't have time to work through a concept presentation before getting to the product. You have a one-second chance, particularly in the trade press, to drag the reader's eye into the body copy of an advertisement. All this conceptual stuff, whilst of much interest to us, was in fact cluttering the advertisements and rendering them ineffective. We learned that you can't mix "concept" or "brand" advertising with product. Yet another rethink was necessary. An example of the "labels" campaign is on p. 229.

THE CURRENT STRATEGY

Third time lucky we got it right. With the cooperation of our lenders, we featured *their* names and logos, these being instantly familiar to mortgage intermediaries. Our logo was cast in the role of the sub-brand, with the strapline "Designed & Distributed Exclusively By ..." preceding it. The analogy that we used to describe this approach is the AMG badge on a Mercedes motorcar. When AMG advertises its styling and enhancement services it first establishes firmly in the readers' minds that the core product is the Mercedes motor car that they know and love. The AMG badge just means that the core Mercedes product will be a little faster, more stylish and more exclusive than the normal showroom product. Likewise, with our new campaign, we were trying to put across the fact that clients would get a mortgage from a popular, well-known lender, but that, if the product was designed and distributed by us, it would be a little more stylish and exclusive.

We first developed this campaign in 1995 and, by and large, have stuck to it since. This is in itself an important factor, because an advertising campaign needs time to work, so long as your instincts tell you that the basics are in place. In 1995/6 we used the same format, namely "Mortgage of the Week". This communicated on several levels. It could be read as our selection of the best mortgage to advertise that week. Alternatively, it might be viewed as the trade press publication's "Mortgage of the Week". Or it might be taken as everybody's acknowledged "Mortgage of the Week". We were happy with any of these interpretations, so long as intermediaries responded to the advertisements! With a weekly deadline to meet we also had to have an easy-to-use format so that we could leave the selection of the product to be advertised the following week until the last moment. Examples of the "Mortgage of the Week" campaign are on pp. 230 and 231.

In 1997 we changed the format slightly. The advertising agency devised a sequence of six advertisements, three featuring strong visual devices and three majoring on the fact that our campaign was being featured on the back page of *Financial Adviser* throughout the year. All six formats were set up on the computer, and we allocated the following week's advertisement into the next format in the sequence. We would interrupt the sequence from time to time with bespoke advertisements, which had the benefit of widening the time gap between a repeat of the same advertisement style, and our sense is that this has been our best campaign ever. Examples are on pp. 232 and 233.

WHY ADVERTISE?

Unlike the advertisements that our sister company, John Charcol, places in the national press, our trade press advertising campaign is not directed primarily at generating enquiries. I have never found an enquiry tracking system that I totally trusted in any event. Such statistics that we have been able to generate on new enquiries directly attributable to our trade press advertising campaign would suggest that we should scrap it. Yet, the more we have advertised, the more our volumes have increased. The point I made in Chapter 5 about new business numbers being the only worthwhile judge of whether or not a marketing or sales action is validated is a core philosophy throughout our business.

The reason we believe our trade press advertising campaign to be so effective for us is that it establishes a substantial presence. When members of our regional salesforce call on intermediaries, or when our customers receive direct mail items from us, they are familiar with the name. It is often said to our salesmen "You've suddenly got a lot bigger lately". This is not a reference to their physical appearance, although some of them probably do lunch too much. It is a reference to a perception that Private Label has "suddenly" grown in size, whereas in fact the difference has been a constant and high-profile advertising presence in the trade press.

We find also that more and more of the intermediaries we speak to are familiar with a particular product we are seeking to promote. They don't necessarily know why they are familiar, but our sale is made much easier because of it. The two main roles of the campaign are therefore to promote awareness of the company, and familiarity with the product being advertised. Of course there will be some calls to our Helpline in direct response to the advertisements, and we are pleased to have them and to send out an introducer pack. But, in our particular case, immediate enquiries are not the campaign's main purpose: rather we focus to a larger extent on the wider new business results at the time in order to assess the impact of the campaign.

> in our particular case, immediate enquiries are not the campaign's main purpose

Supporting an advertising campaign is as important as the campaign itself. Our sales faxes, for example, cross-refer customers to the campaign. Our regional salesforce are given sales aids which support the products being used in the campaign. Copy advertisements get framed and put on the walls at Head Office and the Processing Centre so that staff live with, and get a good feel for, the sales messages and the products being promoted. An advertising campaign must not be conducted in isolation: if used as a core marketing function from which there are other spin-offs, greater recognition and better results will flow.

NATIONAL PRESS

So far I have looked at our experiences in the trade press only. But in the course of researching this chapter, a number of people have been contacted who advertise in the national press. There the objectives are entirely directed towards generating new business enquiries, with choice of media being crucial to ensure that the readership of that newspaper aligns with the type of product being promoted. As Ian Darby, Marketing Director of John Charcol, says: "An effective advertisement for John Charcol can only be judged on cost per response". Simon Tyler, Managing Director of Chase De Vere, endorses the profile point by saying: "The readership profile of a newspaper must be right for us. We never use certain national dailies, for example. As long as you know the market you are aiming at, leads should result."

The aims and objectives of a national press advertising campaign are different in my experience from the objectives we set ourselves for our trade press advertisements. It is even more important that the advertisements have impact and clarity, making the reader stop and take notice. Lucian Camp, Creative Director at Camp Chipperfield Hill Murray, develops this point further with his "IRMA" principle. An advertisement must:

- have **I**mpact

- be **R**elevant

- be **M**emorable

- require **A**ction

The audience being aimed at must feel "that's for me". If they don't, then the advertisement is likely to be a failure. Often this will be because of over-complication and Lucian's advice is that, even if there are six good selling points about the product you wish to promote, choose only one or two to feature in an advertisement.

Some national press advertising will aim to create a lasting image for the advertiser's brand. A good way of judging this is what John Meakin, Managing Director at Corporate Marketing & Advertisement Services Limited, calls "the thumb test". If you place your thumb over the logo of the company in the advertisement, can you still recognise who the advertiser is? The recognition factor is essential to the strategy of brand-building, something that John Charcol has developed by being amongst the largest mortgage product advertisers in the intermediary market. Whether it's the four-line advertisement where lines two and four also read together, or "Dear John", or any of the other innovative campaigns John Charcol has developed (examples of which appear as case studies 1, 2, 4, 18, 22 and 24 in Chapter 4), the core theme is the same, namely to make the advertisements immediately recognisable as coming from John Charcol.

As Ian Darby adds: "The advertisement also has to say something about your business and your service, as well as your product". An innovative, clever advertisement will, inevitably, create the image in the client's mind that your company is innovative and clever. Ben

Thompson, Client Services Director at DMB&B Financial, thinks that advertisements have "attitude". He says: "An advert is just the first point of a long chain setting up expectations for the consumer. The attitude of the advertisement must therefore fit the personality of the provider."

It is important not to expect an advertisement for a mortgage product to persuade somebody to take out a mortgage when they were not already thinking of doing so. For most people, mortgages are boring and a necessary evil. If they are not already thinking about switching mortgages, or buying a new property, they are most unlikely to be motivated to do so by an advertisement. They are much more likely to skim over such advertising on their way to the real news, or the sports pages. Expectation as to conversion rates should therefore be set at a realistic level, with 100 responses to a national press advertisement converting into 20 mortgage applications being towards the upper end of expectations. It is also important when tracking such statistics to take into account that there will be one level of immediate conversion and another along the line, when those without a property in mind at outset eventually find one and decide to go ahead. An advertisement for a spectacular fixed rate, going out just as base rates have increased by half a per cent, for example, will obviously produce better-than-normal results. But it is better to budget for relatively few leads, and a 10–20 per cent conversion at best.

> An innovative, clever advertisement will...create the image...that your company is innovative and clever

Impact can be maximised by the advertisement's position within the newspaper. Budget constraints might require you to take a lower profile slot than you might otherwise have chosen. There are also those who feel that it is better to be in the main bunch of advertisements if you have confidence that your product will shine above the others also being featured on that page. We and John Charcol have tended to take the view, however, that it suits our businesses to be the only advertisement on a particular page, using wherever possible an unusual shape. We have found it possible to negotiate such deals if you allocate a disproportionate amount of your spend to one particular publication. In John Charcol's case it is *The Times*, in which John Charcol appears every week as a strip across the bottom of the Tuesday business section. In our case, it is an unusual A4 solus slot on the back page of *Financial Adviser*. The front and back pages of any publication are read most, followed by pages two and three and the diary plus letters pages. Most publications track recognition of advertisements by readers, and can give potential advertisers data on the performance of any particular slot within the publication.

TV ADVERTISING

Television advertising is beyond the budget of most organisations. Moreover, it is the ultimate medium for the subliminal sell. TV advertisements interrupt customers when they are in relaxed mode. They are intrusive and can plant a message into the subconscious. But that message is rarely retrieved there and then. It is retrieved when the customer bumps into that product on the supermarket shelves, or in the high street. Most of the experts spoken to when this chapter was researched had great praise for the Halifax Building Society TV advertising campaign, which features a large number of people standing in a formation that builds up the shape of a house. But nobody expected a customer, having seen this advertisement, to leap out of his armchair and make a note to ring the Halifax the next day. When next faced with the choice of selecting a mortgage provider, however, the customer will have in his subconscious an image of the Halifax as big and confident and a brand leader.

The experts also felt the Cheltenham and Gloucester's "No Strings" TV campaign to be very good, effectively getting across the message that their particular mortgages had none of the associated fees and expenses a customer would ordinarily incur when taking out a mortgage. Direct Line was also mentioned by the experts as having conducted a highly successful name awareness TV campaign, both in respect of their "red telephone" original device and the "Direct Line challenge" by which the company invited the more traditional mortgage providers to compare their terms with those offered by Direct Line.

COMMERCIAL RADIO

Commercial radio should not be ignored as a potential medium, particularly as it offers the opportunity for market segmentation. For example, John Charcol ran a successful campaign for its 100 per cent product on Capital Radio, where the listening profile aligned well with first-time buyers. Conversely, Jazz or Classic FM can present different markets respectively for products which are perhaps a touch off the wall, or more sophisticated. Again, it is an intrusive medium which is best combined with a poster, direct mail or a national press advertising campaign. Its big limitation so far as financial services products are concerned is the fact that a long list of regulatory information has to be read out at the end of the advertisement. Such information can fairly easily be accommodated in a footnote to a national press adver-

> advertising will only work... with those who have already decided to buy

tisement, but in the context of a radio advertisement it becomes a turgid list of boring facts that no one understands. It is extraordinary that even in this age of communication the regulators continue to ignore the fact that too much information means less understanding on the part of the consumer. Or rather, perhaps they do realise this, but are seeking to "cover their behinds" in the amount of information they require to be given, as opposed to seeking a formula that will actually warn and inform the consumer.

When contemplating any form of advertising, the choice of agency is very important. The agency must understand your business and know your market. A long period of preparation and planning is necessary, and expect it to take time for the campaign to develop. Be ready to refine it as the weeks tick by, and remember that advertising will only work on behalf of a mortgage product with those who have already decided to buy. I have not set out to write the ultimate textbook on the role of advertising: there are plenty of those in existence from individuals more expert than I. If there are just one or two pieces of interesting information derived by the reader from the words so far used then I will be satisfied. The same applies to my thoughts and experiences with public relations and direct mail, which have certainly emerged in our business life as probably more important even than advertising.

PUBLIC RELATIONS

I mentioned a few pages back that an advertising campaign needs to be supported if you are to get the best out of it. And you can give no greater support to an advertising campaign than through good public relations. We will always announce a product first in the trade press, before we then go on to advertise it. These publications get bombarded with press releases each day, so we try to give a news angle so that the journalists have a reason to report the product launch in the news pages, rather than to confine the mention to a few sentences under "product news". For example, we launched one fixed rate with a lead-in commenting on how quickly its predecessor had sold out, thereby indicating increasing public concern with rising mortgage rates. We launched our "Mortgage of a Lifetime" product on the back of the stories then circulating about the desire for lenders to take a "year one hit" when offering cashbacks, rather than amortising them over the first few years which tended to distort a profitability comparison between lenders. You need to explain why your product is a news item, rather than an information item, to stand any chance of getting greater coverage.

If you do get coverage then an article is worth ten times an advertisement. Everybody knows that the latter has been prepared by the company promoting the product, trying to push that deal forward in its best light. But an article from a journalist is accepted as independent and, therefore, represents a much greater endorsement. We work very hard at trying to turn our product launches into news items, which involves a certain amount of holding back. For example, we do not press-release every product so that we at least give ourselves a chance of holding the attention of journalists, on the basis that we only press-release information if we feel we have something interesting to say.

In order to stand any chance of getting decent press coverage, it is necessary to maintain a relationship with the journalists. This means being on hand every week to take a call about what is happening in the market. You need to give your time freely and openly to the journalists to help them write their stories, not looking for personal quotations unless the journalist wants to handle the article in that way. If you can build up a relationship of trust and cooperation, then at least the journalist knows who you are when you call to try and place one of your own stories. This process can be very hard work given the fact that the people specialising in mortgages on the trade press publications tend to change round every few months. But I have always found that a fairly regular presence in the trade press builds a profile foundation from which advertising, direct mail and other marketing activities can benefit.

An important fact to bear in mind, however, is that journalists have a job to do. If a story comes up which might be critical of your company, an established relationship might guarantee an opportunity to discuss the matter whereas the publication might otherwise have just printed the story. But it does not guarantee good coverage! Journalists are there to report the good and bad news, and the good ones will always do so irrespective of personal relationships, as we found out when we had our little local difficulty in 1995 over the Preferred Introducer remuneration campaign. It is also the case that, however much you spend on advertising, the publications keep the journalists and the advertising sales staff well apart. So if the worst thing you can do is to assume that a good relationship with the journalists will insure you against bad coverage, the next worst thing you can do is to quote your advertising spend as a threat.

Over the ten years we have been in business, from that initially "leaked" launch through to the present time, we have enjoyed an outstanding profile in our target market, the trade press. The profile foundation this has given us has contributed enormously to our new business growth. But we do not take it for granted and we understand the rules. With those caveats I would recommend any company seeking to expand its business in the intermediary sector of the mortgage market to focus primarily on having an effective PR set-up (in-house or via a good agency) as a foundation on which advertising and direct mail can build.

DIRECT MAIL

As Lucian Camp says: "The difference between "junk mail" and "post" is targeting". Genuine post is, by definition, personal, because it is a written item from the sender addressed solely and specifically to the recipient. Direct mail, although it may be individually addressed, is a message intended to be seen by a large number of people. That's why, to be effective, it must be targeted. Luxury, expensive products mailed to low-income households is worse than useless: it is offensive.

Direct mail items must be personalised, credible and create a desire to read. You must achieve a quality feel. Your direct mail item will be amongst many that the recipient will have received that week and must therefore be as memorable as possible. This is the age of choice and, certainly in the case of mortgages, there's absolutely no reason why the recipient of a direct mail item needs to buy your product. As with an advertising campaign, realistic expectations must be applied to response levels. Typically, about 1–2 per cent of those mailed would respond, although I have known of better results in unusual circumstances.

CAMPAIGNS DIRECT TO THE CUSTOMER

We use direct mail in the context of marketing our mortgage products to intermediaries. But we have worked with many of our larger intermediary customers on campaigns that they have conducted direct to their client databases. We have found that the best results are achieved when the letters have been timely (e.g. promoting a fixed rate mortgage at a time when the press are discussing interest rate rises) and featuring one product only. There should be one, clear, simple message with an urgent call to action. Presenting individuals with a choice of mortgage products that they didn't ask for in the first place is not, in our experience, likely to get a good response.

Most direct mail campaigns to client databases with which we have been involved have promoted remortgages. Unless you are using a commercially purchased database of those who have recently registered with estate agents as being interested in buying, there is no way of knowing when people on your own client database are looking to move home. But so long as you know that the recipient does have a mortgage, there is always an opportunity to persuade that person that they might be better off switching to another lender.

There has to be immediate and obvious benefit to the clients to persuade them to act. It might be possible to get somebody to transfer from a variable rate loan to a fixed rate loan at the same rate, without any consequential saving in the monthly payment. But we have not experienced much success in this area. The most successful direct mail campaigns that we have been involved in alongside our customers have been where the product being recommended *has* permitted a substantial saving in the monthly payment for those paying at the full standard variable rate with their existing lender. The best results are achieved if the mailing also removes as far as possible one of the biggest barriers to making a change like this, namely costs. A fee-free switch from a variable rate to a fixed rate where the latter is less than the former, and in an environment where interest rates are rising, is the best combination we have found.

Our experience is that client databases up and down the country are in pretty bad shape. Commercially purchased databases can be better segmented. The better the targeting, the better the effectiveness of a direct mail campaign. We were involved with one intermediary customer, for example, that was able to deselect Halifax customers from a particular remortgage mailing at the time when the customers would have lost their entitlement to free shares in the run-up to the Halifax conversion if they had remortgaged. Acting responsibly, the intermediary concerned did not wish to encourage existing Halifax customers to make that switch, not least because it was not possible to determine whether, and to what extent, they would have been disadvantaged by making such a move (since nobody could at that time safely predict the ultimate share price).

It is important to ensure that nobody's time is wasted by large numbers of inappropriate enquiries being generated by a direct mail campaign. If the remortgage product is not available to those who have been in arrears, or with a low percentage of equity, a simple phrase within the body of the letter can act as a filter. For example: *"If your mortgage represents no more than 80 per cent of the estimated value of the property, and has been paid on time, then this new deal is just right for you!"*

The fact is that the vast majority of people mailed will not respond to the suggestion that they should change their existing mortgage arrangements. For the small percentage response rate you are seeking, you have to grab their attention. You are trying to keep your mailing letter as short as possible, whilst being chatty and direct. It is part of our service to intermediaries that we will always help them with advertising and direct mail campaigns, and we have a stock of standard letters which they might like to use (subject always to the intermediary concerned obtaining his own legal and regulatory advice). One such standard letter we use is featured on p. 234, and asks the recipient to consider why discounts and cashbacks are being offered to *new* customers when they, as an existing customer, are paying their mortgage on time and are just as deserving of these incentives. If you can create a reaction by this approach then you may have made a start on convincing the customer to take your direct mail item seriously.

> It is important to ensure that nobody's time is wasted by large numbers of inappropriate enquiries being generated by a direct mail campaign

Don't expect customers to fill out complicated forms. It is almost certainly best not to send an application form with the initial mailing letter. The idea is to whet the appetite and to prompt a telephone call which can then fill in some of the details. Hopefully, an interview will result at which the form can be completed with you (the intermediary or the lender's representative) in attendance. Better still, if the application form in question is already programmed into a computer system, the details can be keyed in as the customer gives them on the telephone, with the final form then only requiring a signature. Filling out forms is just as much a barrier to switching a loan as the payment of up-front fees.

The tone of the direct mail piece should be just right for the target market. Technical jargon should be avoided at all costs, but it is just as important not to get too colloquial. You never know who you might offend. Professional copywriters working freelance and within advertising agencies are widely available. The impact on the response rate will be significant if the wording of the direct mail item is clear, readable and urgent, and it is a mistake to cut back in this crucial area. Also, research has shown post scripts to be the most remembered part of a direct mail item: always reserve this to re-emphasise your most important sales message or call to action.

Database checking is a key element in this exercise. Getting someone's name and address spelt correctly is very important. A sloppy salutation will, in the minds of recipients, reflect a sloppy company, and there will not be much motivation to buy. I have always remembered an incident very early in my career where a customer of a building society I worked for had a title along the lines of Brigadier John Fotheringham-Chumbley, or something similar. Whatever the name actually was, it was too long to fit onto the first line of the

At last, we reveal the people behind five years of mortgage innovation.

After working behind the scenes of the mortgage industry for five years, it goes against the grain to shout.

But to the surprise of our advertising agency, we've grudgingly accepted that the milestone of our fifth anniversary (and, by chance, our first £1 billion of new business) is a good moment to summarise what we stand for.

Private Label is unique. What we're not is a centralised lender – or indeed a lender of any kind. What we are is a mortgage marketing and distribution company. Which means that our success depends upon our ability to develop mortgage ideas which are innovative, practical and relevant to your customers' needs.

And despite market conditions, that's exactly what we've done, time after time.

It would be bad manners to boast about the number of new products we've brought to the market. Suffice it to say that every time we do so, we provide a competitive edge for everyone who works with us.

That means our lenders (who, these days, are mostly big building societies).

It means the growing number of life offices which distribute our mortgages (today there are about twenty, including many of the country's biggest names)*.

And, perhaps above all, it means financial advisers.

Just think about it. Through up to 20 life companies, you can offer your clients products with unique benefits. Products which they can't find anywhere on the High Street and products which come with a guarantee from the lender never to cross-sell.

Five years and one billion pounds later, we think we can safely say that the concept works. And so, rather than linger in the spotlight, we intend to return to the shadows, and get on with developing the products that'll give you the edge during our second five years.

Which may be a disappointment for our advertising agency. But it's definitely good news for you.

PRIVATE LABEL MORTGAGE SERVICES LTD. BRETTENHAM HOUSE 14–15 LANCASTER PLACE LONDON WC2E 7EB TEL. 071–379 5232

*SOME OF THE TWENTY INSURANCE COMPANIES WHICH DISTRIBUTE OUR PRODUCTS ARE AS FOLLOWS. ACUMA LIMITED ALBANY LIFE ASSURANCE COMPANY LIMITED; AXA EQUITY & LAW LIFE ASSURANCE SOCIETY PLC; BRITANNIA LIFE LIMITED; LAURENTIAN FINANCIAL GROUP; LEGAL & GENERAL ASSURANCE SOCIETY LIMITED; LIFE ASSOCIATION OF SCOTLAND LIMITED; MGM ASSURANCE SOCIETY; PROLIFIC FINANCIAL MANAGEMENT PLC; SCOTTISH PROVIDENT INSTITUTION

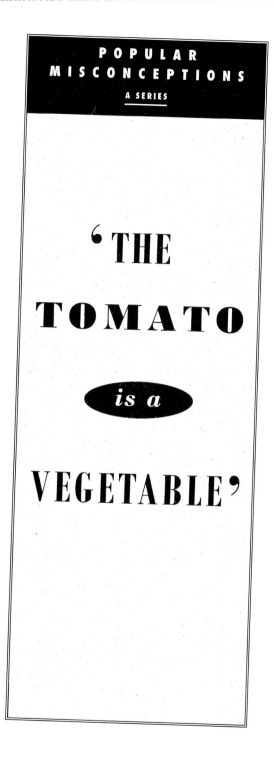

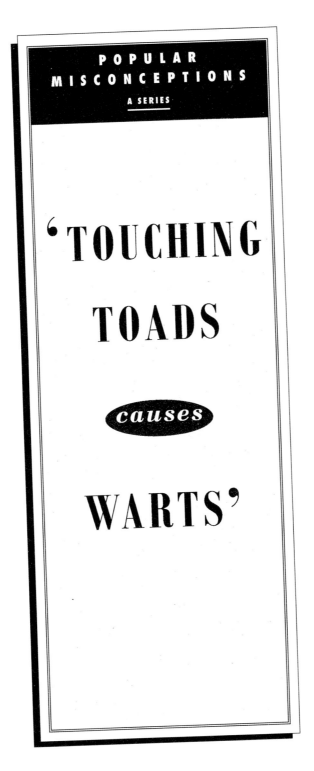

POPULAR MISCONCEPTIONS
A SERIES

'PRIVATE LABEL *is a* LENDER'

- Private Label is a specialist mortgage design and distribution company: no one else in the market does what we do.

- Private Label is not a lender of any description: our products are funded by banks and building societies, exclusively for the intermediary market.

- Our products are innovative yet practical and cannot be sourced by your clients directly in competition with you.

- All our products are backed by a "no cross-selling" guarantee.

- You can access our unique products via our distributors using one simple application form.

- We are paid by the lender on a success basis for our design and distribution activities.

- Private Label's products offer you the opportunity to access major lenders with exclusive, innovative yet different mortgages to offer your clients.

MORTGAGE DESIGN
AND DISTRIBUTION

POPULAR MISCONCEPTIONS

A SERIES

'HOUSEHOLD NAME LENDERS CAN ONLY BE ACCESSED *via* THE HIGH STREET'

Many clients today demand that you recommend only "household name" lenders. Understandably, therefore, this has led to a return to more business being done in the High Street. But, of course, this carries the attendant risks of customer security, and of the client, having learned about a particular product from an adviser, then going and purchasing it directly from the lender.

Private Label presents you with an alternative to that process. Our product designs are funded by the very "household name" lenders which your clients demand. But they are not available in the High Street. Indeed, they are available exclusively via mortgage advisers and come backed with a no cross-selling guarantee from the lenders.

Whether you're recommending short or long term fixed rates, a discounted variable or a 100% mortgage with no deductions, they're all there in our product range. So help us to help you in today's competitive environment - it's an opportunity you cannot ignore.

PRIVATE LABEL CHARTER

- We are a specialist mortgage design and distribution company
- We are not a lender of any description
- Our product designs are funded by banks and building societies
- Our products are designed exclusively for the intermediary market
- Our products cannot be directly sourced by your clients
- Our lenders guarantee no cross-selling
- We guarantee to regularly offer you exclusive mortgage products

MORTGAGE DESIGN AND DISTRIBUTION

Your home is at risk if you do not keep up repayments on a mortgage or other loan secured on it

Written quotations available on request. This advertisement is for use by authorised intermediaries only and must not be given or distributed to potential borrowers. Loans subject to age and status of applicants and to type and value of property. Security will be required. Limited funds available. All products other than "Variable" must be reserved, for which a non refundable £35.00 booking fee is payable. For loans in excess of 75% of purchase price or valuation, whichever is lower, a mortgage indemnity guarantee premium or higher percentage advance fee will be charged by the lender. The above APRs are variable. The fixed rate products are fixed to 1 January 1996 and 1 January 1998 respectively.

1 FIXED 1996
Top 20 Building Society — 6.99% (APR 8.4%) (rate dependent on LTV)

2 FIXED 1998
Top 10 Building Society — 7.99% (APR 8.4%) (rate dependent on LTV)

3 100%
Top 10 Building Society/Bank — 8.55% (APR 10.4%) (average illustrative rates)

4 VARIABLE
Top 10 Building Society — 6.34% (APR 8.3%) (rate dependent on LTV and loan size)

FOR FURTHER INFORMATION SIMPLY RETURN THE COUPON BELOW OR TELEPHONE:

TELEPHONE
071 404 6966

To: Private Label Mortgage Services Limited 14 Great Queen Street, London WC2B 5DW
I would like to know more about your exclusive mortgages. Please send me further information.

Name:

Company:

Address:

Postcode:

Tel No: Fax No:

POPULAR MISCONCEPTIONS
A SERIES

'ALL IFAs *are* RICH'

- IFAs face some significant challenges in the mortgage market.

- Clawback, endowment saturation, commissions disclosure and clients' reluctance to pay fees may persuade some IFAs to abandon the mortgage market altogether.

- This would be bad for the mortgage industry. It needs a thriving IFA sector. So, in a very modest way, we are trying to do something about this trend.

- With our new HEDGEMASTER mortgage we're paying IFAs a fee of 0.4% of the loan, up to a maximum of £1000 per completion.

- No clawback. Quick payment. Greater flexibility over what you sell or charge to your clients.

- Help us to help you by supporting HEDGEMASTER.

Private Label

MORTGAGE DESIGN AND DISTRIBUTION

Private Label Mortgage Services Limited
14 Great Queen Street
London WC2B 5DW
Tel: 071 404 6966

POPULAR MISCONCEPTIONS

A SERIES

'INTEREST RATES *are* PREDICTABLE'

HEDGEMASTER is a new mortgage alternative for your clients. Funded by a top 10 building society, it's a variable rate (currently 7.99%, <u>APR 8.6%</u> - but this will reduce if mortgage rates fall) captured within a 2% band until 1 January 1998. During that long period the rate cannot rise above 8.99%, but it can fall to 6.99%. In between, it's guaranteed to always be the lender's standard variable rate.

Thus, if interest rates continue to fall, your clients <u>win</u> because they'll be undercutting many of the long term fixed rates available today. But if interest rates rise, your clients also <u>win</u> because they'll have purchased long term rate protection very cheaply. And if they're fed up with <u>winning</u>, there's only one month's redemption interest payable (during the period to 1/1/98 only)!

What's more, if your clients select the lender's competitively priced payment protection or buildings and contents cover for the capped period, we'll pay you today's cash equivalent of the commission in the form of a fee of 0.4% of the loan, up to £1000 per completion.

PRIVATE LABEL CHARTER

- We are a specialist mortgage design and distribution company
- We are not a lender of any description
- Our product designs are funded by banks and building societies
- Our products are designed exclusively for the intermediary market
- Our products cannot be directly sourced by your clients
- Our lenders guarantee no cross-selling
- We guarantee to regularly offer you exclusive mortgage products

MORTGAGE DESIGN
AND DISTRIBUTION

0.4% of the loan to you, up to a maximum of £1000 per completion

If you would like to offer your clients a hedge against medium term interest rate movements, whilst having the opportunity not to charge a fee for the advice, then help us to help you by supporting HEDGEMASTER. Call us today or contact any branch of the following insurance companies: Scottish Life • Legal & General • General Accident • Axa Equity & Law • Britannia Life • Guardian Royal Exchange • or

Call Private Label direct on: 071 404-6966

FOR EXCLUSIVE
DESIGNS FROM
MAJOR LENDERS,
LOOK FOR THE
PRIVATE LABEL.

Each one of these market-leading mortgages is funded by a major building society.

But they're only available through us.

Why? Because we designed them. Since 1987, that's been our business: designing exclusive mortgages from major lenders. And since they're distributed only through intermediaries like you, your clients don't have the option of going directly to the lenders to buy them.

With over £2 billion of new business generated, twelve major lenders ready to fund our ideas, and three consecutive industry awards for Most Innovative Lending Organisation, there's no doubt that it's a winning formula.

For more information, call our Intermediary Helpline now on 01483 454460. We look forward to giving you our exclusive attention.

01483 454460

The intermediary's exclusive label

Mortgage of the week

£150 introducers' payment per completion

- GENERAL ELECTION CAP
- Initial rate 6.74% (APR 7.1%)
- Rate can't exceed 7.95% first 5 yrs
- Low redemption charge
- Ultimate "both way bet" for pre-election interest rate protection

FUNDED BY

BRADFORD & BINGLEY
BUILDING SOCIETY

Designed & Distributed Exclusively by

Private
Label

MORTGAGE DESIGN
AND DISTRIBUTION

Call now on 01483 454 460

Mortgage of the week

- Rate reductions *guaranteed* each year until 1999 – 6.99% / 5.99% / 4.99% Step-Down Fixed Rate

- The money markets are still predicting rate rises through 1999; this product sends rates in the opposite direction

- Lender's underwriter based at our Processing Centre for speedy case approval and offer issuance

(APR 7.1%)

FUNDED BY

BRISTOL & WEST BUILDING SOCIETY

Designed & Distributed Exclusively by

MORTGAGE DESIGN
AND DISTRIBUTION

Call now on 01483 454 460

Mortgage of the Century

An incredible 10% package of benefits into the next century for a typical £50,000 loan, comprising:

- 2% Discount for first 3½ years   (7%)

- Refunded valuation and reservation fee covered by initial £500 cashback   (1%)

- Second cashback of £1000, in December 1999, to celebrate the Millenium   (2%)

- To 95% LTV purchase and remortgage. (98% LTV with fees added)

- Lender's underwriter based at our Processing Centre for speedy case approval and offer issuance.

Exclusive corner.

Designed & Distributed Exclusively by

Private Label

MORTGAGE DESIGN AND DISTRIBUTION

Call now on 01483 454460

Funded by

HALIFAX

MORTGAGE
SERVICES
LIMITED

We put this offer on the back page to save the best till last.

£150 introducers' fee

- 5 year Fixed & Capped
- Fixed at 6.99% to April 1999; then
- Capped at 7.99% to April 2002
- Fixed rate certainty when needed most
- Capped rate flexibility next three years
(APR 7.3%)

Funded by BRADFORD & BINGLEY
BUILDING SOCIETY

Designed & Distributed Exclusively by

Private Label

MORTGAGE DESIGN
AND DISTRIBUTION

Call now on 01483 726161

Draft

THIS DRAFT LETTER IS PUT FORWARD AS A MARKETING IDEA, WITH NO RESPONSIBILITY ON OUR PART. ANY USER MUST TAKE ITS OWN LEGAL AND COMPLIANCE ADVICE BEFORE IMPLEMENTING. THE ATTACHED TYPICAL EXAMPLE SHOULD BE USED ON CONSUMER LETTERS.

Broker ⟶ Client

[date]

Dear

£1,800 cash and a 2% mortgage rate reduction could be yours!

Pick up the weekend papers and you'll read about discounts and cashbacks available to *new* mortgage borrowers. You've probably wondered who's subsidising such generous give-aways. Well, if you are an *existing* mortgage borrower paying your lender at the full variable rate, then I have to tell you that it's <u>you</u> providing the subsidy!

You may think that, as a long-suffering up to date mortgage payer, you are just as entitled to a generous discount off your mortgage rate, and/or a cashback. We agree! And if you transfer to our new mortgage funded by a "top ten" building society at no cost, we'll give you both.

This new mortgage has been negotiated providing a limited amount of funds at **5.25% (<u>APR 5.5%</u>)** representing a discount of 2% off the standard variable rate for the first year of the loan. That's a saving of £100 per month on a £60,000 mortgage. And to enable *existing* mortgage borrowers to take advantage of this offer, we have additionally negotiated a 3% cashback payment, representing **£1800** on a £60,000 loan.

The cashback will cover most borrower's costs in moving their mortgage across, with a useful lump sum left over, <u>plus</u> a valuable monthly saving in the form of the 2% discount.

We will do all the paperwork for you, and there is no fee for our services. So, for little effort, and no cost, you could improve your mortgage position in a matter of weeks. Please call us today so that we can confirm eligibility and set the wheels in motion.

Yours sincerely,

[A named person]

PS: Please act quickly, as we only have access to limited funds

Draft client database mailing letter.

PROCESSING
CENTRE

Mr A N Other
Any Company
Other Street
Any own
Other County
A12 B34

11 April 1997

Dear Mr Other

Mortgage of a Lifetime - New Product

Replacing Mortgage of the Century, which closes for new reservations after close of business Monday 14 April 1997, is the virtually identical Mortgage of a Lifetime - details enclosed.

We have retained the popular combination of long term discount plus two cashbacks, offering an incredible benefits package worth 12% at the minimum loan size.

The product is called Mortgage of a Lifetime because lender giveaways are currently much lower than they were when we launched Mortgage of the Century in June 1996.   Compared with today's benchmark, Mortgage of a Lifetime is therefore <u>even more competitive</u> than its predecessor.

So please keep those applications rolling in!

Yours sincerely

Tony Fisher

Tony Fisher
Marketing Manager

PRIVATE LABEL
PROCESSING CENTRE
Dukes Court, Duke Street, Woking, Surrey GU21 5XT.
Telephone: 01483 726161 Facsimile: 01483 726767 DX Number 2950 Woking 1.

The Private Label Processing Centre is a division of Private Label Mortgage Services Limited.
Registered in England No 2096862. Registered office 14 Great Queen Street, London WC2B 5DW.

Laser-signed letter, personalised to every introducer.

Page 1 of Product Portfolio Guide

BRITANNIA BUILDING SOCIETY
6.99% FIXED TO 1.1.2002

LTV:	Up to £200,000 = 95%, £200,001 - £450,000 = 85%, £450,001 - £1,000,000 = 75%, £1,000,000 + by arrangement.
MULTIPLES:	3 + 1 or 2.5 joint.
LOAN SIZE:	£15,500 - £3,000,000.
MIG (OR EQUIVALENT):	75.01 - 80% = 4.00%, 80.01 - 85% = 4.75%, 85.01 - 90% = 6.5%, 90.01 - 95% = 9.5%, 95% + = 10.15% (minimum £100). Rates shown are inclusive of Insurance Premium Tax. Fee can be added outside of income multiples. If added at 95% LTV this pushes loan into 95%+ band.
REPAYMENT METHOD:	Repayment <u>or</u> Interest Only (including Endowment and Pension) or combination.
ARRANGEMENT FEE:	£295. Can be added within LTV and income multiples.
GENERAL INSURANCES:	None compulsory.
TERM:	10 - 30 years. For interest only loans the maximum term may be extended to 40 years if a repayment vehicle is in place, linked to the maturity date of the loan.
DEFINITION OF INCOME:	100% of basic, 100% of guaranteed and 50% of regular additional income. 100% of secondary income if secondary employment is permanent and job held for at least one year. Secondary income may be added to primary income before applying multiples. No minimum period of employment. Applicant(s) must be in permanent employment with any gaps in employment satisfactorily explained. Contracted employees may be considered if the current contract is for a minimum of 1 year and there is 6 months left to run.
LOAN PURPOSE:	Purchase and Remortgage.
LOCATION:	England, Wales, Northern Ireland and mainland Scotland.
SOME UNACCEPTABLE PROPERTY TYPES:	100% timber construction or timber framed with no brick skin. BISF steel frames, pre-fabricated reinforced concrete, poured or shuttered concrete, system built, no-fine construction (except Wimpey), Easi-form construction (except Laing) and high alumina cement. Flats in blocks with more than 6 storeys. Properties with agricultural restrictions. Unexpired lease less than 25 years plus the term of the mortgage at application.
LOCAL AUTHORITY: (including Right to Buy)	Houses only not flats or maisonettes. A maximum advance of 100% of the DPP plus the costs of any anticipated home improvements, providing the total amount does not exceed 75% LTV. A retention will be made for the home improvements.
SELF EMPLOYED:	Those holding 25% or more of the issued share capital. 3 years certified accounts, accountant's certificate, or Inland Revenue approved accounts required.
AGE:	Minimum 18 years primary and secondary applicant. Maximum 75 years.
REFERENCES:	Credit Search. If not on the Voter's Roll, 3 months' original bank statements and an explanation will be required. Credit Score. Employer's reference. 3 years' audited accounts or accountant's certificate. Lender's reference or satisfactory statements in lieu, in the form of last annual statement <u>plus</u> last 3 months bank statements showing payments to lender. Bank reference (loans over £200,000). Valuation report (panel). Proof of residency and identity also required post offer.
REDEMPTION:	180 days' gross interest for full or partial redemptions prior to 1.1.2003. Normal terms thereafter. Portable.
SOLICITORS:	Applicant's if known to the Society.
APPLICATION FEE SCALE (INCLUDING VALUATION AND RESERVATION FEE):	Each application must be accompanied by a cheque for the correct application fee, as read from the scale reproduced below. Included within the fees shown are the costs of obtaining a valuers' report on the property being offered as security and a £45 reservation fee. The full fee must be submitted with each application. **Applications submitted without the correct fee, or with no fee at all, will not be looked at until the correct fee is submitted.** The fee is based on the purchase price, or valuation in the case of remortgages, as follows: up to £50,000 **£240**; up to £100,000 **£270**; up to £150,000 **£290**; up to £200,000 **£340**; up to £250,000 **£370**; above £250,000 by negotiation. If an application is rejected, cancelled or withdrawn, the following refunds will apply: • at initial assessment stage (which includes a basic credit search). Full refund. • after initial assessment and prior to valuer incurring costs. Full refund less £45 reservation fee and £50 administration charge. • after the valuer has incurred costs. Nil. **NB: The application fee can also be paid by Access, Visa or Mastercard. The applicant(s) must call the Mortgage Helpline number below to make use of this facility.**
WHAT TO SUBMIT WITH APPLICATION:	• Lender's last original annual statement plus 3 most recent original bank statements, or a cheque payable to existing lenders for provision of a reference (call the Helpline for appropriate figure). • If not on the Voter's Roll, 3 most recent original bank statements, plus an explanation. • A cheque for the correct application fee (see scale above), payable to the Private Label Processing Centre, unless the applicant has already called the Mortgage Helpline and paid the application fee by credit card.
INTRODUCER PAYMENT:	We will send a cheque to the Introducer **at the end of the month following the month in which completion takes place.**
CONTACT:	All enquiries and applications to the Private Label Processing Centre, Dukes Court, Duke Street, Woking, Surrey, GU21 5XT. Tel: **01483 726161**; Fax: **01483 726767**; DX No. 2950 Woking 1.

(1) This material is intended for use by authorised intermediaries and professional financial advisers only. It is not intended as an advertisement complying with the Consumer Credit Act and as such must not be given or distributed to potential borrowers or otherwise used to promote or advertise the products referred to; (2) Every effort has been made to ensure that the content of this publication is accurate and up-to-date at the time of going to press. However, the lender(s) referred to herein may alter the terms and conditions of their mortgages at any time and (3) The detail shown is only a summary of the full criteria. Reference should be made to the full lending criteria for a definitive description of the lending terms. If in doubt, applications should be discussed direct with the underwriters before an application fee is expended or other costs incurred.

Page 2 of Product Portfolio Guide

database, so somebody had the bright idea to shorten his title to "Brig". Unfortunately, the database input was not checked and the customer came into the branch absolutely fuming. A mailshot we had sent to him had been hand-delivered by the postman, who was laughing all the way up our customer's drive. The Brigadier, who was only five foot six inches tall, took possession of an envelope addressed to "Big John Fotheringham-Chumbley"!

Another important direct mail item for those looking to leverage their client databases is the company newsletter. Through this medium – perhaps mailed to clients quarterly – general topics can be discussed (e.g. the impact of self-assessment or what is happening to house prices), intermingled with product pitches. The customers feel valued by virtue of receiving the newsletter, and this is a good background against which to promote your sales message. We use this device ourselves with our intermediary database, via our quarterly *Newsline*.

More important to us than the occasional direct mail campaigns we help to arrange in partnership with our mortgage intermediary customers is our own direct mail campaign from us to the intermediaries themselves. As I explained in Chapter 5, we conduct our own campaigns centrally when launching mortgage products, plus members of our regional salesforce are encouraged to undertake a few mailings each per year to their own databases. The techniques and experiences I will be sharing in this area will hopefully be of interest to any organisation seeking to serve the mortgage intermediary market.

DATABASE MANAGEMENT

It was in 1993 that we started seriously to gather information about mortgage intermediaries for our database. Prior to that, the distribution of our product information had been a rather simple affair. We dealt with a panel of insurance companies and referred enquiring intermediaries back to one of those offices in order to find out about the products and to get the application forms. Insurance companies moving out of this role led to us undertaking the pre-offer processing ourselves which, in turn, led to us taking business from the intermediary market at large. We therefore had to introduce some kind of database management.

As an outsourcing company ourselves, our natural instinct is always to look down this route first. We therefore used a marketing agency to maintain our database and fulfil mailings, whilst maintaining a separate fax database via a specialist multi-fax issuance company. A third database was naturally being built up by virtue of the mortgage applications which were now coming to us from various points around the market. But the three different databases did not speak to each other, and it was a manual affair to update all of them. Rather like our experience in delegating the pre-offer processing of mortgage applications, there are some functions which can only effectively be undertaken in-house. With the help of Michael Kelly's software company, Dunstan Thomas, we developed our own database management system which integrated all three. But we left the fulfilment of mailings with the agency as this *is* an efficient and cost-effective outsourcing function for most small to medium-sized companies.

The constraints of our previous database management system amounted to more than the fact that we had not automatically captured for our database intermediaries who had undertaken business with us. We also had the problem of details that *were* being recorded coming onto the database on an ad hoc basis, without suitable cross-reference. We could not send an individually addressed letter to anyone on the database because we did not have all of the entries in a consistent form with the individuals' Christian names. We therefore had to send out our product portfolio guides without an accompanying letter, which just about doubles the likelihood of your communication being binned without being read. Moreover, our mailings in any event took a bit of a scattergun approach, since we were not at that time auditing the database on a daily basis and could therefore never be sure that individuals were still with the companies being mailed. All of these issues had to be taken on board as we wrote our new database management system.

> our mailings in any event took a bit of a scattergun approach

There was no choice but to start from scratch. We hired teams of people to telephone everybody that we had on the database at the time to see if they were still with that company, and still wished to be on the database. As we had not always recorded telephone numbers, we had to first contact Directory Enquiries. It was a long-winded affair, but, eventually, we arrived at a standing start position. From there we could build a database, by the automatic transfer of information from our Processing Centre in respect of new entries, plus referrals from our regional salesforce. We now have a person dealing with the database management full-time, and each and every entry/correction goes through several levels of checking so that we record consistent details including type of company, address, key contact name (including Christian name), telephone and fax numbers, unique identification number and numbers of items to be mailed or faxed. The latter is key because, in our experience, if you have 15 salesmen at one life company branch on the database, it is more cost-effective to send those contacts 15 individually addressed envelopes than it is to send 15 product guides to one person and hope that he or she will distribute them. Conversely, when it comes to sales faxes, there is nothing more annoying to a busy life company branch than to have its fax machine clogged up as 15 identical faxes come through. With the fax medium you therefore have little choice but to target one individual, asking them to distribute. An integrated database management system has to have the flexibility to pick up on these issues.

The new system meant that there was no question of the mailing database held by the marketing agency being up-to-date in circumstances where the fax database held by the multi-fax company had not yet been corrected. We were working off one, clean database, downloading the correct information to the mailing house or the fax company (as appropriate) every time we needed to send something out, using one system as the source. Not only did this make our commu-nications more targeted, direct and up-to-date, it also meant that our mailing items could be individually addressed.

> database management is a daily, full-time affair

Our experience endorses general research in this area in that it is several times more likely for a communication to be read if the letter is addressed to an individual, and looks like a normal business letter. If there is no signature at the foot, however, much of the impact can be lost. This problem was solved for us by our marketing agency, who can produce 12,000 individually addressed letters for each mailing including a laser-printed signature in script in the appropriate place. This is the best compromise to get as close to an ordinary business letter in the context of a bulk mailing, and an example of the sort of letter the agency produces for us is on p. 235.

The mistake that many companies make is to have a one-off clear up of their database, without acknowledging that database management is a daily, full-time affair. Every day – particularly if you are dealing with mortgage intermediaries – your database becomes out-of-date. People leave the industry, join the industry and change companies, and hardly any of them notify you of the fact. Every member of our regional salesforce and call centre has large supplies of our database update forms readily to hand. The simple and clear one-pagers can be completed in seconds by ticking/deleting the appropriate points, leaving only the new details needing to be written in. If you want your database to be as up-to-the-minute as possible, it is necessary to minimise the work involved for those who have to complete update forms. It is a straightforward business practice that we certainly didn't invent: the simpler the forms, the more likely they are to be used. We encourage all staff to be vigilant about updating the database following any information they receive. But this is, of course, absolutely vital for the regional salesforce who come across instances daily of individuals no longer being with companies and so on. We expect our salesforce to be sending through database correction forms most days.

At the end of each month, the marketing department sends each member of the salesforce his or her "new" database, reflecting the month's changes. Flagged on that printout will be any new entries captured by the Processing Centre. This would be a mortgage intermediary who had submitted a mortgage application to us, or applied for an information pack, where the computer could not match those details with an entry already recorded. This is a most important lead for the salesman. If a new entry arose due to the submission of a mortgage application then the salesman should already have picked this up via the daily applications sheets mentioned in Chapter 5. These represent a key sales tool. However, the salesman would not ordinarily know who had applied for information packs, and this database report therefore fulfils three purposes. First, it forces the individuals concerned to "audit" their databases and correct any situations where, for example, they remember that John Smith has now left XYZ company. Second, it provides an opportunity to go back to those who have applied for information packs recently, to ask if there is any further information they would like to receive. Third, it prompts a check just in case a new user *was* missed from the daily applications sheets.

In addition to staff vigilance and monthly audit, we also use the simple, additional device of having our return address on all envelopes in which mailings are enclosed. In a busy product launch month we may, for example, send out three mailings over a space of six weeks to our full database. Despite their close proximity, we will still receive anything up to 50 return envelopes *per mailing*, in respect of people who have "gone away" or "left the company". With no return address on the envelopes, recipients would tend to just bin items addressed to people who were no longer at that address, or at that company, the result being that we continued to meet the expense of wasted mailings. With a return address on the envelope, it is much easier for people to write "gone away" or similar and just put the sealed envelope back in the post. This process helps to keep our database as up to date as possible.

Having your own database management system also gives rise to a number of other statistical opportunities. To support our marketing efforts we are able to pull off database reports categorised by introducer group types, for example IFAs, tied agents, life company direct salesmen and so on. We can also produce data in postcode order, alphabetical order of individuals or by company name. Our mailings can therefore be more targeted and, very often, we will have a full database mailing go out where six different categories of company have each had a slightly different sales message, normally on the post script of the accompanying letter.

We do not input "cold" information to our database. Everybody on the database is either with a company that has signed up to do business with us, or has actually introduced business to us, or has applied for an introducer pack, or is an individual that one of our salesforce has met and who has agreed to have his name go on the database for future updates. I see no benefit in having people on the database who have not either asked or implied that they want to be there. We always mail by first-class post and the cost of downloading the appropriate disk, having the letters individually produced, alongside the cost of printing and fulfilling the printed product information going out, cannot be justified if it is sent to someone who is not interested in receiving it. The people who are recipients of your communications must have demonstrated some degree of predisposition towards your company and its products, otherwise you will simply annoy.

SALES FAXES

Sales faxes are a completely different communication medium from a mailing letter, but with just as important a role to play in the communication mix. Because each exclusive product we run is based on a pre-agreed tranche of funds controlled by our computerised reservation system, we are able to update our customers when a tranche is running out. We achieve this by use of the multi-fax facility at 75 per cent usage (first warning), and 90 per cent usage (final warning). Because application fees can be paid by credit card, this normally leads to a wave of credit card bookings, with the result that the final 25 per cent of any particular tranche will be used up in a fraction of the time that the first 75 per cent got allocated. We always therefore prepare ourselves for the onslaught when we issue a 75 per cent usage warning on a particular product.

The result is that, whilst we have to close out on popular products every month of the year, we do so in a way that positively assists our customers to plan their business lives which, in turn, is only possible through the multi-fax facility. There is nothing more frustrating for an intermediary than to have fixed up a customer interview for the weekend, only to be told on Friday morning that they have two hours in which to get the application forms into the local branch. If they had received a fax warning that the tranche was running out they could have done something about it.

Sales faxes are an important new part of the "direct mail" family. You are much more constrained for space, and an unsolicited fax can be just as irritating to the recipient as an unwanted direct mail item, if not more so. However, so long as you reserve this particular medium for urgent information that an intermediary wants to know (for example the close out of a successful product, or the launch of a new one) then the sales fax is normally well received. We also use the medium to give intermediaries an up-to-date sales angle. For example, if that day's headlines predict an immediate base rate rise, we use that to demonstrate why intermediaries should be calling their major clients and recommending one of our fixed rates.

> within the hour, some six thousand individuals will have received the desired communication

We sometimes follow up sales faxes to understand the reaction of the intermediaries who receive them, and have found that long-winded communications trying to put across complicated points are the ones that receive a negative reaction. A sales fax should therefore always involve lots of floating space and deal in headlines only. Of course, any communication medium should be self-contained, because the effects of summarising a particular product detail can subsequently be held against you. If you are summarising and paraphrasing important product points, a warning should be included that individual client recommendations should not be undertaken based on this fax and, instead, reference should be made to the full product portfolio guide. Sales faxes also have to contain the usual warnings regarding the Consumer Credit Act.

We will download to the multi-fax company the database entries we wish to receive a particular fax and, within the hour, some six thousand individuals will have received the desired communication. The agency provides a report of numbers and entries which were engaged at the first attempt, with the service standard being that three further attempts will be made in order to get the fax through to that particular number. We all know that technology is changing our personal and business lives in ways that cannot be predicted. We certainly cannot remember what business life was like before the facility to multi-fax our database, although it is by no means a certain mechanism for getting your message through.

I mentioned that sometimes we undertake some sample research in order to learn more about the effectiveness of our sales faxes. Through this process we have certainly surfaced the important information that the briefer the fax, the more likely it is to be remembered. An interesting additional point, however, is that faxes giving relevant information are more often remembered than those seeking to make sales points. To prove this we sent two faxes on subsequent days to exactly the same database, one giving a warning about a product that was selling out, the other recommending a different product where we had plenty of funds left. Research showed that significantly more people said that they had received the information fax, even though we knew that all of those researched received both faxes. We therefore decided to undertake a small research exercise in which we asked people whether they had received a fax that we had not actually sent. Well over one third of those researched said that they had received it, but had not had a chance to look at it! The net message is that any organisation plays a relatively small part in its customers' daily business lives, the customers being so busy that they will often tell you anything they think will help to end the telephone call. A healthy respect for not overstaying your welcome in the attention span of your customers, plus a healthy cynicism for some aspects of research, are the net messages we draw from these various exercises.

> technology is changing our personal and business lives in ways that cannot be predicted

SUMMER POSTCARD

Just as we have experimented with different forms of advertising, so we are also looking to push out the frontiers of direct mail. As we brainstormed our marketing activity one summer, we hit upon the idea that everybody – at one point during that summer – would receive a holiday postcard. We therefore decided to re-create the old "seaside postcard" approach and use it to promote a mortgage product we had available at the time. Of course, these days, it is not possible to be as "saucy" as one would like, for fear of giving offence. Some of the illustrations and copy put forward by the agency, and countered by our own sales team, were a source of much amusement. However, we decided on a relatively subtle approach, the first example of which is illustrated on p. 236 promoting our 4.99 per cent short-term Bradford & Bingley fixed rate product.

CHRISTMAS CARD

The postcard idea seemed to go down well, and was even mentioned as a diary piece in *Financial Adviser*. We therefore decided to give it another go in September of the same year, by adopting the same theme, but as a Christmas card. The idea of sending out a Christmas card in September caused a degree of amusement amongst our intermediaries, and we were able to put across a message relating to our then 4.75 per cent short-term fixed rate that, if intermediaries acted quickly, they could give their clients a happy Christmas by completing on the new mortgage by 25 December. The Christmas card can be seen on p. 237.

Although we felt this to be a helpful, humorous and different approach to communication, we knew that it could also become tiresome if "overcooked". The problem with humour in any communication medium is that once the joke has been used a few times, it then becomes irritating, even though you might have laughed in the first instance. We therefore decided to give the postcard idea a rest for a while, until resurrecting it in the summer of 1997 to advertise our "Mortgage of a Lifetime" product, an illustration of which appears in Chapter 5 (p. 191). The key message is "Don't be scared to be different". We are always prepared to try out new styles and concepts in communication if this will promote product usage and/or make us more memorable in the eyes of our customers.

PRESENTING PRODUCT INFORMATION

Sales faxes and accompanying letters can only paraphrase a mortgage product. At some point, you have to put in front of your customers a detailed product guide. We have spent, quite literally, millions of pounds developing and evolving a form of product presentation which maximises both sales and information, mainly for use as a direct mail item. Of course, our product guides are also a point-of-sale tool which could equally have been discussed in detail in Chapter 5. However, as the main bulk of any given print run is mailed to our database, I will discuss the issues, and share the relevant information, in this chapter.

The Legal & General Mortgage Club is one of the most successful insurance company mortgage programmes ever, arranging £3 billion of mortgages each year. In fact, research undertaken by Paragon Mortgages, and released in June 1997, showed that the Mortgage Club was the most regularly used multi-lender programme amongst mortgage advisers, pushing Private Label into second place. As we are part of the Mortgage Club I am not sure of the extent to which there is a double count in these research statistics. But I can certainly endorse the notion that the Mortgage Club is well organised, well run and a major success.

What has this to do with the presentation of product material? Well, each year Legal & General carries out a detailed survey amongst Mortgage Club members who, in our experience, do not pull any punches when criticising things they don't think are right. In the most recent Mortgage Club survey, undertaken in January 1997, we were in first place amongst all the mortgage providers on the Mortgage Club scheme (which includes most of the major lenders) in the area of product presentation. So this is a fairly long-winded way of saying that the position to which we have evolved is worthwhile, although it has taken us some pain and expense to get there.

Our first attempt at summarising a product appears as case study no. 19 in Chapter 4. In fact, throughout the various case studies illustrated in that chapter, you will find different examples of the way in which we have presented products, with the date against each case study indicating the evolutionary stage we had by then reached. Our current product portfolios are comprehensive two-sided documents where each word, space and comma is designed to achieve a particular purpose. I have therefore included on pp. 238 and 239 both sides of an up-to-date, July 1997 product guide, to which the reader may find it helpful to refer as the various comments below unfold. I have chosen this product because it has not previously been mentioned in this book, and also because the Britannia 6.99 per cent Fixed 2002 product featured created a new record for the company in July 1997 when it sold £70m in just 14 working days.

The concept of having one stand-alone document per product is something that has been developed to suit our sales strategy. I know that many lenders adopt a booklet or leaflet approach, where all of their products are included within one display. Many insurance companies produce ream after ream of product listings on behalf of all of their panel lenders. We produce the latter for information and administration reference only. But we find that one guide per product, although the most expensive route, is the way to maximise focused selling.

I have already covered in Chapter 5 how we pre-qualify our sales calls with regard to the sort of products an intermediary is currently selling. We use the age-old listening techniques at point of sale to narrow down still further the products we intend to promote. This should eventually lead to one, or a maximum of two, product portfolio guides being produced in the sales situation, i.e. less paper for greater clarity. Just as important, it enables each product to be covered in some detail so that an intermediary knows exactly where he stands. Most of the summary information I have seen from lenders does not provide the intermediary with the sort of criteria that he needs in order to ensure that a client does qualify for the product recommended. This, in turn, leads to poorly presented applications and disappointment. Moreover, it can lead companies like ours – in the middle between lender and intermediary – exposed to all kinds of complaints and requests for compensation if the product guide is not comprehensive. But it is only possible to make a product guide comprehensive if you have one guide for each product.

In conjunction with our marketing agency, we have developed eight principles to which our product information has to adhere:

1 Product guides must have a quality feel, be visually attractive and clear. You have a one-second chance with busy mortgage intermediaries in order to gain their attention. The document you give them must not look daunting, and must encourage them to read on. So long as you adhere to the eight principles, don't hesitate to give the guides a "lick of paint" from time to time, and the reader will see from our Britannia Fixed 2002 product guide that our latest "lick of paint" includes the "zoom" effect by which the product title comes out of the page towards the reader. Your product guide will be given the importance that you attach to it: if it is a scruffy, photocopied piece of information it will not receive the same attention as a glossy, high-quality document. We always produce quality glossies on artwork paper using a large variety of bold colours, the effect of which cannot, unfortunately, be fully captured in a black and white book.

2 Summarise the key facts. It should be possible to mention the key facts relating to a product in no more than half a dozen bullet points. These should be so summarised, on the front page. Having attracted your reader to the document in the first place, you should try and establish within the first 30 seconds or so of their reading what the product actually delivers. If there is an intermediary payment then this is a particularly key fact, which we separate from the main list and show prominently on the front page.

3 **Summarise the key selling points alongside the key facts.** To be accurate, and strictly factual, often means to be boring. How to sell a fact is not the same as restating the fact itself. Alongside each key fact on the front page, normally in a different typestyle for contrast, we give intermediaries an indication of why and how we think that particular fact can be used as a selling point. This always represents our first attempt at the sales script for a new product being launched, and will often reflect our research leading up to why we developed that product in the first place.

4 **There must be a call to action.** There must be no doubt in the intermediaries' minds as to where they can call in order to get further information, to obtain an application form, or discuss a specific case. Our Mortgage Helpline number appears prominently on the front page of each product portfolio guide as a large "call to action".

5 **Ensure that, visually, your product portfolio guide is instantly associated with your company.** There is no point in product information adopting an approach which is inconsistent with the advertising campaign which might, for example, have prompted the enquiry for the product information in the first place. If an intermediary is predisposed to your company and its products then you want to build on that by ensuring that your distinctive style can immediately be recognised in new product information. On our current product portfolio guides we therefore include the logo of the lender, alongside our own, reinforcing the "AMG" badging effect that I discussed earlier. An interesting by-product of this is that, following the Legal & General Mortgage Club survey mentioned above, one of the other Mortgage Club lenders decided to copy our style of product presentation because we had won first place in the survey. The result was that we received quite a few calls from Club members asking about our "new product", and commenting that they did not know that we had added that lender to our panel. This was not, of course, our product, and we politely asked the lender concerned to use a different style. We also used that incident as the catalyst to change our own presentation, now incorporating the current "zoom" effect.

6 **Present comprehensive, relevant criteria detail in a consistent format.** On the reverse of the product portfolio guide, we list the product criteria information which research has shown to be the most relevant to a mortgage intermediary when deciding whether a client qualifies for the product being recommended. We produce this information on behalf of each lender using the same headings in the same order every time. An intermediary used to dealing with us therefore knows exactly where to look in order to test whether he is wasting his or his client's time.

7 Repeat in the product guide all information regarding customer fees payable. We publish our application fee scale in a comprehensive format separate from our product portfolio guides. For a long time, we worked on the assumption that this should be sufficient, and an intermediary should be able to read the two alongside each other. The fact is, however, that mortgage intermediaries are bombarded with information. If they kept efficient filing systems on behalf of all of the products they were told about then they would need to operate out of a warehouse. In addition to all of the product criteria, therefore, you have to make it as easy as possible for mortgage intermediaries to access your products. For this, they want only one document in their possession when interviewing customers. We therefore reproduce our application fee scale, and the circumstances in which refunds are allowed, on each product portfolio guide.

8 You must specify what to send with an application and where to send it. This is an extension of point 7 above. It was only about a year ago that we started to include a checklist of what to send with each application, again assuming this to have been known or understood by our customers. As the market gets ever busier, however, it is not realistic to expect mortgage intermediaries to interpret a lender's criteria as to what paperwork they will require with each application. We therefore now spell this out on each product portfolio guide as well.

These days, our product presentation is often praised. We are rarely criticised by an introducer on the basis that he did not know about a certain key fact relating to a client's suitability for the product he was advising on. But it has taken many years of experience to arrive at this point. Using one guide per product is more expensive, but it avoids the problem of rendering an entire document out of date by the withdrawal of one particular product on a multi-product guide.

Of course, criteria can change after a product has been launched, but before it has been fully utilised. We have experimented with stickers covering this point, but have found that the only realistic way to deal with this is to "bite the bullet", scrap the existing versions and print afresh. As we are regularly mailing our full database, it is often possible to have such reprinted product guides included as a "free ride" on a mailing that was going out in any event.

USE OF PRODUCT PORTFOLIO GUIDES AS KEY FEATURES DOCUMENTS

The current product portfolio guides are prepared for intermediaries' use only and are not to be shown to customers, as they are not intended to be compliant with the Advertising Regulations of the Consumer Credit Act. But with mortgage regulation being extended to cover the work of intermediaries, hopefully via the CML's new Mortgage Code, our mind has been turning on the production of a key features document which would be of use to mortgage customers. Such problems as have occurred in relation to the promotion of mortgage products by intermediaries have often been the result of a misunderstanding at point of sale. It would be a relatively simple matter of ensuring that our product portfolio guides complied with the Consumer Credit Act by printing the Annual Percentage Rates in a more prominent fashion than the nominal rates, and adding a fully worked example in the box on the second page substituting for the normal disclaimers. With procuration fee disclosure inevitable as part of the new Mortgage Code (a concept which we support), there would be no need for many more significant changes to our existing guide. The tricky point is how to get these guides into the hands of customers in a cost-effective way.

> The tricky point is how to get these guides into the hands of customers in a cost-effective way

Virtually all printing these days is done from a computer screen. It would therefore be relatively easy to give insurance companies, and intermediaries who understand technology, a disk relating to each product. Guides for use by customers could then be run off in as many quantities as the recipient required. Whereas a mortgage intermediary needs one glossy from us in order to sell the product to 20 customers, he would need 20 guides if they were to be used as quasi-key features documents. These could be cost-effectively printed off a disk by an intermediary, but would be prohibitively expensive for us to print and send out. We are currently wrestling with this problem and have no solutions to offer at the time of going to press. But our starting point is a little more advanced than most because we have evolved the concept of one guide per product, and have embraced the eight principles noted above.

WRAP-UP

Advertising, public relations and direct mail have key roles to play in the marketing of mortgages. Under the "direct mail" heading lie a multitude of different communication media, helped by technology and your own creativity. Private Label has developed a whole set of guidelines and experiences relating to sales faxes, and has never been afraid to try different types of communication media such as the humorous "summer postcard" idea. The way in which products are presented also needs far more thought than has typically been allocated to it by many lenders and lending organisations. Mortgage products very often receive attention and usage in direct proportion to the thought and expenditure invested in their presentation. The successful mortgage intermediaries are very busy and over-supplied with information: this presents clear challenges of relevance, targeting, clarity and visual attractiveness in whichever communication medium you are contemplating.

Ultimately, however you are putting your product across to your chosen customer, the overriding rule is that its relevance to the recipient must be more important than its relevance to you. As Ben Thompson of DMB&B Financial concludes: "Bad marketing tends to come in circumstances where the recipient's point of view is *not* to the fore".

7

PRE-OFFER PROCESSING FOR GREATER SALES

T he best definition of marketing that I know is, "Getting the goods in the right place at the right time and making a profit". This simple phrase demonstrates that the marketing discipline covers pricing, positioning, profitability and delivery. In the preceding three chapters I have taken the cycle through from initial research to the point at which the product is presented to the end buyer – typically a mortgage intermediary in our case – for consideration. This chapter assumes that the product has been selected, and deals with the delivery of the final link in the chain, namely the mortgage offer.

A Mars bar is an example of a product which is all "instant satisfaction". A few bites and it's gone. There are no ongoing benefits. By way of contrast, a motor car is an example of a product that embraces both instant satisfaction and anticipated long-term benefits. Consumers gain pleasure both from the immediate delivery of the car, plus the benefits they expect to accrue over time. It is often felt that a mortgage belongs in a third category, namely a product which delivers only long-term benefit with no immediate satisfaction. I have never subscribed to this theory. I believe that a mortgage fits into the second category, with the offer of advance being the item that creates the immediate satisfaction. The rest of this chapter deals with getting that offer of advance into the hands of customers as quickly and efficiently as possible.

As in previous chapters, I will be drawing mainly on Private Label's experience, although the research net has been cast wider in order to secure a diversity of opinions around the industry. The techniques employed, and the lessons learned, will hopefully be of interest to any company using or providing a pre-offer service, or perhaps contemplating doing so.

Our experience is in serving the intermediary market, and it would be wrong to assume that all of the points made in this chapter were relevant to operations dealing directly with the consumer. It is my experience that mortgage intermediaries are not only more demanding on behalf of the consumers they represent, but also that they are more demanding of companies like us than they would be in the more traditional setting of dealing with the lender direct. These are caveats which must be embraced by the reader in order to get full value from this chapter.

SOME GENERAL POINTS ABOUT SERVICE

Research commissioned by a leading customer service management group shows quite clearly that price alone no longer attracts customers. All evidence points to the emergence in this country of a generation of consumers who are no longer willing to turn the other cheek and put up with poor service. Even more importantly, there is an increasing culture of telling others if service has been poor. It is estimated that unhappy customers tell up to nine other potential customers about their bad experience yet, in many industries, management has not embraced this change in consumer attitudes. In the research mentioned above, for example, approximately one third of consumers placed efficiency at the top of their list of requirements in the service arena, with friendliness and politeness well down the list. When managers and customer-facing staff were asked the same question, the former put friendliness first and the latter put politeness first. It is no wonder that the British do not enjoy the worldwide reputation of the Germans or the Japanese for business efficiency.

The consumer accepts politeness and friendliness as the absolute norm. There are no prizes for being polite and friendly, because that is the benchmark. There are severe brickbats, however, for *not* being polite and friendly. Having established the minimum attitude required, all focus should then be on efficiency. In the same research, just over half of consumers felt that service was more important than price, and as many as two thirds said that they would take their custom away if they did not feel they were getting the right service. There is no doubt in my mind that – assuming "leading edge" commodity pricing to be an ever-present factor in the market – service will be the next frontier on which the battle for competitive advantage will be fought. The winners will be those companies that understand the importance of listening and responding quickly to their customers' demands in this area.

> even in this fiercely competitive and over-supplied mortgage market of ours, a lender with an outstanding product rarely achieves a quick take-up if it has a reputation for poor service

Whilst a good feeling about service is not easy to define, customers are nevertheless pretty good at recognising it when they get it, and when they don't. These various factors are well illustrated by the fact that, even in this fiercely competitive and over-supplied mortgage market of ours, a lender with an outstanding product rarely achieves a quick take-up if it has a reputation for poor service, with intermediaries never able to get through on the telephone and with offers of advance taking an age to be issued.

Good service has both "hard" and "soft" elements, the hard being the quantitative and the soft being the qualitative. Good service might be answering the telephone within the first three rings (the "hard" element). But this will be of little use if callers are then frequently referred to the wrong extension, or the response is curt or abrupt (the "soft" element). Taking another example, it might appear to be good service to answer all letters within two days, but this is of little use if the responses are unintelligible, or do not deal directly with the points raised. To stand any chance of meeting customers' increasing demands in the area of service, it is important for any business to have clearly defined service standards transparent to staff and customers.

SERVICE STANDARDS

It is only by defining standards that we can measure how well, or badly, we have done. This is important from the perspective of internal monitoring and control, and also when dealing with external queries. The service standards should be published to customers in simple, summary form. But they must also be realistic.

There is no benefit in setting out the service standard of assessing every mortgage application within three hours of receipt, when a company offering a central processing service has no control over whether it receives 10 or 100 applications that day. Published service standards should therefore be competitive and acceptable, but nevertheless cut the business some slack to deal with peaks and troughs.

I have known some companies to feel that the publication of service standards is all that is necessary to make staff work to them, and make customers believe in them. But there is no point in publishing service standards without introducing the infrastructure behind them that will: monitor control and correct; identify and deal with training needs; and provide the forum for feedback and discussion. These are all hard lessons we have learned over the years and later in this chapter I cover the various techniques we use to maintain our service standards. But it is first necessary to look at the structure of a modern, centralised pre-offer mortgage processing operation before moving on to how those various functions are knitted together and made to work as a whole, delivering that all-important immediate satisfaction measure, the mortgage offer.

WHY UNDERTAKE PRE-OFFER PROCESSING AT ALL?

In our particular case, we had no choice. I have already covered in Chapters 2 and 3 the fact that, when our business was first launched, the insurance companies through whom we distributed our product designs carried out the pre-offer processing, dealing directly with the lenders. But the recession put paid to that, and the only practical way we could keep the show on the road at that time was to perform the pre-offer processing function ourselves.

From that decision flowed a number of benefits including, but not limited to, improved service, switching, on-site underwriters, technology links with lenders, and so on. Providing an efficient pre-offer service to both lenders and distributors is now as fundamental a part of our business as product design. It also means that we control every aspect leading up to the delivery of the mortgage offer, including the provision of draft offer checking facilities for a number of our lenders. At present, the offer of advance is not issued from our office, but that will come.

Over the years, a number of companies – variously described as "Design", "Distribution", "Wholesaler" and "Packaging" companies – have tried to combine all or some of these various techniques in competition with us. But I have not come across any organisation that provides the sort of comprehensive service that we offer to a standard of a 98 per cent offer strike rate, which is the average we achieve with most of our lenders. Some have decided to opt out of the pre-offer process altogether, selling it as a merit that intermediaries deal directly with the various lenders. But this is not for us. I cannot give up control of the crucial pre-offer process and maintain the sort of volumes we seek. There is too much potential for dissatisfaction arising from matters outside our control, but for which we would be punished, for us to consider that route. The more we study the techniques of pre-offer processing, the better we get at it. But we are acutely aware that we can get a good deal better still.

The most fundamental lesson that we have learned is that you can only handle 1500 telephone calls a day, 5000 items of post a week and £100m of mortgage applications a month (our typical 1997 volumes) through specialisation of the key tasks involved in achieving that all-important mortgage offer.

SPECIALISATION AS A GENERAL CONCEPT

When we launched our Processing Centre in 1994 we had a flat structure. Reporting in to one manager was a team of people, all of whom were required to undertake the same tasks. At the first sign of volume, this system blew up. We therefore revisited this structure, and called in consultants to advise us on the specific issue of telephone calls. The result was a specialisation not just of each function, but also of the type of work that an individual handles within that function, so as to align growing experience with growing complexity of work. Knitting this structure together in our organisation is now a career path and communication forum which allows staff to understand each other's work and to progress to other functions, whilst overlaid on top is a system of quality control, audit and supervision. It is this structure that I will now explain in greater depth. For convenience, I will use the job titles that we employ. However, it is the specialist function that the person carries out, rather than the job title, which is of the main importance.

> The result was a specialisation not just of each function, but also of the type of work that each individual handles...so as to align growing experience with growing complexity of work

Although I support the specialisation of functions, I prefer to keep structures as flat as possible, because this promotes ownership and communication. A simplified version of our pre-offer processing organisation structure therefore appears below:

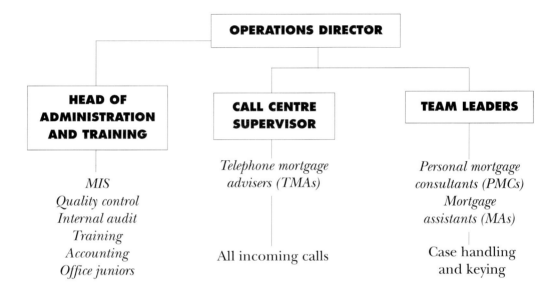

Under the overall control of our Operations Director, the three groupings deal with case handling, call handling and back-up functions, keeping the latter away from interrupting the focus of the people who deal with our customers. The key link is at the control, audit and training level where the Head of Administration provides the structure for the team leaders to audit and control, and then "checks the checkers", whilst maintaining the necessary feedback mechanisms to target training at individual areas of need.

The danger in separating out the functions in this way is the lack of communication, and perhaps even rivalry, between the specialist functions. We counter that by having a common grading structure, different types of meeting involving all staff, and a constant flow of movement between the functions. For example, one of our PMCs has progressed from office junior through MA to her current position underwriting mortgage applications. We have TMAs who are now PMCs, and MAs and PMCs who are now TMAs. At first glance, this may seem a small domestic matter out of context in this sort of study. But, in fact, it is a crucial element to achieving success through specialisation, the latter being vital to achieving an efficient pre-offer processing service which will, in turn, generate greater sales.

TEAM LEADERS

It is a Japanese principle to break down large operations into small, easily manageable component parts, and it is one that works. We have different teams aligned with our sales regions, each headed by an experienced person whose sole responsibility is to allocate the day's applications amongst their team and subsequently to monitor, control, check and support the work on those applications. Ad hoc cases are pulled from the system by the Team Leaders and assessed as to quality of work, training needs and so on. On-the-job training support is given within their teams, and the Team Leaders liaise with customers and our regional salesforce on difficult

> any operation seeking maximum efficiency must be a meritocracy

cases. As a matter of course, MAs telephone intermediaries every five working days to update them on the progress of the applications they have in with us. But the Team Leaders themselves call if the case reaches 20 working days, so that a full assessment of why it has taken so long can be undertaken. That particular level of review is then confirmed in writing to our customer, the mortgage intermediary.

The Team Leaders are the first rung of the management ladder within our Processing Centre staff, with these positions normally filled by internal promotion. However, there is a degree of outside recruitment to underline the fact that any operation seeking maximum efficiency must be a meritocracy. Only the best people are able to secure the important jobs irrespective of whether they are internal or external candidates. If capacity is the same in each team then it is easy to compare each Team Leader's results with another, and a high-volume operation is thereby broken down into bite-size chunks.

One mistake that we made early on was to assume that one lender was as easy to deal with as another. In fact, there is still diversity between lenders in terms of the complexity of their lending criteria and their approach to different lending situations. Moreover, we act for some lenders who want to fund a product in a quick burst over a short space of time and then take a rest. We therefore decided to take all of the more difficult and occasional lenders out of the mainstream and dedicate a team of our most experienced people to deal with applications for those particular lenders. We also added all self-employed applications to this "attack team" so that, in the core of our business, there would be every opportunity for applications to proceed smoothly. If a case fell within the responsibility of the "attack team" then, by definition, it had the potential to cause difficulty and/or delay, and we over-communicate on those cases. In a sense, we are creating two production lines rather than slowing down the majority as a result of the awkward shape of the few.

PERSONAL MORTGAGE CONSULTANTS (PMCs)

PMCs are the individuals who look after a set number of applications from receipt to lender hand-off. The individual PMC's personal number forms part of the application number allocated to that case, and the PMC then "owns" that particular application throughout its time with us. PMCs are underwriter level and experienced in the criteria of the lenders on whose behalf they act. The service standard is for an assessment to be made of the application within 48 hours of receipt, but this is normally achieved on the first day, with every item of post, and every development on the case, coming under the individual scrutiny of the PMC. This is one structure that we introduced when we launched our Processing Centre in 1994 and which we have never changed. There is nothing more likely to cause inefficiency and error than to have several people trying to deal with the same application. Ownership and consistency are essential and introducers really value this approach.

It is important to align the experience of the PMCs both with the quality of application being received, and the number of cases allocated to that individual each day. This was a mistake that we made originally, in assuming that all PMCs could cope with the same capacity and that all applications were the same. This resulted in a disparity of performance which threw out our capacity model. We therefore had to sit down with a blank piece of paper and start again. The result was three grades of PMC. Grade three PMCs are typically newly-promoted MAs or new recruits, and are given just three new cases a day, for below 75 per cent loan-to-value business (sub-MIG) only. On a typical 16 working day cycle to lender hand-off, this creates a pipeline of about 50 applications per PMC. Grade three PMCs do not have MAs and ease themselves into the job by personally handling all follow-up communication calls to the introducers. After a period of time and monitoring, a grade three PMC will be expected to be promoted to grade two.

A grade two PMC handles six new cases a day up to the maximum loan-to-value of the lender served by that particular team. Although this doubles the pipeline, grade two PMCs have an MA to key the cases initially and deal with all of the intermediary communication call-outs. In due course, grade two PMCs are expected to acquire sufficient experience for promotion to grade one.

Grade one PMCs are our most experienced group. Although their capacity remains at six cases per day, grade one PMCs will be expected to handle more complex business. Only grade one PMCs can work with cases where the applicant is self-employed or in the "attack team" dealing with the more complex, difficult or occasional lenders. We would expect our grade one PMCs to be the main pool from which we recruit Team Leaders.

PMCs assess and become familiar with each application from day one, and then work with their MAs to get the application to offer stage as quickly as possible, including maximum communication with the introducer. It would not be possible for PMCs to undertake this specialist function if they were constantly interrupted by chase-up telephone calls, which is why a completely different department deals with that aspect of our business. Although PMCs can only make themselves available on the telephone to deal with the most urgent or detailed of individual queries, it is nevertheless of comfort to introducers to know that one person is focusing on the same application from start to finish and owning the turnaround time between receipt of application and its hand-off to the lender. Although we do not underwrite on behalf of lenders, the quality of our decision-making has to match that of the lenders for whom we act, so only experienced people can be recruited to the PMC position.

> it is nevertheless of comfort to introducers to know that one person is focusing on the same application from start to finish

A vital part of the decision-making process is the initial assessment of a case by a PMC as to what is required to make it acceptable to the lender. There will inevitably be some points of clarification and additional paperwork necessary to satisfy the lender's criteria. But the PMC must get this "shopping list" right first time. Nothing is more likely to produce a complaint from a mortgage intermediary than two "shopping lists", the second one appearing when the first one has been satisfied. We have to ask our lenders to back us on this, so that they don't come up with their own list. In this sense the PMCs undertake a highly pressurised job, which is one of the reasons that they could not perform this function if they were interrupted by incoming telephone calls.

MORTGAGE ASSISTANTS (MAS)

The MA position was born when we realised that we could not maximise capacity through the PMCs if the latter were also chasing references and calling out to introducers. We therefore decided to recruit a team of more junior level people who would work alongside the PMCs and key the applications in the first instance, then communicate to introducers that the application had been received, noting in that call any outstanding information required as soon as their PMC had carried out the initial assessment. After this task is completed the remainder of the day is split between chasing outstanding references and calling introducers with their five-day updates. A computer-generated report each day shows the applications by case manager due for a five-day telephone review. The MAs call the introducers and remind them that we are pressing on with the application, whilst noting the outstanding information still awaited. We have found this approach to be the most popular way of communicating progress to intermediaries, and it heads off quite a few incoming telephone calls and potential complaints whilst also building interpersonal relationships.

We have tried various methods of communicating progress to intermediaries. At one point we faxed overnight a weekly update of all applications in the course of process by way of a computer screen dump. But follow-up research showed this to be an unpopular method of communication: moreover, it actually increased the telephone calls we received the following day. In our experience, introducers like telephone contact and plenty of it when they are dealing with a company like ours rather than directly with the lender. When introducers get used to the fact that they will be called once an application has been received, and then thereafter with a progress report every five working days, they will be more inclined to use a service like ours. Such a system also ensures that no application gets misfiled or not looked at because of the five-day computer-generated update report, which is actioned as a priority under the supervision of the Team Leaders.

Paper references are a throwback to the past, and an area in which the processing of mortgage applications has hardly progressed over the last ten years. It is about time that paper references were dispensed with now that higher level credit searching, and mature credit scoring systems, are in place. We believe that this will happen in the near future. Meanwhile, most lenders insist on paper references and in only a very few number of cases do these come back quickly from employers, landlords or lenders. It is therefore a key part of the MA's job each day to chase such references in respect of cases handled by their particular PMC, and this chase-up is under-taken every two days. We warn those we are calling that we will be chasing again in two days and there is some evidence that this proactive, almost nagging, approach does speed up response times. But the key message here is that any company engaged in pre-offer processing will be judged by the speed with which offers of advance come out, whereas it lies in the hands of others as to how quickly references are responded to. There is therefore no choice but to follow up the initial reference request and chase it every two days, producing a high burden of extra cost which we absorb in the MA function.

The other major advantage of splitting the functions between PMCs and MAs is that, in unexpected surges, it is possible to recruit temporary staff to the MA role. This can be done fairly quickly and will ensure that we maintain maximum pro-active communication with our customers, including the important reference-chasing function. We could bring in, say, 20 temporary MAs at fairly short notice and train them in a morning, leaving the PMCs to underwrite. Any centralised pre-offer processing service must plan for unexpected surges, and our structure always has one eye on that possibility. When it happens, there is only a major problem if your customers aren't being communicated with. It takes no technical training to chase up references and to read out update messages to introducers, which experienced MAs can source in a "surge" situation and pass to the temporary MAs for action.

CALL CENTRE SUPERVISOR
I touched on the issue of incoming telephone calls above and in Chapter 3. This is the main problem with pre-offer processing. Introducers are not interested, nor should they be, in a service provider's peaks or troughs. It is tough that 200 applications arrive one day, and 50 the next, and even tougher that you get over 50 per cent of your daily telephone calls between 10am and midday and between 3pm and 4pm. Our mortgage intermediary customers want their particular query answered when they call and it is up to service providers to meet that level of demand or fail in this market.

The technology, training and specialism now available in telephone work are an industry in themselves. As already described, we soon realised that the PMCs looking after the applications, and the MAs making outgoing calls of various descriptions, were not in a position to take the incoming calls as well. A call that interrupts somebody undertaking a clerical function can double its disruptive effect when the recovery time is taken into account, representing the lag between the end of the call and the recipient's ability to recover sufficient concentration to return to the task in hand. The sophisticated techniques now required to deal with the technology, and the high volume of calls, meant that specialists were required, the most important of whom is the Call Centre Supervisor.

The first thing that the specialist external consultants advised us to do was to have a separate department linked by a glass wall to the main office, but enclosed to assist the management of noise volume. The desks should be carefully configured with maximum light and so that no one was facing the wall. In the centre, fully visible to and from the various telephone advisers, should be the Call Centre Supervisor armed with an Automated Call Distributor (ACD). Not only does this machine allocate calls to the next available person, it also provides instant supervision and daily statistics. It enables service standards to be delivered and for staff to be measured against those service standards.

Each of our telephone operators uses a headset so that the telephones are not constantly ringing in a way which would make the working environment impossible. In our particular case, we have 16 operators available at a maximum standard capacity of 100 calls per day. But as soon as the ACD shows more than five calls waiting there is a loud speaker system by which the Call Centre Supervisor can ask everybody to log in by category, e.g. "Can all MAs now log into the telephone system until further notice?" With one particular fixed rate close out we had to have 30 people log in at one point, such was the number of calls coming in per second. Of course, this is still relatively modest in relation to some of the direct telephone operations we have visited, where calls can be

> A call that interrupts...a clerical function can double its disruptive effect when the recovery time is taken into account

upwards of 5000 per day. But, at 1500 calls per day, we are still busier than some of the outsourcing call centres we have also visited.

We programme into our ACD a maximum limit of 3 minutes for incoming calls or "busy" periods, with 5 minutes on outgoing calls, before the supervisor's screen turns red against that individual's name. If somebody makes their telephone "busy" for more than three minutes (perhaps because they are sending out an introducer pack), or if incoming and outgoing calls trip beyond the maximum time programmed into the computer, then the supervisor becomes aware. No immediate action is necessarily taken unless a trend develops, in which case the Call Centre Supervisor will have a word with the individual concerned. Meanwhile, the ACD allocates the calls evenly in rotation to the rest of the operators, who show up blue on the screen when they are available. At any moment in the day, and always at close of play, the ACD delivers up statistics showing how many calls have been received and what the service standard has been in relation to the speed of answering those calls. The number of calls taken by each operator is recorded for assessment against the bonus programme, with the speed of call-answering forming part of the overall team bonus calculation.

One of the areas that the consultants advised us strongly against was a telephone system that is answered by the computer. We have all come across such systems and they are infuriating. If you call a number regularly you have to listen to the same script time and time again. People do not like talking to a computer, and they do not like having to wait before they can dial the number of the extension they require. Although such systems have certain advantages, they are extremely unpopular and are not user-friendly. Despite the progress of technology, it is our experience that people want to speak to people, the telephone being the preferred method of communication.

The Call Centre Supervisor is a crucial position for us to fill given the level of incoming calls. It is a key management appointment where specialist telephone skills must be combined with an in-depth knowledge of the company, its products and of mortgages generally. In addition to being responsible for the performance of the call centre, the Supervisor must also undertake telephone interviews for new recruits. One of the first lessons we learned is that, if you are recruiting for a telephone specialist position, then the first interview must be conducted by telephone so as to establish the candidate's telephone manner. It takes a certain type of individual to spend all day on the telephone wearing a headset and dealing with all manner of incoming mortgage enquiries, and there is a fairly high turnover in this stressful role. Recruitment is therefore a live, ongoing process for the Call Centre Supervisor.

Just as the Team Leaders carry out internal monitoring and control, so the Call Centre Supervisor has to undertake similar tasks in respect of the achievement of service standards. This is not limited to managing the calls by the minute and using the statistics provided by the ACD system. The Call Centre Supervisor is also required to listen in to a certain number of calls each day to ensure that the information being given is accurate (the "hard" element of service), whilst being delivered in a confident, friendly manner (the "soft" element). In this way, training needs are surfaced and all staff are kept on their toes.

TELEPHONE MORTGAGE ADVISERS (TMAS)

The position of TMA is perhaps the most difficult we have ever recruited for. There is no way of knowing in advance the content of a particular telephone call. It might be the most simple criteria-checking enquiry, or the caller may require a decision in principle on a complicated potential application. A third option is a chase-up on an existing case where something unusual has occurred. We soon realised that our TMAs would have to possess a level of competence which would enable them to deal with all such calls, whilst demonstrating an excellent telephone manner.

The consultants advised us that we should aim our recruitment at those seeking specialist telephone work, preferably with some experience of customer service. Knowledge of mortgages was low down on the list. We were sceptical at first about this approach, but it has proved to be the correct one. Our induction course and supervised training allow new staff to be brought sharply up the learning curve, and there are always enough incoming calls to present newcomers with a sufficient level of diversity to help them gain confidence and knowledge. The key with this crucial front line position is to ensure that the TMAs have smiling voices at 5.30pm as well as at 9am when the call centre opens up.

> We consistently exceed our benchmark standards in the call centre

Our TMAs are at the same level in the company as the PMCs. They need the same level of underwriting knowledge and training. They are dispensing that knowledge through telephone work rather than working on individual cases. In order to persuade callers that they need not interrupt the individual PMCs, it is necessary for the TMAs to prove that they are able to answer all queries confidently and competently. This places great emphasis on the computer system, which has been designed to provide look-up help screens which explain exactly what the status of an application is at any given point in time. Moreover, the real time memo facility enables one TMA to be taking a call from a valuer saying that the vendor is on holiday, for example, keying this information as it is being received, so that another TMA taking a chase-up call on the same case can see the message and give it out immediately to the intermediary concerned. In order to provide an efficient service it is important that everything is recorded onto the computer as soon as it is known, which presents particular challenges with post.

The volume of applications we handle means that over 1000 items of post are received each day both in the morning and in the afternoon second post. As soon as postal items are received they are distributed amongst the TMAs who key them onto the system as having been received, but not looked at by the relevant PMC. As soon as the PMC has assessed the item of post the relevant comment is entered onto the computer, e.g. "tick" (meaning approved and satisfactory) or "queried" (meaning that some further points have been raised). A memo point expanding on the latter will then appear for use by the TMAs. If an introducer is chasing whether a particular item of post has been received, it is not necessary for TMAs to leave their position in the call centre and search through piles of paper. If it is not on the computer screen then it has not been received. If it has been received it is on the computer screen and the TMA can say at a glance that it will be looked at shortly or that it has been looked at already.

Although the vast majority of situations can be catered for by the systems I have described, it is always necessary to provide for the unusual. This might be a dissatisfied introducer, where it clearly is going to be necessary for the Call Centre Supervisor, the PMC or the relevant Team Leader to become involved and take the call. Or it might be a situation so unusual or individual that it needs to be taken out of the mainstream. The TMAs are trained to look out for this and ensure that, ultimately, the callers go away satisfied. If this involves speaking to someone other than a TMA then we must respond to that demand rather than impose our own will.

There are many areas in the growth of our Processing Centre where we feel that we are only halfway along the learning curve. But our call centre is one area where we are starting to become reasonably satisfied with progress. We have a "queuing" message that cuts in after eight seconds, followed by an answerphone (with a one-hour call-back facility) after 30 seconds. Our aim is to answer 75 per cent of calls before the first message and 95 per cent of calls before the second. This point is then built into the qualitative part of our bonus programme for the TMAs, which is covered in greater depth later in this chapter. We consistently exceed our benchmark service standards in the call centre and, although there is no room for complacency in any service business, I never see a complaint that we have failed to answer an incoming call in a speedy or helpful manner. The TMAs all give their Christian names in a welcoming message, instilling both warmth and confidence into the initial contact, with the supervision, training and systems back-up ensuring that we can deal with the vast majority of calls there and then.

HEAD OF ADMINISTRATION AND TRAINING

Anything which could reasonably be described as back office, or back-up work, is taken out of the customer-focused teams. Too often, organisations have people who are trying to provide a service to customers also undertaking tasks for the company's management. It is inevitable that such tasks are given a greater priority than serving the customer, not least because the boss is no doubt pressing for the task to be completed. Yet there is nobody more important to an organisation than the customer: if back-up tasks need to be undertaken then those not involved in customer interface should pick this up.

For example, faxes have to be received and sent. They must be linked with files and referred to the relevant PMCs. Call-back messages from the answerphone must be transferred from the call centre to the relevant individual, colour-coded to indicate when they should be returned. Files need to be photocopied and introducer packs need to be sent out. All of these tasks are picked up by the office juniors, who come under the supervision of the Head of Administration. It is a mistake to confuse customer and non-customer work.

In order to integrate office juniors into the overall structure, and to ensure that they embrace the same goals as everybody else, we include such staff in the bonus programme. We also make a point of ensuring that office juniors get an opportunity to undergo formal training so that they can pursue a career path with the company. Good training is an "everyday" requirement, but, once again, it should be supervised outside of the structure for dealing with customers.

Our basic induction course involves familiarisation with the company and the various departments, spending a short time in each. Our "introduction to mortgages" course comes at the end of the induction period and is effectively a "crammer" in a number of different aspects related to mortgages. Once newcomers have emerged from both courses they then go through a period of supervised on-the-job training before finally being allowed to work unsupervised. Given the inevitable peaks and troughs in the lending industry, I have seen too many examples of temporary staff arriving in the morning and dealing with detailed work within an hour of arrival. This helps nobody and will simply serve to harm the reputation of the organisation concerned. Recruitment has to be pitched at the peak level for the year and started as soon as the year begins, so that you are fully staffed to the peak level by the end

> there is nobody more important to an organisation than the customer

of the first quarter. In this way you will have time for training to ensure that customers are not being practised on by new and inexperienced people. The Head of Training should be involved in the recruitment of new staff wherever possible, since that person will be the first port of call in the journey from new recruit to valuable employee.

We provide four levels of training in addition to the "induction" and "introduction to mortgages" courses:

1   Information is shared, and case studies are analysed, at the regular weekly meetings;
2   Lenders visit our Processing Centre regularly and undertake training on their own criteria, particularly when changes occur;
3   Specialist in-house courses are arranged, such as when the Chartered Institute of Bankers came to our Processing Centre and undertook a training course on the interpretation of accounts; and
4   Our staff are regularly sent on external courses across a range of management and processing disciplines.

In connection with point four in the above list, two mortgage qualifications are currently being prepared by the Chartered Institute of Bankers. The Diploma in Mortgage Lending is more relevant to our processing staff, although we will also review the syllabus of the Certificate of Mortgage Advice and Practice, which is the qualification being developed to link up with the new Mortgage Code when it is extended to cover the work of intermediaries. We do not give mortgage advice to the public and do not wish any confusion or misinterpretation to arise in this area. Nevertheless, we need to understand what our introducers are going to have to go through and may get our key staff qualified in this area to assist our understanding of the job our customers undertake.

Accounting is yet another function that comes under the title of Head of Administration. Valuers and introducers have to be paid, queries have to be resolved, incoming cheques and credit card slips need to be accounted for and so on. Once again, this is part of our philosophy of keeping back-up work away from the customer-focused personnel. Where the two areas do cross over, however, is in relation to internal audit and quality control. The Team Leaders, and the Call Centre Supervisor, are required to check the work of their direct reports. The internal control function prescribes the means by which this has to be done and then "checks the checkers".

Examples have already been given of where the Call Centre Supervisor listens in to certain calls at random, for example, and the Team Leaders pull a certain number of random files for audit each week, sending their reports on these cases to the Head of Administration and Training. The latter also undertakes spot checks of files, and deals with the whole raft of computer reports which flag up applications that have taken longer than the norm to process or where the lender has taken more than 72 hours to issue the offer of advance. It is no good presuming that a system will work efficiently. There have to be layers of check and audit which underpin and validate the system, whilst surfacing training needs, because the customer will be a harsh judge. And, in the mortgage market, there is no harsher judge than the busy mortgage intermediary, who can always place the same application several times over with other organisations.

The final function that falls to the Head of Administration and Training is the provision of statistics. We wrote our bespoke software so that any field keyed could be retrieved by way of an ad hoc Management Information Statistics (MIS) report. Thus, we can call up real time how many applications a particular introducer has done with us over a year. Alternatively, we can analyse how much below 75 per cent loan-to-value business several introducers have given us. The number of MIS reports we can produce is infinite, and essential to assessing individual relationships, planning marketing activity or just providing back-up information to help our lenders. This information should be readily available in flexible format, but not provided by people whose job is to provide a service to the customers.

This detailed analysis of the various functions involved in our Processing Centre is really a case study of one approach (i.e. ours) that produces fairly good results in a high volume environment. Others will have a different approach. But the intention throughout this book is to share our direct experience in a way which will hopefully help those involved now, or potentially, in the various mortgage market disciplines covered by each chapter. In the remainder of this chapter I examine briefly a number of separate topics, all of which are relevant to the efficient pre-offer processing of mortgage applications.

IT STRATEGY

The ability to process mortgage applications to pre-offer stage relies absolutely on good software. Any company undertaking or contemplating this role must have an IT strategy. Many of the larger lenders will already use mainframe-based systems. For the smaller player the choice is off-the-shelf or bespoke software. There are some advantages to the former, but, ultimately, we felt that our needs could only be met by bespoke software. Moreover, this particular course – which is not necessarily cheaper – leaves the door open a little wider to future developments. The market is changing so rapidly that future flexibility is just as important as meeting current needs.

In our particular case, we needed a system which could hold each lender's criteria so that the application could be validated by the computer as part of the initial assessment process. Each lender has slightly different angles on its criteria and there is nothing more frustrating to an intermediary or mortgage applicant than for a mistake to be made in the initial assessment, which is only discovered by the lender when the papers are presented for formal offer consideration. Our system prevents that from happening. It also permits validation of an application amongst all of the lenders and products we have at any one time, to permit instant switching between lenders should that be necessary or desirable. As all lenders accept our common application form, valuers' panel and pre-offer processes, switching between lenders is a vital component of our pre-offer service. This facility has been made all the more important by the withdrawal of delegated authority from the high street such that all applications, whether submitted locally or through a processing centre like ours, ultimately get underwritten by the computer anyway.

> The market is changing so rapidly that future flexibility is just as important as meeting current needs

The software must make as many of the fields pre-coded as possible, with lots of "help" and "look-up" screens. In this way, you can eliminate from mortgage processing the mindless, wasteful job of the specialist computer keyer. We employ no such people because we can key an application in several minutes as part of the initial assessment since the free format element is minimised. We have written our software so that individuals are forced into performing certain checks on the work they are carrying out before being able to move on to the next stage. Checklists appear within the system to help in this process. Warning signs appear if input data does not match the lender's criteria, for example, and the quick address system reduces the keying-in time for an address from about 40 to approximately 12 keystrokes. Our software also seeks validation from the intermediaries by way of the initial acknowledgment letter of certain matters we have keyed to the system, such as to whom the introducer fee is payable, and where that fee should be sent. The system allocates application and reservation numbers from the many different fixed and limited issue tranches we are running at any one point in time and captures important database information, updated daily for use by our marketing department.

A clearly defined, well thought-out and highly specified IT strategy is essential to good pre-offer processing. If the route of bespoke software is selected, the results from your chosen software house will be directly related to the detail on your specification. Our latest software took four months to specify from a team working virtually full time, with the results already proving why this was the right thing to do. The next stage is to interface our system with that of our lenders so that there can be data hand-off. The whole point of our approach to mortgage design, distribution and pre-offer processing is to save more costs for the lender than we need to run our business or pay our introducers, so that there is the maximum amount left to be recycled into the customer product. Linking our computer system with that of our lenders will be another important step along this road.

A theory which we have not validated in the area of technology is providing screen-based updates for intermediaries. We have put modem links into a number of key, volume distributors so that they can achieve the same end result, but our experience is that hardly anybody uses this facility. We have actually been in the office of one of these larger intermediaries where the administration teams have preferred to call to get an update on a case rather than move over to the next desk and look it up on the PC. This is why we have so far ignored the Internet for screen-based updates and have evolved our strategy around the telephone, with regular calls out supporting a facility to take a large volume of calls in.

Our software is already flexible enough to take the downloading of an application form via a modem link. You would think that we would be the ideal choice for such an approach, since we are one of very few organisations to offer a short, simple common application form acceptable to a number of lenders. Yet our research indicates that hardly anybody currently wants this facility: indeed, a pilot keying exercise in our sister company, John Charcol, revealed that it took almost twice as long to fill out an application form on a computer screen than it did to handwrite in the various answers. There is no doubt that everybody is becoming more comfortable with computers, and there is also no doubt that as younger people come into our industry, and older people exit, there will be more demand for such technology links. But, when evolving an IT strategy, it is important not to let the computer experts – who are, by definition, the boffins – encourage you to develop facilities that are too far ahead of those actually in demand by your customers. There is no substitute for constant research and feedback amongst those who give you business.

Technology really scores when it automates, and makes more efficient, functions that support rather than substitute for human contact. For example, we download to our bank direct from our computer system the introducer payments we make each month, and the bank sends out automated warrants plus counterfoils, debiting our current account in the process. This has replaced the manual drawing of £100,000 worth of cheques each month, and is a good example of where flexible bespoke software can link with business partners to produce spectacular time-saving results to the benefit of all.

ON-SITE UNDERWRITERS

Another development that has massively improved our service has been lenders siting underwriters at our Processing Centre. Because there are no pre-submission queries, and post-submission chase-ups, the capacity of each underwriter to approve offers is doubled if they are on-site rather than based in their own offices. Moreover, once the day's application packages ready for offer have been approved (or otherwise), we are able to raise grey-area queries on applications we have recently received so that less time is subsequently wasted. Our offer turnaround time has been greatly improved, and the service has been extremely popular amongst our distributors, thereby creating its own extra volume. Although our customers do not speak directly to the lenders' underwriters, our staff have access, and this is better access than can often be obtained by intermediaries when dealing with lenders locally, not least because the underwriters we need have to be senior people with larger mandates. Although the concept of an on-site underwriter is only really relevant to a multi-lender high volume programme like our own, the principle of listening to customer demand, and giving them their requested greater access to decision-makers, is so relevant to a customer-orientated business.

PREMISES DESIGN

The physical layout and design of the premises where pre-offer processing is carried out will be very important to efficiency and workflow. Surroundings significantly influence the attitudes of staff and how valued they feel. This will, in turn, reflect the way in which they interact with customers. We spent a great deal of time considering the design of our Processing Centre, hiring design specialists to help us create the right environment.

We had to ensure that all staff had easy access to files and product information, with screens between desks high enough to help to reduce background noise, but low enough to maintain air and light flow and an integrated open plan office feeling. Desk management, where all wires are out of sight, is essential to help maintain a tidy environment which, in turn, enables your internal control function to enforce tidy, well put together mortgage files. Our Operations Director can therefore get a feel of the "mood" of the entire office, and of the general work flow, in one glance, whilst the individuals are able to undertake their work efficiently in a smart, colourful air-conditioned environment which makes them feel valued. The call centre, for reasons already covered, needs to be a self-contained unit, separated from the main area by a glass wall so that it is still evidently part of the same overall team. The message is that if you want to maximise your efficiency, which is what customers demand, then office design is an element that cannot be treated lightly.

> Surroundings significantly influence the attitudes of staff and how valued they feel

STAFF INTEGRATION AND PERFORMANCE

Cross-communication is particularly important in an environment like ours. The sales team put the mortgage products in front of the intermediaries they call on, but the processing team have to deliver against each intermediary's expectation as to the efficient processing of the resultant application. This is why we place great emphasis on communication between the sales, marketing and processing departments, and also between the different areas within our Processing Centre.

Every fortnight, Godfrey Blight, our Managing Director, addresses the call centre staff (who have the main contact with our customers) on the current sales position and sales strategy. Prior to a product being launched, Tony Fisher, our Marketing Manager, briefs the entire processing staff in small teams on why that product is being offered, where it fits against the competition, how much business we expect and why we think it is a good deal. Similarly, before any sales fax is sent out, a prior briefing session is undertaken by Tony explaining the purpose of that particular communication and what message we are trying to put across. The intermediary reader will, I am sure, recognise many situations where the sales department of a particular lender has put out a communication which, when followed up, is "new news" to those on the processing side.

In addition to the weekly briefing and update sessions that each Team Leader has with his or her own teams, there are full staff meetings once a week out of working hours to discuss the overall performance of the Processing Centre. This gives our Operations Director an opportunity to convey certain messages for the week, whilst encouraging cross-communication between various Processing Centre departments. It is at these particular team meetings that we surface all complaints using case studies.

There is no doubt that people complain more these days, and there is also no doubt that the serial complainer is emerging within our society. But any customer-focused organisation cannot afford the luxury of trying to second-guess whether somebody is a serial complainer or genuine. Every complaint must be regarded as a de facto fail on the part of the organisation in that the reality of the delivery has failed to match the customer's expectation.

Our formal complaints procedure ensures that every complaint is dealt with by a senior manager within a specific time frame. But, additionally, any file on which there has been a complaint is brought to the weekly team meetings and pored over to establish how that complaint could have been avoided. Nine times out of ten it is a question of better communication of what we have been doing rather than a change required to our various internal systems, although the latter is by no means uncommon. If approached responsively and constructively, complaints can be a very positive feature in ensuring that your procedures and general approach are constantly revised and updated, and we publish a complaints hotline for our intermediaries to use if they should ever feel that our published service standards have been breached. The bigger problem for any business is the customer that votes with his feet rather than raising an official complaint.

Another area where organisations can sometimes let themselves down is to assume that it is only the sales side of the business that needs an incentive-based bonus programme. The Processing Centre staff are in the front line of an important volume-based activity where reputations can be won and lost with customers. Every member of our Processing Centre staff is therefore part of a bonus programme, which reflects quantitative and qualitative goals in line with our approach to service standards generally. For example, the Processing Centre overall has to achieve a certain number of mortgage offers in a calendar quarter to create a bonus pot for that quarter. If a pot has been established, both PMCs and MAs then receive a bonus based on a percentage of salary only if the cases assigned to them have achieved a target average turnaround time between receipt to lender hand-off. Similarly, the TMAs only qualify individually if a certain percentage of the calls received by the unit have been answered before the first recorded announcement. Office juniors and support staff receive a bonus based on the overall Processing Centre performance. The better-performing staff earn a bonus for that quarter where under-performers do not. But the slate is wiped clean for the next quarter where the positions could, feasibly, be reversed.

It is absolutely essential in my view to align the financial interests of Processing Centre staff with the service requirements of the customers they serve, thus enabling those who provide service excellence to our customers to enjoy the financial benefits of their performance.

WHAT NEXT IN PRE-OFFER PROCESSING?

Pre-offer processing is still too paper-based. With higher level credit searching and mature credit scoring systems now in place, there is no need for all these paper references. Mortgages should be offered within seven days or sooner, and paid out immediately thereafter, relying on title insurance. I expect that development to be with us very shortly.

As the Internet becomes more widely used, interaction between users and providers should permit mortgage application forms to be completed on screen and in an interactive way. That is very much a medium- to long-term development.

Naturally, I believe there to be a long-term future for multi-lender programmes like ours who can continually integrate their service with a given number of lenders so as to offer easy application switching and genuine choice to customers, recycling the cost savings of that approach into product opportunities for the customer. The idea of multi-lender organisations acting as some kind of coordinator, with each intermediary dealing direct with a lender, as favoured by some of our newer competitors, is not something for which I see a great future.

WRAP-UP

Private Label is a specialist company, and some of the techniques we employ are applicable only to our type of business. Equally, however, some of the processes, techniques and lessons learned in this chapter could be of value to anybody involved in the pre-offer processing of mortgage applications. If you get service right it will create greater sales. If you get service wrong then, even with a market-leading product, you will not maximise your mortgage sales.

CHAPTER

8

WHAT NEXT?

For the final chapter, I have rung the changes. Throughout the book so far, the reader has heard my views and my experiences. It is about time – so you may feel – that we wheeled on some real experts! This book has focused so far on the factors affecting the mortgage market over the past ten years. I have therefore asked 14 eminent people interested in, and associated with, the mortgage market to state their views about the major mortgage-related factors over the *next* ten years. The contributions differ in length and in tone, because they are printed here unamended and unedited. But building societies, banks, insurance companies, major brokers, direct operations, networks, estate agents and consumers are all represented. I sum up at the end, but what now follows are the 14 contributions (in alphabetical order, naturally).

WHAT NEXT?

PETER BIRCH, CHIEF EXECUTIVE
ABBEY NATIONAL Plc

Home ownership as a proportion of all housing tenure has risen from 10 per cent in 1914 to 47 per cent in 1961 and now to 67 per cent in 1997. One of the key issues is that this is now a mature market with little prospect of significant further growth in the proportion of owner occupation.

Only 20 years ago, the majority of mortgages were provided by building societies with an average market share of around 80 per cent in 1980. As a result of a combination of competition from banks and centralised lenders, and the wave of conversions to plc status, building societies are likely to account for less than 20 per cent of the mortgage stock by the end of 1997. The building society movement has consolidated considerably this century. There were 2145 building societies in 1910 falling dramatically to 125 in 1987 and falling still further to 78 in 1997. By 2000, this figure may be as low as 50.

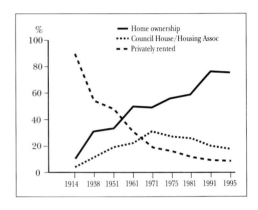

The 1980s saw a jump in the volumes and value of the mortgage market, caused in part by a reaction to fiscal change and an expectation of continued house price inflation, as well as other factors such as people having the opportunity to buy their own council homes. The market in the 1990s has been much more mixed, with only a gradual increase in volumes and values in the mortgage market after a significant downturn in the period 1989–91. This gradual increase is unlikely to accelerate, partly because the percentage of home ownership is unlikely to increase to any great extent. In addition, the tax regime is becoming more neutral towards home ownership with declining MIRAS, higher stamp duty and a reduction in the state support available.

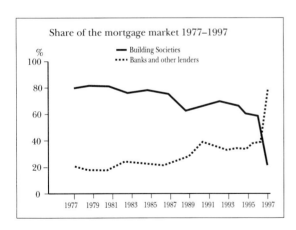

The near future will see a great deal of change in the market, though much of it will involve a continuation of existing trends. MIRAS benefit is likely to continue to be eroded and inflation is likely to remain in the 2–4 per cent range. The total UK mortgage market will probably stabilise with net growth advances at around £25 billion per annum in today's terms with around 1.5 million housing transactions per year. The move towards increasing telephone mortgage sales will continue, reaching a 10 per cent market share in the near future.

Peter Birch

Building societies will virtually disappear with perhaps one or two more demutualisations and many more mergers/acquisitions as, over time, the board and management of the remaining societies change or retire. It is estimated that banks will provide 90 per cent of all UK mortgages, with new lenders such as retailers and insurance companies providing the main competition. Mortgages are likely to be securitised in order to free up capital. Finally, although absolute percentage market shares will change, the leading mortgage providers of the future will continue to be the principal players in the market today. Abbey National is committed to retaining its position as one of the foremost (and best respected) mortgage providers.

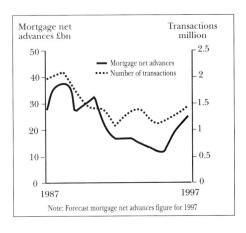

Note: Forecast mortgage net advances figure for 1997

WHAT NEXT?

MIKE BLACKBURN, Chief Executive
HALIFAX Plc

Just 20 years ago there was "a mortgage" and "the mortgage rate". No variety – any colour so long as it was black. Then market regulations changed and the inevitable occurred. More products, more price competition, more suppliers, some riskier lending. Nerves of steel were needed through the house price slump of the early 1990s – but interestingly there was no suggestion of rolling back regulation. The competitive market had arrived and was with us to stay.

What of the next decade? Competition in the mortgage market puts the focus on the customer. The customer may not yet be King – because prudent lending doesn't let him buy his palace – but he is certainly Crown Prince. What this will amount to is a far wider range of mortgage products, virtually tailored to individual needs, with a strong emphasis on value for money and on flexibility. Technology, and the long-awaited improvements in the actual house-buying process, will speed up and simplify transactions. But apart from simple and, probably, "pre-scored" applicants, there will still be a need for face-to-face mortgage selling. Not only will the regulators expect this, the very range and complexity of products will make telephone or even PC-based selling a dubious proposition – certainly for first-time buyers and the inexperienced.

> Despite the gloomsters, buying a house is and will be quite exciting. But getting a mortgage will never be fun

The high cost of technology and distribution, and growing economies of scale, will lead to more industry consolidation. But this will not reduce competition. A wide range of lenders will still bid for a market which will certainly grow (4.4 million new households by 2016) but by no means as rapidly as in the 1970s or 1980s. And with EMU we can expect cross-border European competition in the various mortgage markets.

Who will be the winners? Those who run tight ships, keep their costs down and offer the keenest pricing. Those who sense and respond to changing market needs and have the technology and resources to launch new products quickly. Those with the distribution systems that customers find most convenient. And those with a solid reputation for fair dealing.

Despite the gloomsters, buying a house is and will still be quite exciting. But getting a mortgage will never be fun. What the best players need to do is ensure that the borrower gets a cost-effective deal that meets his own particular needs – with as little hassle or worry as possible. No rocket science in that. Leave the hassle for choosing the curtains!

Mike Blackburn

WHAT NEXT?

ADRIAN COLES, DIRECTOR GENERAL
BUILDING SOCIETIES ASSOCIATION

Over the last three or four years there has been a general recognition that the four decades to 1990 represented an extraordinary period in the development of the mortgage market, which can no longer be characterised as the norm to which we will return. Inflation, which in the past destroyed the value of mortgage debt taken on by borrowers, is now much lower. Government has

> The sale of council houses and the liberalisation of the mortgage market are one-off events that cannot be repeated

almost withdrawn support from the owner occupied market. Private renting is once again a viable option and demographic change, in particular the impact of the one-third reduction in the number of births in the United Kingdom between the mid-1960s and mid-1970s, will continue to have a profound effect into the next century. The sale of council houses and the liberalisation of the mortgage market are one-off events that cannot be repeated.

Consumers too are changing. On average we live longer and spend a greater proportion of our lives living alone. We are more likely to suffer a period of unemployment. We will enter the labour market in our early twenties rather than our mid-teens, leaving full-time education with substantial loans to repay, and are much more likely to retire in our mid-fifties than mid-sixties. In financial services we will less and less see branches as the appropriate method of contact with financial institutions. The post, telephone, Internet, ATMs and intermediaries will take an increasing share of distribution.

For the mortgage lender these trends represent powerful challenges. The winning institutions will be those that can translate the economic and social changes into product designs that reflect not only short-term consumer appeal in an ultra-competitive world, but also incorporate longer term features that will be able both to match potential changes in households' circumstances and which are easy to understand. This will not be an easy package to put together, but the prizes for those institutions that get it right, and their customers, will be immense.

Adrian Coles

WHAT NEXT?

MICHAEL COOGAN, DIRECTOR GENERAL
COUNCIL OF MORTGAGE LENDERS

Lenders will need to survive and prosper in an environment where financial assistance for owner occupiers (such as mortgage interest tax relief) will have been removed. The government will also further limit its role as funder of a safety net for borrowers in difficulties, either by capping the amounts or limiting the period over which income support for mortgage interest will be given. This will increase the onus on lenders, in conjunction with insurers, to reintroduce an effective safety net for borrowers. The prospect of possession figures returning to the levels of the early 1990s during the next recession will be politically unacceptable. The government will expect lenders to demonstrate by their actions that possession is only taken as a last resort.

The structural changes and rationalisation in the financial services sector, in particular amongst mortgage lenders, will continue apace. The leading players of the future will primarily be bancassurance groups, although a few committed mutuals, direct operators and retailers may be able to remain serious competitors on price and/or service. The winners of this competitive battle of the future will be those lenders which can build relationships with their customers which last. Deeply discounted and other low start products will become less attractive, not least because of criticism of the effect on borrowers of long lock-in redemption periods at a time of high interest rates.

Retaining brand loyalty will be ever more difficult as customers see their mortgage like any other commodity. A lender which is perceived as more interested in obtaining new business through preferential offers, rather than looking after and thus retaining loyal customers, will be less able to sustain its position. Changing a loan (whether moving house or not) will become as quick and easy as buying and selling a car.

Lenders' selling practices will have to be more focused on the real interests and particular needs of each customer, either to avoid intrusive statutory regulation or because of its introduction. The provision of an advice service to borrowers on the suitability of the lender's products to fit their personal circumstances will become the norm amongst all major lenders.

A key issue for the mortgage industry dealing with a Labour Government which equates self-regulation with self-interest will be demonstrating that it can deliver effective consumer protection. If it does, the limit of intervention may be to give statutory backing to the Mortgage Code. Otherwise, new, detailed conduct of business requirements will be imposed on lenders in a revised Financial Services Bill.

Convergence of regulatory organisations, as already announced, will be matched by a move to a single statutory Ombudsman Scheme for financial services and the introduction of a federal structure for more formal links between, and control over the costs of, different financial services trade associations.

> The winners of this competitive battle of the future will be those lenders which can build relationships with their customers which last.

Michael Coogan

WHAT NEXT?

IAN DARBY, DIRECTOR
JOHN CHARCOL LTD

It is 13 years since I started my career in the mortgage industry, and it has been a period of unprecedented change. I believe the next ten years will see the momentum continue, and the market will look different to its present structure.

Ten years forward those institutions with strong brands, and large client bases, who have chosen to form strategic alliances with large financial institutions, will have firmly established themselves as players, challenging the safe territory hitherto occupied by the banks and building societies. The speed of arrival of the Virgins and Sainsburys of this world will have taken many of the competition by surprise, and I am sure that many more new entrants will follow, and indeed prosper.

I suspect that flexible mortgages will form the basis of a significant percentage of new mortgage business, with borrowers demanding a core mortgage product adaptable enough to meet the continually changing labour market and their increased financial awareness of future needs. This will accompany, I hope, a radically different service proposition, which by and large doesn't exist in today's market. Our clients often comment on how inefficient and time-consuming our industry makes the whole borrowing process, which regrettably does not engender client loyalty. In ten years' time borrowers really will have grasped how tradable a commodity a mortgage is, and the financial institutions who have worked hardest on establishing an ongoing relationship and high service levels will have to focus less on aggressive new product offers.

> I suspect that flexible mortgages will form the basis of a significant percentage of new mortgage business

I believe it is inevitable that there will be further consolidation within the lending sector, and the number of societies and indeed banks offering mortgage products will reduce. However, I hope and suspect that the mutual will survive as a concept, which would certainly be advantageous to the consumer, providing healthy competition.

Technological changes are bound to be significant, with clients demanding a real choice in how their affairs are handled and, indeed, how they can access lenders. Most lenders and intermediaries will have to offer a full direct process, together with Internet facilities to ensure that they are providing a choice of how a client deals with a company.

Ultimately I believe that the mortgage market will be fully regulated, that MIRAS will have been removed, and that, in many cases, a fully qualified intermediary market will be the first port of call for most clients.

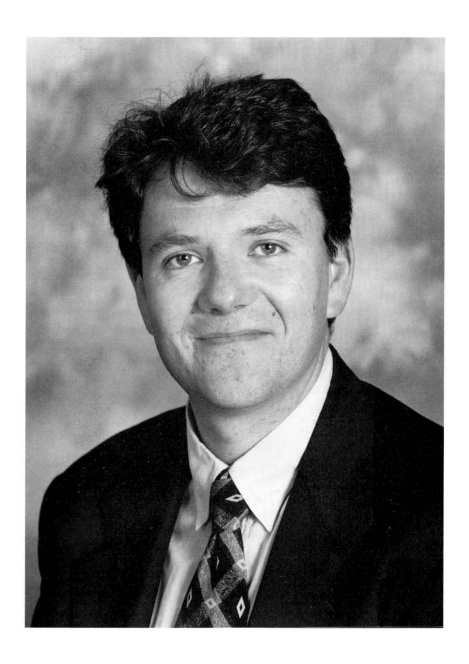

Ian Darby

KEN DAVY, Chairman

DBS FINANCIAL MANAGEMENT Plc

All the major political parties are committed to the concept of private home ownership. This commitment, coupled with the still predominant wish of most people in the UK to "own their own home", provides the mortgage market with an underlying stability probably unequalled anywhere in the world. The saying "an Englishman's home is his castle" may no longer be entirely accurate, but recent traumas of negative equity have failed to undermine our fundamental belief in the value of a property-owning democracy.

The mortgage market is nevertheless about to undergo major changes as a result of increased regulation of both the marketing and arranging of mortgages. The initial restructuring which will result is bound to be painful, but it will nonetheless force the mortgage industry to fully embrace increased professionalism, which in turn will undoubtedly help the intermediary market to flourish.

> recent traumas of negative equity have failed to undermine our fundamental belief in the value of a property-owning democracy

The parallels with the regulatory moves in the life and pensions industry are clearly apparent. The consumer's increasing desire for independent and impartial financial advice has expanded the IFA's market share despite dire predictions of its demise. I believe it is inevitable that in future qualified advisers providing high quality independent mortgage advice will have a major impact in the new world of regulated mortgages.

The paradox is that though in general the opportunities will increase, how can the small firm hope to take full advantage of them or perhaps even survive in this new market-place? The increased demands of research, examinations, continued training and the countless other requirements which flow from regulation will add significantly to the small intermediaries' operating costs.

This is a similar environment to that which provided a platform for the growth of networks within the financial services arena, and will lead mortgage-orientated intermediaries to consider the benefits of joining a network. In particular, networks which offer comprehensive mortgage support facilities are certain to become increasingly sought after. This will allow mortgage intermediaries to continue running their independent businesses whilst enjoying the essential support needed to provide their clients with the standard of advice and service that a properly regulated market demands.

Another dynamic change within the grasp of the mortgage market is that of technology. The major benefits that the computer age can deliver to lenders, intermediaries and clients must be harnessed if we are to take full advantage of the opportunities the coming decade will bring. Historically, the mortgage industry has clung to its paper-based systems, but a new breed of technology-minded intermediaries are already starting to create the catalyst for change.

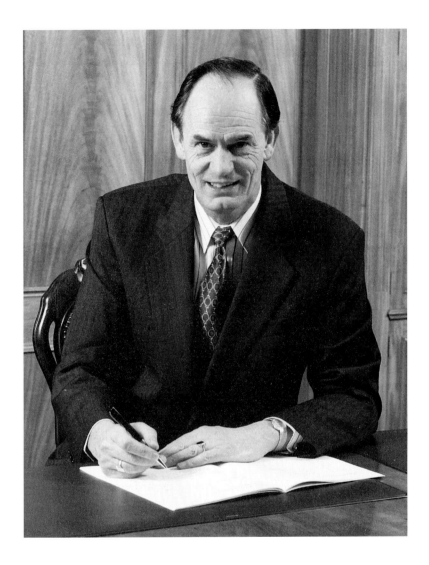

Ken Davy

For the increasingly financially aware consumer a particular benefit of technology will be reflected in the design of new mortgage products. By taking account of the consumers' requirements more closely, products which match the client's expectations can be delivered more effectively. As a consequence, the mortgage market of the future is likely to be a properly regulated market served by professional independent intermediaries with the added benefits and cost and service that technology provides.

This bodes well for a decade of positive change within a secure and stable marketplace.

WHAT NEXT?

HUGH DUNSMORE-HARDY, CHIEF EXECUTIVE

NATIONAL ASSOCIATION OF ESTATE AGENTS

I believe that the recession in the housing market which occurred between 1990 and 1995 has brought about a fundamental change in people's philosophy to home ownership.

There is no doubt that the high level of price inflation which occurred between the mid- and late 1980s led people to move more with short-term investment in mind than the long term security of owning a family home. The subsequent collapse in the market, which saw property values fall by up to 40 per cent in some parts of the country, sent a stark message to many who had regarded owning a home as a one-way ticket to increasing personal wealth.

It is now more noticeable that people's attitudes have returned to the fundamental reasons for home ownership in that it provides security and some prospect of long term investment which can be capitalised in later life when the accumulated equity within the home provides a cushion to supplement living standards in the years of retirement. In other words, the adage that a home is for nesting and not investing has now become the focus of most people's reasons for owning a home.

Evidence in 1997 shows that there is far less property coming to the market and this will be a likely trend for the future, with annual volumes of transactions often less than was witnessed on an annual average during the 1980s. With the reduction and ultimate removal of MIRAS, the tax advantages associated with taking a mortgage will no longer encourage people to gear up their mortgage borrowing to maximum levels. Indeed it will probably encourage a higher percentage to consider paying back their mortgage as soon as possible and treating it much as a conventional HP debt.

Moving costs within the United Kingdom as a percentage of transaction values are considerably less than those within Europe, which provides scope for the government of the day to look at this area as a means of raising revenue. We have already seen the first steps in this direction through the Government's increase in stamp duty levels. This, I believe, will be likely to continue and, as a result, may well deter a rise in the volume of housing transactions in the future.

The trend will be towards a far greater level of remortgaging for home improvements, on the basis that people will be more considered in their choice of property to allow for future domestic needs. I can also see a need for greater flexibility in mortgage products, perhaps moving more towards the transportable mortgage concept with the mortgage attached and available with the property, thus avoiding the need for multiple valuations/surveys and an easier process that will be more focused on the buyer's ability to reach the mortgage repayments.

It has also been argued that the market is driven from the bottom up and that the first-time buyer is the key to the general buoyancy of the market at

Hugh Dunsmore-Hardy

all price levels. We must not overlook that many first-time buyers had their fingers badly burned and are still paying the consequence of the recession. Furthermore, with the recent news of a greater move towards placing the burden of higher education on students through student loans, it is foreseeable that many young people will start their working life carrying with them considerable debt which may well make it difficult for them to consider becoming home owners at such an early stage in their careers. This is therefore another factor in support of my overall view that estate agents and those engaged in the property market, together with mortgage lenders, will have to be competitive in fighting for a "larger share of a reduced cake".

> the adage that a home is for nesting and not investing has now become the focus for most people's reasons for owning a home

WHAT NEXT?

As the consumers of the future face increasingly hectic lives, convenience and ease of use will drive people to the direct channels of delivery as their point of choice and away from the traditional High Street face-to-face interview. Customers will regard their custom as there to be won rather than accepted by the lender. The success of Direct Line in the financial services market has already shown that this trend has started and will continue at an increasingly fast pace. This will lead to a massive shift in the structure of our industry. The end of mutuality is already in sight, it won't happen overnight but at the end of the ten-year period the process of consolidation will leave a market dominated by large, strong financial groups who can deliver the products through the channels the customers want.

Increasing regulation will force a new wave of products that will follow in the blue print of Direct Line's simple and transparent mortgage product. The practice of using a mass of loyal customers paying standard variable rates to subsidise new customers and offer loss leading deals in an effort to grab market share will have ended. Customers will have woken up to the fact that they can choose their lender and move their mortgages frequently and to the lowest cost, highest value provider.

The appearance of new entrants will also add to the increasingly competitive market. These entrants, both from financial and non-financial backgrounds, will take time to get their products right but the convenience of the new delivery channels they will offer will have a significant effect.

> Customers will have woken up to the fact that they can choose their lender and move their mortgages frequently and to the lowest cost, highest value provider

The consumer of the future will also have to develop an increasingly large portfolio of financial products to enable them to provide for their future welfare and their families' education as the state reduces its support. This will encompass pension provision, long-term health care and income protection, and the mortgage product will need to contain the flexibility to be part of this portfolio and cope with the changing situation of the consumer's lifestyle.

The success of Direct Line Insurance in taking the motor insurance market from under the noses of the big insurance companies in the 1980s has shown how a seemingly static market can be turned on its head, and this process is being repeated in the financial services market. This process will be ignored by the market at its peril. Only the companies who respond to the challenges will succeed. The provision of transparent flexible products through direct banking, whether it is by the telephone, Internet or home banking through interactive television, is the future.

Stephen Geraghty

WHAT NEXT?

JIM GILCHRIST, Director
SCOTTISH LIFE ASSURANCE COMPANY

Removing the lemming approach! I see the introduction of regulation to the mortgage market, the greater use of technology and further improvements to product design assisting in the education of the mortgage buyer. We need to produce simple and more flexible quality products, that reflect market conditions, which smooth the ups and downs that have plagued the market in recent years.

Mortgage buyers are like lemmings which tend to blindly follow current trends and ignore the future. They seek financial benefits now and do not plan the course of the next few years. This has left borrowers vulnerable to adverse change and often locked in to severe redemption penalties.

> We need to produce simple and more flexible quality products, that reflect market conditions, which smooth the ups and downs that have plagued the market in recent years

When the Standard Variable Rate (SVR) fell to record low levels, many borrowers opted for "cashbacks" and "discounts". But, historically, money markets reverse every few years, which will leave many borrowers questioning the wisdom of their earlier decision, and repaying interest significantly in excess of the earlier cash benefits. If they had bought a fixed rate, then they would have seen real and tangible benefits. The reverse situation applies when interest rates increase. Many borrowers buy into fixed rates ignoring the fact that the trend will reverse at some stage and they may be left paying more than SVR.

Some lenders have been happy to follow public demand, because if the public are wrong (which they usually are), the lender makes more profit. Lenders do not offer fixed or discounted rates in order to make a loss!

The way forward has to be a greater understanding of the new "flexible" mortgages. The opportunity to select a monthly payment level that allows the overpayment of capital and interest, as market conditions and personal circumstances demand, will ultimately benefit borrowers and lenders. Regular mortgage reviews and advice from the lender or intermediary are essential, together with good design and sensible fee and redemption levels.

Only in this way can borrowers have confidence in the mortgage market. Lenders will then have happier customers, and not dissatisfied lemmings.

Jim Gilchrist

WHAT NEXT?

JOHN HEAPS, Chief Executive
BRITANNIA BUILDING SOCIETY

Is it too radical to suggest that the obituary columns will some day soon carry an entry relating to the demise of the traditional mortgage? Certainly the current mortgage scene is facing many pressures that may combine to change our views as to why we need a mortgage and what we want the mortgage to do for us when we get one.

Mortgage professionals of all kinds will be presented with a set of new challenges in the way that mortgages are designed, marketed, sold and administered. We have moved from a supply-led market, through deregulation, into a demand-led scene in which we have witnessed an explosion in product types and lenders. Mortgage marketing in this period has been dominated by a focus on rate. The basic purpose of the mortgage has not been explored.

During the next ten years mortgage marketeers will see consumers facing factors that will challenge the basic purpose of house acquisition. For a start there will be a shift in the pattern of the family unit towards increasing numbers of single family units. People will be expected to carry a far greater burden of the cost of providing benefits currently available from the state. At the same time the continuing rise of the "nanny" state, and the tendency to direct us as to how to conduct our lives, will increase the social pressure to provide for a greater range of needs.

Technology will help in marketing products, especially in the information sources available and the complexity of regulatory compliant detail that will need to be given. The mortgage of the future will compete for shelf space in this complex world as part of an integrated approach to financial arrangements tailored to meet individual needs. Mortgages will be viewed as the line of credit they present to the borrower and the extra services they can buy as a result, rather than just a means of buying a home.

> We are...seeing the beginning of the end of the conventional mortgage

This emphasis on features of flexibility does not mean increased margins for product providers. Competitive pressures, including a range of new entrants, will see to that. As the sale of mortgages becomes more specialised there will be a move towards fee income rather than interest margin as the main reward. We may even see the long anticipated development of markets based on securitised mortgage books and mortgage-backed financial instruments.

We are today seeing the beginning of the end of the conventional mortgage. The next ten years will see a different contract emerging in which the consumer's needs other than home provision will feature strongly. Just as deregulation offered current mortgage designers a range of options, this new approach presents a new set of exciting opportunities for tomorrow's product designer and marketeer. They had better be ready for the challenge!

John Heaps

WHAT NEXT?

MIKE JACKSON, CHIEF EXECUTIVE

BIRMINGHAM MIDSHIRES BUILDING SOCIETY

I can give you a cast-iron guarantee that there will be a series of key events that will affect the mortgage market over the next ten years, and that they will be more dramatic than any we have seen in the past. Some of these events are apparent, others speculative, but when they will happen is open to question. However, we can consider the 2007 marketplace ....

A mortgage is now as much a commodity as a motor insurance policy became in the mid-1990s, with new competitors entering the market, often in strategic alliances with other players. The remaining traditional lenders from the previous century have experienced the arrival in the market of homebuying accounts from organisations whose roots are in other fields. What they do have in common is a passion for delivering key customer benefits in our buyer-empowered society.

Few customers favour a visit to a High Street outlet for their needs. Interactive technology has been harnessed to fulfil the needs of the buyer, and has provided the international software and communications giants with the opportunity to become key players in the provision of mortgage finance. By linking with business partners who have demonstrated a strong focus on excellent service, bespoke products are created which are tailored to individual needs, and which are upgraded on any house move. The borrower has become the security as much as the property, and accesses any additional funds that may be required, within a pre-agreed loan-to-value related limit, by plastic, PC or phone. These changes have meant a focus on first-time buyers by intermediaries, and the establishment of financial agreements with providers which reward ongoing retention as well as attraction.

> A mortgage is now as much a commodity as a motor insurance policy became in the mid-1990s, with new competitors entering the market

The winners are the consumers, and those organisations able to retain them. The desire by providers in the 1990s to build relationships has proved successful by those who were truly committed. This has been reflected in the expectation that the customer is a partner whose full dealings are considered in the price that they pay for their mortgage as a segment of one. They expect, and receive, transparency in their dealings, and can download information on a range of factors. These will include the daily cost of interest on their outstanding balance and "what if" scenarios on changing the structure of their borrowing, or when the European Central Bank makes yet another change to ECU funding rates.

The next ten years will provide a stimulating environment in which to be part of the industry delivering homebuying products. Birmingham Midshires has a structure and outlook which deliver customer service excellence, and we have the foundations on which to build our part as we look forward in prosperous partnership.

Mike Jackson

WHAT NEXT?

SHEILA McKECHNIE OBE, CHIEF EXECUTIVE
CONSUMERS' ASSOCIATION

Competition amongst mortgage providers is intense at the moment. The mutuality/Plc debate has kept mortgage rates in the headlines. But two factors will drive further rationalisation which will be bad news for consumers.

Some of the banks are sitting on substantial pots of money. Part of this will be used to enhance shareholder value by buying back shares, but much of it will be used to increase market share in the retail financial services market. The banks will try to increase their market share through the purchase of smaller players, or a merger with larger rivals, who have attractive mortgage books. The same process of rationalisation will also be seen in the building societies' sector. Societies will merge either to further improve efficiency to aid competitiveness, or to increase market share to appear more attractive to predators.

Whatever the banks do, they know that they will have to remove their rivals in the mutual sector. If they succeed – and without protective measures the odds are that they will – then that will be the end of effective competition for the banks. The threatened destruction of mutuals is probably the most pressing financial crisis facing consumers today. Of course, competition will continue to exist. But what will happen is that there will be what the Consumers' Association (CA) calls a "levelling down" of competition.

On a macro-economic level, there is every chance that we will see a repeat of the boom/bust housing cycle. The new administration hasn't yet put any constraints in place to slow down demand. The price levels for the new stamp duty rates are simply too high to have any real knock-on effect. However, it is much too early to say if we will see the same frenzy as we did in the 1980s. Much of the boom prices recently is down to an imbalance between supply and demand, and is specific to certain regions and sectors of the market. We have yet to see the same crazy prices being paid for small single person units whilst decent, mid-range properties are playing catch-up to some extent. Although, at some stage, demographic and social pressures will reassert the demand for single person units which will provide a platform for further growth.

The impact of inherited wealth from housing on the economy may well be over-estimated. Much of this wealth will be absorbed by the costs of providing long-term care for the increasing numbers of elderly in society. One thing is certain, we will see more cherry-picking by mortgage providers. We will see the development of two distinct categories of consumers paying differential rates. One tier will be existing homeowners with secure employment who are perceived to be low risk. They will buy direct from mortgage providers – charges will be relatively transparent – and will be able to make informed choices.

However, at the other end, mortgage providers will extend the use of "flexible", tailored mortgages for a second tier of consumers who are deemed to be a higher risk, or have intermittent employment patterns. These consumers will, rightly or wrongly, come to rely on intermediaries to find a mortgage which suits them in an increasingly complex market. This two-tier approach will be a feature of the

Sheila McKechnie

mortgage market for years to come, and is one of the reasons why CA has made the inclusion of mortgages under the revised Financial Services Act (FSA) one of its priorities. Buying a home is one of the biggest, if not the biggest, financial commitment many consumers will make in their lifetime. It needs to be regulated now under the FSA.

It is likely that we will see a number of measures to make buying a home much easier. The whole process is more traumatic than it need be. The new Government has announced that it will examine the entire process to look at the possibility of ending gazumping and such things. This is a good thing – as is the introduction of one-stop shops covering all aspects of purchasing a home. CA has been campaigning for this since 1985, but we are well aware that, unless handled properly, "bundling" of services could be bad news for consumers. This all leads back to the FSA. Without proper legislation, and disclosure of information, comparison of bundled and unbundled services will be nigh on impossible.

WHAT NEXT?

ROBIN PHIPPS, DIRECTOR

LEGAL AND GENERAL ASSURANCE SOCIETY Ltd

Despite relatively high "owner occupancy" in the UK, I expect the mortgage market over the next ten years to be an attractive market for both competitive lenders and professional intermediaries. The next few years will benefit from the remaining "unwinding" of pent-up demand amongst first-time buyers who delayed buying during the recession of the early 1990s. As prices rise, I believe the market will also benefit from an ending of reluctance among many to move.

On the supply side, no doubt the next ten years will bring further consolidation amongst mortgage lenders and I expect numbers to reduce. However, competition will remain intense, fuelled in no small way by new providers such as supermarket banks and "direct" lenders with different pricing, technological and distribution strategies.

Notwithstanding the upward trend in UK interest rates in 1997, reduced global inflationary pressures are likely to lead to a relatively low interest rate environment over the longer term, providing a generally stable basis for mortgage rates.

Innovation in mortgage product design will gather pace as lenders compete to deliver mortgages best suited to changing customer requirements. I expect to see a growth in "flexible mortgages" as customers seek to integrate their mortgage with other family and personal financial requirements, such as banking, personal loans and savings. Technology will change dramatically over the ten-year period. Customers and intermediaries will access lenders electronically and this will become a key method of achieving competitive advantage.

Distribution will remain a vital issue for mortgage lenders and intermediaries. I expect an increasing minority to buy "direct". But the majority will continue to seek advice and explanation from lenders and/or intermediaries. Standards of mortgage advice required by customers and regulators will rise, leading to increased staff training costs for lenders, and probably the disappearance of many "part-time" mortgage intermediaries. It will become increasingly important for lenders to compete for business from professional mortgage intermediary networks.

A mortgage is likely to remain central to the finances of most UK adults. Increasing competition is likely to deliver customers greater choice and value. This market is key to Legal & General and we will continue to play a leading role in it.

Robin Phipps

WHAT NEXT?

CHRISTOPHER RODRIGUES, CHIEF EXECUTIVE

BRADFORD & BINGLEY BUILDING SOCIETY

There is an old adage that the only thing certain about the future is that it will be uncertain. While, ten years from now, the majority of Britons will still live in homes with mortgages, many will have different mortgages meeting different needs, supplied by different people through different channels and on different financial terms.

These changes in the mortgage market reflect three major trends that are evident throughout the consumer financial services sector:

1 Customers are getting smarter: they realise they have a choice of repayment vehicles and are increasingly rate sensitive. They are also getting older, which means that the great house-buying post-war baby boom is getting to the end of its traditional 30-year mortgage.

But an ageing population means that the equity-release mortgage is likely to come back into fashion. This is particularly true given the apparent inability of the public sector to provide full pensions and lifetime health care for a growing ageing population.

2 Competition is getting tougher: as barriers between different parts of the financial services sector come tumbling down, the traditional mortgage providers are facing some tough competition. Whether or not you believe many people will buy their mortgages as their margarine, the major retailers have powerful databases and are intent on being a force in the market.

At the same time, companies who manufacture mortgage repayment vehicles such as the PEP and Endowment Policy providers would like to sell mortgages with their products as opposed to vice versa.

We are also seeing a growing number of consumers choosing to use professional mortgage advisers. This reflects an understandable consumer trend to seek help when faced with an extraordinary diversity of product choices.

And, last, but not least, the defection of some major building societies into the banking sector has polarised the battle between the mutual building societies and the Plc banks. At the end of August 1997, loyal customers with a variable mortgage rate paid almost 1 per cent less with the Bradford & Bingley than with the Halifax or Abbey National.

The impact of this growing competition is that consumers have a real choice to make when deciding how to go about buying their mortgage and who to get it from.

3 Technology is changing the mortgage business: in the past, getting a mortgage was simple. You went to a building society branch and applied. Now you can use the telephone; see a specialist salesperson in your home; get a mortgage by mail; go to your supermarket; log on to the Internet; or even go to a building society branch.

Christopher Rodrigues

The theory is that soon, everyone will buy their products direct and branches will be dead. However, I believe, as Mark Twain might have said: "reports of their death are greatly exaggerated". The more likely outcome is that we will see mortgage customers using a mixture of channels. Their choice will depend on what is most convenient to them and where they are in the mortgage process.

Whatever happens, over the next ten years, one thing is clear. The consumer will be the winner.

There are some common themes to our experts' comments and predictions which are worth highlighting. In the analysis that follows, the views expressed are my own.

MORTGAGE REGULATION

The likelihood is that there will be statutory regulation of mortgages sooner rather than later. But, in my view, this will be to appease the lobbyists rather than promote the interests of consumers. My strong belief is that a voluntary code, adhered to strictly by all lenders, is the right way to proceed. The reader need look no further than the calculation of the Annual Percentage Rate (APR) under the Advertising Regulations of the Consumer Credit Act to see what chaos can be caused when statutory regulation proves to be too inflexible to quickly resolve an emerging problem.

The problem with statutory regulation is that those in charge of policing it can never give practitioners a definitive view. They can tell you what their current interpretation of the law is, but always with the caveat that, ultimately, only the courts can decide what the law really is. Practitioners therefore have a situation where they never really know whether they are inside or outside the law. This rumbles along effectively enough until somebody challenges the position and a case comes to court, as happened under the Consumer Credit Act Advertising Regulations.

A lender was challenged on its policy of assuming that the initial fixed rate offered to the borrower would be the rate to apply for the rest of the mortgage term. At that time, the interpretation of the Office of Fair Trading was that the lender's prevailing base variable rate should apply at the end of the fixed rate term, and be reflected in the APR. The lender won this case, effectively overturning the practice adopted by those policing the Advertising Regulations. All lenders therefore had to change their practices and, when advertising, assume the continuation of the initially offered interest rate for the remainder of the mortgage term.

One particular lender then offered a large short-term discount, producing a low initial customer rate. In accordance with what was then considered to be the established practice, this lender quoted an APR on the assumption that the initial rate to be paid by the borrower would continue for the remainder of the mortgage term. This lender was prosecuted and, notwithstanding the earlier case, was found to be guilty of incorrectly stating the APR. The court in the second case decided that, on a variable rate loan, a lender needed to take into account how likely it was that the initial rate to be paid by the customer would continue for the rest of the mortgage term. As the second case related to a variable rate loan, however, confusion arose as to whether this new ruling also affected fixed rate loans, since many of the principles put forward to support the second decision applied equally to all types of loan.

A situation was then created where nobody really knew the right way to calculate an APR, and this situation prevails as this book goes to press. New legislation is going to be necessary to clear this issue up, which will be delayed in order to take account of forthcoming European Directives on the issue of advertising credit. So the consumer is left without any consistent formula for comparing the true cost of one loan against another, with practitioners helpless to address that confusion.

Had there been a voluntary code dealing with the question of calculating APRs then the problem could undoubtedly have been resolved by industry practitioners within a couple of weeks. The mortgage market is dynamic and ever-changing. It is impossible for anybody to lay down in advance a framework of rules that will not produce anomalies and unforeseen circumstances as new types of product and delivery systems develop. The rules therefore need to be flexible enough to respond quickly in order to protect the consumer. I believe that this can best be delivered by way of a voluntary code, so long as lenders accept that the greater good of the industry comes before individual competitive advantage, meaning that the Code must be policed and implemented rigorously.

A compromise might be statutory backing for the Mortgage Code which has been introduced by the Council of Mortgage Lenders, shortly to be extended to cover the work of intermediaries. But my expectation is that there will be full statutory regulation which will take many years to settle down, and which will produce its own degree of chaos. The price of implementation will inevitably be borne by the consumer, and the theorist will win over the pragmatist once again.

TAX ENVIRONMENT

The UK mortgage market over the last ten years has been assisted considerably in its development by a favourable tax regime: tax relief on mortgage interest, low stamp duty levels, Capital Gains Tax exemption on the sale of the primary residence and housing benefit support for mortgage payments in times of need. Over recent years, however, these tax advantages have gradually started to be eroded. It may not, therefore, be safe to assume that the mortgage market will perform over the next decade as it has over the last.

Tax relief on mortgage interest is gradually being reduced by the classic stage-by-stage method. The change each year is considered marginal, when viewed against the current position. When viewed against the starting point, however, where tax relief at the highest marginal rate was offered on all mortgage interest, it is a massive reduction. Perhaps this is right, to even out the interests of those in the privately owned and rented sectors respectively. It used to be the view that home ownership led to independence, responsibility, harder work, a sense of worth and family and so on, which would have other benefits around the economy. That appears to be an unfashionable view, assisted by the misery caused to many homeowners in the 1991–95 recession. The balance probably lies somewhere in the middle, but – for those planning to continue their careers in the mortgage market – the assumption must be that mortgage tax relief will disappear fairly quickly.

> home ownership led to independence, responsibility, harder work, a sense of worth and family

There seems to be an inevitable drift towards adopting some of the cultural approaches already in place in Europe, where, generally, home ownership is not, and never has been, considered to have the same level of importance as we have given it in the UK. I believe that this will lead to increasing stamp duty and, possibly, to the introduction of Capital Gains Tax on house sales. I think we can also expect to see changes to Inheritance Tax which will also significantly impact the housing market, since the privately owned house is normally the most valuable asset of the average person.

Without underpinning via income support for mortgage interest, lenders and borrowers will have to be more cautious. I remember, back in the mid-1980s, reporting to my Citibank superiors in New York that the favourable tax regime, and the commitment to home ownership by the British, presented a not-to-be-missed opportunity for a foreign bank to exploit in the UK mortgage market. The picture has radically changed since then and, whilst there are still opportunities, they need to be assessed against the background of purely commercially related factors. Part of me welcomes the changes as the market growing up, and approaching natural saturation levels. But having started my career in what was then a building society movement, I do mourn the loss of the special place which home ownership had in the hearts of government and of the British people (although 77 per cent of households still see it as their preferred tenure, nevertheless).

Give your name, address and social security number in the United States and the mortgage is either yours, or it isn't. Credit scoring and other credit assessment techniques have reached such a level of sophistication that your propensity to go into arrears can be predicted with amazing accuracy. If you cannot get a loan from the mainstream lenders, there is a highly active sub-prime lending market prepared to offer you terms which are a little more expensive, but which nevertheless allow you to obtain a loan. Decisions are quick, unemotional and largely correct.

In the UK, many lenders have adopted the worst of all worlds. Most of the major players have now introduced various forms of credit scoring and higher level credit assessment, thereby introducing some of the pain associated with turning people down for a loan based on factors which the applicants cannot control, namely the lender's secret credit scorecard. However, these lenders have doubled the pain by continuing with the long-winded paper reference chase, which often leads applicants to hang around for weeks whilst a mortgage offer is issued (up to 23 working days on average, according to some benchmarking studies I have seen). Over the next few years this must change.

Already some lenders have sufficient confidence in their credit scorecards to do away with paper references. But few are making this known publicly. I believe that this will change rapidly so that we get nearer to the way things work in the United States. Some lenders claim that they are waiting for their credit scorecards to mature, so that delinquency statistics can be compared over several years. But if someone is an innate bad payer then he is statistically likely to go into arrears within the first year of the loan. People who pay initially and then subsequently get into arrears are normally victims of circumstance, such as divorce, redundancy and so on. I know of no credit scorecard that can predict with any accuracy the propensity of people to get divorced, or suddenly to be made redundant, based on character and status profiles. It is therefore perfectly possible for lenders who have introduced credit scoring over the last few years to now be brave enough to dispense with expensive and time-consuming paper references. People should be able to receive an instant, subject-to-valuation, mortgage offer based on the initial computer check.

Some of the more forward-thinking lenders are also looking at the possible demise of the house valuation. Building societies are, of course, required by law to obtain an independent valuation on each property taken into mortgage. But this does not apply to banks and non-building society lenders. The application of a property index, perhaps supported by a drive-by, could well replace the independent mortgage valuation. If all the valuation fees paid by borrowers were, instead, provisioned against losses directly caused by the property not being what the lender expected, there would be massive profits for both lenders and borrowers. The fees would reduce, the lenders would be fully protected, but – importantly – mortgage applicants would get their loans, and be in a position to exchange contracts, much quicker than is currently the case. This is what is needed to modernise the application process and mitigate the incidence of gazumping. And I am sure that it will come about during the next ten years, although at a much slower pace than I would like.

As more of our land becomes registered, so Title Insurance can replace the long-winded pre-completion legal process. There is therefore no reason why the whole mortgage cannot be paid out within seven days of applying. Lenders rightly view such developments with caution, just in case there are hidden pitfalls. The strength of the companies providing the Title Insurance will, of course, be as significant a factor as the extent of the cover itself. But as consumers get more sophisticated they will demand better service. As I said in Chapter 7, on the assumption of an ever-present need for leading edge commodity pricing, service will be the next frontier on which competition is based.

The sub-heading "Delivery" also embraces direct-to-the-consumer techniques. Telephone applications for mortgages have not taken off quite as well as many predicted, largely because the call has to go on for about 20 minutes as the form is filled out, with the paper form then requiring a signature. After all that there is the normal long-winded paper chase. But as soon as we as an industry establish a workable system for the electronic signature, and get our act together in computerised credit assessment, telephone applications are bound to pick up when the customer can make one brief telephone call and receive a definitive mortgage offer in response. This method of applying for a loan will not suit everybody, because they will realise that bargains can be obtained by shopping around. But this will suit a certain section of demand where speed and convenience are more important than trying to squeeze out an extra quarter of a per cent.

Everybody has their own predictions as to how interactive TV will change our lives. Some predictions rely more for their credibility on science-fiction thrillers than they do on commercial credibility. But it seems likely that, within the next ten years, most middle class homes will have access to the "big screen". The feeling is that this screen will be a normal window to the house rather than a screen taking up a whole wall, with the glass capable of being used for its normal function of allowing light into the room, or alternatively as a replacement for the TV. On this screen the consumer will be able to call up the "virtual mall" and direct his or her own image down the high street, popping into sites to do some shopping. Interaction with the supplier, backed up by a Switch or credit card, will allow purchases to be effected from the armchair, probably with next-day delivery.

The extent to which this will impact financial services products is hard to predict. People often need comfort and reassurance when conducting their most important financial purchase, which can best be delivered face-to-face. Misunderstandings which occur in the application for a mortgage can have repercussions many years down the line. My own feeling is that this development will bring about significant long-term changes in the delivery of mortgages to the consumer, but at a slow, cautious pace, that is nothing like the speed with which the computer boffins would have you believe that people will become comfortable with this technology.

FUTURE OF INTERMEDIARIES

In the mid-1980s there was a rush for institutions to buy estate agents. This would, so it was argued, be the end of the road for the traditional mortgage intermediary, as lenders would now control the first port of call in the house-buying process. In practice, the competition which ensued actually increased the amount of business handled by mortgage intermediaries, as customers turned to them for advice in sorting out the choice.

When direct telephone-based selling companies burst onto the scene in the late 1980s, the demise of the intermediary was again mooted. But there are now so many telephone-based providers of motor insurance, for example, that a new type of intermediary has been spawned, namely the direct providers' broker. These companies sort out the best direct quote from a range of direct suppliers, with customers increasingly turning to them for advice as to how to sort out choice.

Despite all the predictions to the contrary, the influence of intermediaries in the mortgage market has grown, currently accounting for an estimated 50 per cent of UK mortgage demand. The bigger, better intermediaries now take a larger market share, with ownership of a substantial and recognisable brand becoming just as important for intermediaries as it is for the product providers themselves. But, whilst the Mortgage Code, and the training/examinations it will bring with it, will increase the market share for the big boys, and bring about the demise of some smaller players, I do not believe that the overall influence of intermediaries will diminish that much. Indeed, I am sure that the professionalism of intermediaries will substantially increase.

All the time that supply exceeds demand in the mortgage market, there will be fierce competition. Customers know that loans cannot be compared on rate alone. Factors like fees, redemption penalties, the lender's policy on further advances, the lender's track record on setting variable rates and so on are all matters where the good mortgage intermediary can help the customer avoid dangerous pitfalls. If you believe in the continuance of over-supply and competition in the mortgage market, all precedent indicates that you should also believe in a powerful distribution role for the intermediary.

A well-trained and qualified intermediary sector, abiding by the principles of the Mortgage Code is of more value to the consumer than many acknowledge. All lending organisations know that the good intermediary is a hard taskmaster, not prepared to allow bad or unsuitable products to filter through the net. This, in turn, keeps lenders on their toes. So, not only do I expect the intermediary sector to thrive and prosper, I also hope that it does, in everybody's interests.

NEW PLAYERS

"That'll be £34.50 for your groceries, and £301.27 for your mortgage" says the Sainsbury's check-out clerk. Why not? The bigger organisations in the UK have been able to bank with themselves for a long time. Their treasury people can access the world's money markets as easily as any bank, and it was only a question of time before the middlemen started to be cut out. Sainsbury's bank is here today, and I am sure that it will be offering mortgages tomorrow.

It will be fascinating to see how this development proceeds. If Sainsbury's has to repossess a borrower, or turn him down for a loan, will the resultant publicity have a negative effect on its supermarket sales? How are Sainsbury's going to compete with the best cashbacks, fixed rates and so on offered by the traditional lenders? It is now clear that Sainsbury's are going to try, and others will follow.

I invited Sainsbury's to make a contribution to this book, but they said that their plans were not quite ready enough. Marks & Spencer Financial Services said that they had no immediate plans to launch into mortgages, and Richard Branson, whilst wishing me the best of luck with the book, said in the friendly and direct style for which he is famous that Virgin didn't want to make a contribution either. So it is difficult to get a handle on quite what the new type of "brand-holder" is thinking about in relation to some of the core challenges they face by becoming mortgage players. Will there be mortgage desks in the supermarkets? How *does* a friendly and successful company like Virgin deal with borrowers in arrears? What is clear is that those looking to get more leverage out of a successful brand will become new players in the mortgage market, and the whole scene will become much more fun because of it.

Some will fail, possibly in spectacular fashion. But some will succeed. It will take time to establish the new concept in consumers' minds, and there will be the ever-present problem of fiercely competitive pricing. Without cross-subsidy, it is hard to see how many new mortgage products could viably be offered by some of the newer players mentioned. If the proposition is going to be an ordinary variable rate, but keenly priced, then this will run the risk of publicity comparing such rates to the discounts and cashbacks offered by the mainstream lenders. I have personally felt for some time that the major opportunity for newer players has rested with the insurance company sector, who are able to potentially cross-subsidise the various streams of income in order to provide a competitive package to a borrower.

For example, there are some insurance companies that can sell a mortgage based on a monthly payment. Within that payment could be the interest on the mortgage, the buildings and contents insurance, MIG insurance, basic life cover and accident, sickness and unemployment protection. The monthly payment quoted could be compared favourably with a typical situation where these various component parts were bought independently of each other. With good marketing and packaging, and an element of cross-subsidy, this could be a winner because, whilst almost everybody knows the going market rate, few know the monthly payment that applies to that rate per £1000 borrowed. Bargains could be made available. The problem is that, typically, the life side of an insurance company doesn't talk much to the general side, and so on.

Kensington Mortgage Company has shown in recent times that it is still possible to create the "virtual mortgage company" by using warehouse funding lines and the securitisation market, subcontracting distribution, pre-offer processing and post-offer administration. As soon as there is anything like a situation where mortgage demand and supply come within sight of each other, there would be a wave of European and international mortgage market entrants able to offer loans at very skinny (but positive) margins over LIBOR. Indeed, there are those who feel that this situation may come about without further supply-side contraction. With a savings war about to develop, led by the Plc vs mutuality battle, now joined by the new players, the mortgage rate has to be a higher margin over LIBOR than currently (so it is argued). That will bring in new players, further increasing supply. Those that argue that supply is about to sharply contract need to have one eye on this particular development when considering the time-frame within which this might come about.

Control of costs and effective treasury management are vital to becoming a winner in these current market conditions. There will be further losers, and we can expect more mergers and takeovers taking players out of the market, just as we can expect newer players coming in. The UK mortgage market is large and profitable, and I do not see any let-up in the current fiercely competitive market over the short term at least.

PLC vs MUTUALITY

Some of our experts have argued that the banks will hoover up the mutuals. Not surprisingly, the mutuals do not agree. I think that this is a battle for the hearts and minds of the UK consumers, with the one-way traffic in favour of the Plcs impacted by the recent vote from the members of Nationwide Building Society to effectively stay mutual. We deal with both types of organisation and see advantages in each. The banks tend to move quicker, without so many apparent constraints. They are more likely to take controlled risks for greater profit and have access to wider capital markets. There is no doubt in my mind that what I call the "consumer banks" will have an increasing influence in the mortgage market.

The one-way traffic I refer to above is the greed factor on the part of consumers, which has brought some mutuals "into play", forcing them to convert or accept a takeover offer so that the members can receive £1000 or so in a windfall bonus. But mutuals persuasively argue that their reserves have been built up over many years. The management team at any one time are only temporary custodians of those reserves, ensuring that they stay intact for future generations of customers. It is neither fair nor appropriate for these reserves to suddenly be dissipated upon the demise of the institution concerned, and this has struck a chord with a few. However, this has not been enough to halt the slide.

"consumer banks" will have an increasing influence

Mutuals have to quickly demonstrate that there is a financial advantage as well. By and large, the leading mutuals have started to be successful in showing customers that they might receive more in terms of higher savings rates, lower mortgage rates and various loyalty schemes than a one-off windfall. I am sure that Nationwide's pricing policy, offering well-publicised differentials below the typical mortgage rate, helped them with their vote. I am equally sure that the banks, in being first to implement mortgage rate rises on top of base rate increases, will assist the move in favour of mutuals.

It is a fascinating battle to watch. Both camps feel very strongly about their positions, as evidenced by the split between the Building Societies Association and the Council of Mortgage Lenders. The BSA/CML was doing a very good combined job, and the two organisations still closely cooperate out of the same London head office. But the protagonists on both sides of the debate insisted that mutuals and banks could not be represented by the same body because their interests were different. The battle is therefore engaged between the, so it is argued, greater commerciality and access to capital markets on the part of the Plcs, versus the lower profitability hurdles of the mutuals, which lead to better rate structures and loyalty schemes.

Our need as an organisation to keep a foot in both camps would have always presented me with a commercial challenge in terms of picking a winner. Fortunately, I am unable to overcome the intellectual challenge of not having the slightest idea. Consumer moods are fickle, and there could just as easily be a backlash against Plcs as there could against mutuals. The winners will ultimately be those who can show that their way makes the consumer better off financially, and media coverage will play a vital part. For tradition's sake, I hope that mutuality does survive as a concept, because the local and regional building societies in particular do a super job in providing a personal service delivered by local people to local people.

FLEXIBLE/LIFESTYLE MORTGAGES

Everybody is so busy talking about this development that they have failed to notice that nobody is buying these products in any volume. Who is going to trade off the definite benefit of an up-front discount or cashback, or a keen fixed rate, against the possibility that they *might* want a few months' respite from the mortgage in the future? In the vast majority of instances I have seen, couples would be better off banking the up-front benefit and using that to subsidise themselves if they want future payment holidays. More than one lender has offered a "Baby Mortgage", offering a payment holiday only if a child comes along. Presumably, the marketing material had to say "Only the fertile need apply"!

It is argued that people change jobs today more frequently than ever, and are more exposed to being made redundant. These are worthwhile lifestyle considerations, if they are built into a standard product range. Unfortunately, as a trade-off for having this flexibility to deal with situations which might never happen, mortgage customers have to give up some of the attractive up-front incentives. I have never enjoyed much success trying to sell tomorrow against today, especially when the events of tomorrow may never happen. Rather than make lifestyle considerations require a price trade-off, I believe that lenders need to embrace lifestyle considerations in the lending criteria they apply to their leading edge products. That is how lenders will truly respond to the consumer demand in this area.

The other type of flexible mortgage allows the home to be used as a line of credit. I certainly see more immediate success for this type of loan, particularly amongst the more sophisticated consumer. The best deal I have seen allows the customer to build up savings by overpaying the mortgage. This has the immediate effect of reducing the mortgage interest charged, thereby delivering to the customer a net benefit which is substantially greater than he would have earned by investing that money in a savings account. The customer also has a cheque book, which he can use to return to himself any or all of the overpayments if his situation should change. An unbeatable net return on the overpayments, an ability to draw them back if necessary, with a line of credit available to the borrower that increases as the property value goes up. This is a bit more like it, offering flexible lifestyle benefits *alongside* the best rates of interest.

Various lenders have variations on this theme, and are pushing them as hard as possible. The problem is finding a communication medium where the customer can be expected to dwell long enough to think through the various implications. Newspaper and TV advertisements aren't really the place, and it is my experience that intermediaries don't always fully understand or agree with the future benefits being offered. This is a marketing problem which will be solved in the end by the lenders concerned, and I certainly believe that the cheque-book mortgage is here to stay. Private Label will participate once we have established in our minds how to deliver such complicated products in the sort of high volume our operation seeks.

WRAP-UP

The only reliable relationship between two indices that I have discovered over the longer run in this market is house prices and real incomes. If you feel that the economy will grow, then you can be sure that house prices will grow with it. This progress might well be patchy, with strong regional differences. But to predict a fall in house prices over the longer term means a negative judgment on the UK economy, which does not seem justified as we look at it in 1997. It is true that home ownership may well be reaching saturation, with 75 per cent often predicted as the ultimate possible limit. But new households are being created at an alarming proportion due to marriage break-ups and other demographic changes. For example, between now and 2020 the number of households in England is expected to grow by 4.4 million. Around 3.5 million of these are expected to come from single person households. With the ability to switch mortgages in-between moving property, I certainly see a healthy mortgage market, substantially in excess of £50 billion per year of gross advances, well into the future.

Innovation and entrepreneurialism will always prevail. Sounds bland and self-serving, doesn't it? But it has been true none-the-less, throughout history. I cannot say that we will be doing in ten years' time what we are doing today, and we will certainly be using our financial resources within the next year to diversify and broaden our service to lenders and intermediaries. But the innovator will always thrive in a dynamic market.

Mortgage pricing has to become more sensible, but I do not see an equilibrium supply/demand situation because of the ease with which new players can come into our market. We welcome more sensible pricing because, without these huge giveaways, innovation becomes the main point of comparison. This is exactly the situation which applied when we launched, and we thrived on it. But I am not holding my breath for the reduction in front-end giveaways. Every time a lender, or group of lenders, attempts to make a step in this direction, their reduction in market share requires them to give even more away when they relaunch, thereby starting the cycle up all over again.

You cannot plan the future by the past. In the preceding seven chapters I have, however, attempted to share some experiences which will at least give the reader some knowledge about successes and failures I have "enjoyed" in meeting past situations. These may be of use to anybody encountering similar circumstances in the future. Nobody knows for sure what is going to happen over the next ten years. This is why I wanted to broaden my approach in Chapter 8 and include comments by leading figures. Readers must draw their own conclusions from the various comments included in this chapter, for there is only one certain thing. Not everybody quoted is going to be right.

In his speech on the Reform Bill in 1866, Gladstone said, "You cannot fight against the future. Time is on our side". We must all enjoy the future: it's the only one we've got. For those involved in mortgages at all levels, I think it's an exciting future.

Index of names

Index of companies and institutions